D0713421

RENEWALS 458-4574

Henry James Goes to Paris

Henry James Goes to Paris

Peter Brooks

Princeton University Press
Princeton and Oxford

Copyright © 2007 by Princeton University Press

Published by Princeton University Press, 41 William Street, Princeton, New Jersey 08540

In the United Kingdom: Princeton University Press, 3 Market Place, Woodstock, Oxfordshire OX20 1SY

All Rights Reserved

Library of Congress Cataloging-in-Publication Data

Brooks, Peter, 1938–
Henry James goes to Paris / Peter Brooks.
p.   cm.
Includes bibliographical references and index.
ISBN-13: 978-0-691-12954-9 (cloth : alk. paper)
ISBN-10: 0-691-12954-1 (acid-free paper)
1. James, Henry, 1843–1916—Travel—France.   2. James, Henry,
1843–1916—Appreciation—France.   I. Title.

PS2127.F7B76 2007
813'.4—dc22
[B]

British Library Cataloging-in-Publication Data is available

This book has been composed in Electra

Printed on acid-free paper. ∞

press.princeton.edu

Printed in the United States of America

1 3 5 7 9 10 8 6 4 2

WITHDRAWN
UTSA LIBRARIES

Library
University of Texas
at San Antonio

this one is for Clara,

---

but also for Anna & Nat & Kate & Preston

Contents

Henry James Goes to Paris

Introduction

This is the story of the young Henry James—age thirty-two—deciding to make a radical break with family, Cambridge, and his native land in order to go become a novelist in Paris. Jump, for a moment, nearly to the end of the story of James's engagement with the Parisian literary and artistic avant-garde. It's Virginia Woolf, in her biography of the Bloomsbury artist, critic, and aesthetic theorist Roger Fry, who recounts James's visit in 1912—he was now close to seventy—to the Second Post-Impressionist Exhibition held at the Grafton Galleries, in London. Here, in what would be a landmark exhibit for Britain, were works by Gauguin, Seurat, Cézanne, Matisse, Rouault, Picasso. Fry took James to the basement for tea, over which James expressed "the disturbed hesitations which Matisse and Picasso aroused in him," while Fry attempted to explain "that Cézanne and Flaubert were, in a manner of speaking, after the same thing."

Woolf's anecdote captures a number of issues. It suggests that James by 1912 was himself considered by the artistic elite—what better representatives of that than Woolf and Fry?—to be an exemplar of the movement from Victorianism to modernism, in fact the person younger generations looked to, and now called the Master, because he led the way into a new kind of fiction. Yet, the comparison of Flaubert and Cézanne, which we may find entirely apt—especially when we think about the late work of these two restless innovators—was perhaps less reassuring to James than Fry intended, in that late Cézanne probably

1

most of all triggered James's longstanding hesitations about Flaubert, offering a cautionary tale in the infringement of certain commitments to representation.

James in 1912 was a modernist master, but one who clung to a notion of representation of the real that he saw as indispensable to the very project of the novel—a project that leads him over and over again to set against Flaubert's practice the more nourishing example of Balzac. So a modernist master who is unwilling to make the leap *beyond* that we see in the work Cézanne did in Provence from 1900 to his death in 1906, and presumably even more so where the experimentation of Picasso and Matisse is concerned. Yet Roger Fry was certainly right in his comparisons. Starting in the mid-1890s, James does produce work that parallels Seurat's *pointillisme* and anticipates Picasso's cubism. It is work that eschews the direct presentation of the story—its characters and its actions—in favor of the play of interpretive consciousness on the action. As in Seurat, the solid outlines of objects give way to a kind of shimmering impression recorded by the eye and the mind. As in Picasso in his cubist phase, the observed reveals different sides and aspects as the observer moves, studying intently that which needs observation, revaluating impressions as new angles of observation open up. Think, for instance, of the unnamed narrator of *The Sacred Fount* or of Fanny Assingham in *The Golden Bowl*, two very different observers who must try to deduce and to interpret from evidence that never stays put, both because they are moving and because the observed itself alters under the observing eye. It's a kind of radical perspectivalism that James brought to the novel perhaps more consistently than any other novelist, which he then made the basis of his theory of fiction expressed in the prefaces of the New York Edition of his works, and which the generation of Woolf and Fry gratefully made their own.

By the time James was sitting in the basement of the Grafton Galleries taking tea with Roger Fry, he was the accomplished master of the three late, great novels of what long ago was dubbed his "major phase": *The Wings of the Dove* (1902), *The Ambassadors* (1903), *The Golden Bowl* (1904), as well as the reflective prefaces of the New York Edition (1907–9). These three novels of the major phase are all highly perspectival. They depend on the play of seeing and the unseen, of knowledge and ignorance, as the very stuff of their dramas. What Milly Theale does not see in *The Wings of the Dove* kills her; and the knowledge of what she knows in her dying eventually sunders Kate Croy and Merton Densher. *The Ambassadors* is perhaps the most obvious example of a perceptual adventure and dilemma, a kind of detective story where the detective, Lambert Strether, eventually gets it all wrong because he's wilfully blinded himself—yet in getting it wrong discovers the perspectives in which it is all right. And *The Golden Bowl* offers a story of finding out and then repressing what you have found in order to use your knowledge in other ways, to alter the very scene of observation.

The perspectival dramas of the last three novels are acute, agonizing, played for the highest possible stakes. Nonetheless they reach us with a kind of high serenity conferred by James's late style, a finish that is perhaps more comparable to an Old Master than to a contemporary such as Cézanne. The more wrenching questions of perspective, of how one sees and how one knows, come just before the major phase, in a series of novels and tales from the mid-1890s into the beginnings of the new century. From approximately the time of *The Figure in the Carpet* (1896) through *What Maisie Knew* (1897), *The Turn of the Screw* (1898), *In the Cage* (1898), *The Awkward Age* (1899), to *The Sacred Fount* (1901)—and then, belatedly, *The Beast in the Jungle* (1903)—James's fiction appears to evidence a radical dis-orientation, a displacement of the observer from a central or frontal position to a marginal one. Following his failed experiment in the theater, he seemed to turn to what the theater could not so readily provide, something that more anticipates the cinema: a severely angled view, a moving post of observation and a shifting field of the observed.

Knowledge had of course always been important in James's fictions, which were indeed often centrally dramas of knowledge—perhaps most notably *The Portrait of a Lady*, where Isabel Archer's discovery of the latent meanings of her disastrous marriage constitutes the core of the drama. Bafflement leading to recognition was perhaps always the principal Jamesian scenario. What seems new in the fiction of the mid- to late 1890s is the emphasis on the bafflement itself, and the difficulty or even impossibility of assuring that the recognition is real, rather than the product of a partial, misinformed, or even unhinged imagination.

James is forced to reflect on the use of perspective in ways that seem to take him beyond Balzac, to the most radical innovations of Flaubert, and toward the painting he never could really appreciate. James's biographer, Leon Edel, notes that after 1895 James seems already to have left the nineteenth century behind, and to be moving toward the fictional experimentation of Joyce, of Woolf, of Proust.

James the modernist is by now so accepted a figure that his earlier work—such novels as *Roderick Hudson* (1875), *The American* (1877), *The Europeans* (1878), *Washington Square* (1880), even the masterful *The Portrait of a Lady* (1881) and *The Bostonians* (1886)—often does seem to belong to a different century, not only literally but symbolically as well. What happened in between this work and the experimental fiction of the mid-1890s—work marked by what we might call a kind of epistemological anguish, the anxious difficulty of figuring out what one knows about other people and the world, and how to know it? Many things of course happened, including, notably, James's attempt to write for the stage, and the bitter disaster in which it ended, in 1895, also the death of his friend Constance Fenimore Woolson by suicide in 1894, and the loss of others, such as Robert Louis Stevenson and his beloved invalid sister, Alice; even the trial and conviction of Oscar Wilde should be factored in as an element in James's psychological evolution. I don't think any biographer has or probably ever will "explain" how James transforms himself during these difficult, often depressed, but also enormously productive years.

As any reader of James, or of Woolf, or of Freud, knows well, chronology is not necessarily straightforward. Things happen, are apparently forgotten, or repressed, and then stage a return to consciousness, a belated influence. It's not my primary intention in what follows to argue that James's transformation in the 1890s is caused by his Paris experience twenty years earlier: I don't believe that this kind of cause and effect are fully determinable in the life and work of a writer. But it is striking that James in Paris in 1875 and 1876—aged thirty-two and thirty-three—encounters the very crucible of the modernism he will later come to represent, even embody. It's even more striking that when he first encounters such emblematic works of nascent modernism as Flaubert's *Bouvard et Pécuchet*, Monet's impression of the sun rising over the Seine in Le Havre, or Whistler's nocturnes, he doesn't like them. He rejects them in favor of something much more conventional and, to our retrospective eyes, far less valuable. He is not yet prepared to see what this work is doing, and the lessons it may hold for his own. To some degree, he will never fully accept it. If he later speaks in high praise of Monet, late Flaubert always makes him uncomfortable. Rightly so, one might say, because he no doubt correctly detects that there is in a book like *Bouvard et Pécuchet* a more radical challenge to the whole enterprise of the novel as representation than James wants to take on. James's modernism will always be tempered by this commitment to a form of representation he tends to exemplify in the person of another French novelist who had died in 1850: Balzac.

Nonetheless, much that he experiences in Paris in 1875–76 will stage a kind of return of the repressed in his work from the mid-1890s on. It's as if it lay for some twenty years in what James called "the deep well of unconscious cerebration" before he was ready for it—before he saw that it could be of use to him, that it was trying to do something similar to what he now felt he needed to do. The wealth of material that James encountered in Paris during his year there may have been too much to absorb at the time. Paris, following the trauma of defeat by Prussia and then the uprising and suppression of the Paris Commune, in 1871, was in a moment of feverish creativity, and James encountered the prime examples of it, in such as the Second Impressionist Exhibit at Durand-Ruel's, and in mixing with writers he worshiped—Turgenev—and others he admired in some descending order: Flaubert, Zola, Maupassant, Goncourt, Daudet. He encountered as well the possibility of a close, possibly erotic friendship with a young Russian artist, aesthete, and devotee of Wagner—whose influence on European music and letters had just been given the consecration of the Festspielhaus in Bayreuth. James missed much of what he experienced—but missed it, I think, only for the time being. It would be back, to shape his own writing in crucial ways.

As I suggested, however, it's not an argument about James's evolution and its causes that most interests me here. It is rather the telling of a story: the story of that year in Paris, from the point of view of the man who at that point was still "Henry James, Jr." Narratives tend to be determined by their endings, what they are headed toward. It may be salutary to try to forget for a moment that Master, and to walk again the streets of Paris with the man who has just seen *Roderick Hudson* to bed and has now hatched the idea for *The American*. Or rather—since it is impossible truly to forget James as he would become—it may be well to try to recreate the experience of the young man in a kind of stereo- scopic view, including the Master as a kind of hovering figure. In any case, what I have tried to do is first and foremost tell the story—the novel of the young Henry James in the somewhat treacherous, but en- chanting, world of Paris in 1875–76.

1. To Paris

From Cambridge to Babylon

The remarkable James family made their home at 20 Quincy Street in Cambridge, Massachusetts, a few steps from Harvard, where William James would pursue his brilliant career. But Cambridge never seemed a solution to Henry James's aspirations—no doubt in large part because of the remarkable family, especially because of the brilliant older brother. He wandered much in Europe as a young man, and made prolonged stays especially in Italy, where he was a passionate pilgrim of beauty. Cambridge in contrast was bleak, parochial, aesthetically and socially thin and cramped. He felt an exile on native ground. Then he decided to try New York, his birthplace, where in 1875 he spent "a bright, cold, unremunerative, uninteresting winter," churning out book reviews for the *Nation*, while his first substantial novel, *Roderick Hudson*, began its serial publication in the *Atlantic Monthly*. Back in Cambridge in mid-July, he decided that he needed to get away again, this time to the old world, and this time to stay. But where? Italy did not seem like a permanent solution. "I wanted something more active"—something like New York without its hard, crass edge. Then in the family home in Quincy Street the answer came: Paris, the place of writers and artists, of the life of mind and spirit, of freedom from family and constraint, and the place where writing novels was taken seriously.

The decision was radical. Here was a young writer (age thirty-two), author of two novels (the first, *Watch and Ward*, a slight affair), of travel sketches and book and art reviews, who wrote in English to a public nourished on Hawthorne and Dickens and Thackeray and George Eliot, whose fledgling career depended on the literary establishments of Boston and New York, making a decision that he could find his place of work in a foreign culture, in a kind of chosen alienation from home ground. But unlike many a later writer seeking refuge in Paris from American provincialities, James felt himself at home in France and in French culture. He claimed that his earliest childhood memory—from his second year—was of the Place Vendôme, with its Napoleonic column; and another family trip when he was thirteen had lasted well over a year, with schooling for the children in Paris and Boulogne-sur-Mer; there was further education in Geneva. He also spent some months in Paris in 1872. He spoke and wrote French perfectly. And he had been reading French authors from an early age.

It's a fact often neglected by his critics and biographers that James's understanding of his profession as a "romancer," as he often called it, derived (as the word suggests) from the French almost more than from the English. From all his voracious youthful reading, the model of the novelist that repeatedly, persistently emerged was not an American or an English exemplar; it was Balzac. It was probably Balzac's Paris that lured James abroad more than anything else. He was like one of Balzac's ambitious young men arriving in Paris from the provinces, to make their way by the power of the pen. The first of the five essays he would write on Balzac—more than on any other author—appeared in the New York magazine *Galaxy*, dated December 1875, just after his arrival in Paris.

Henry James, Jr.—as he signed himself at this point in his life—was intent on living from his pen, as a professional writer, in the manner of Balzac. His travel writing, collected in *Transatlantic Sketches*, published in April 1875 by J. R. Osgood in Boston, was proving a modest commercial success (it quickly sold over a thousand copies); he looked forward to royalties from *Roderick Hudson*; he produced literary essays in addition to book reviews—he planned a volume on French poets and novelists—and before setting out for Paris he proposed to the *New York Tribune* to write fortnightly letters from Paris. Through the good offices of John Hay (the future Secretary of State), he was engaged by Whitelaw Reid, publisher of the *Tribune*, at $20, gold, per letter—less than he had hoped for, but enough to give him the sense that he had a job as a journalist.

He had always resisted any career or profession other than literature. His family was well-off, from the fortune accumulated by his grandfather William James in Albany, in merchandising, banking, and real estate. His father, Henry James, Sr., who dabbled in philosophy and literature, wished his sons to have time and leisure for experimentation before choosing a career. Yet the family fortunes were compromised at times by the bank panics and recessions that periodically afflicted the American economy. (The Paris sojourn in the mid-1850s transferred to the less expensive Boulogne-sur-Mer because a bank panic severely reduced the family income for a time.) Moreover, money never came without strings attached, especially since the bookkeeping fell to his mother, who indeed was Henry's banker for many years, collecting royalties for him and surveilling his expenditures from the letter of credit provided by his father. There would be allegations of family hard times—Henry's sister Alice became a chronic invalid, the younger brothers Wilky and Robertson were not worldly successes—and reproaches of extravagance, particularly with London tailors. Henry James seems early on to have internalized a sense of guilt about money, and a determination to make it on his own—through writing.

He embarked on the Cunard liner *Bothnia*, bound for Liverpool, on October 20, 1875. It turned out that Anthony Trollope was on board—a novelist James never liked, whom he described personally as "the dullest Briton of them all," but whom he admired for his sheer professional persistence in writing every day on the rough crossing: "He drove his pen as steadily on the tumbling ocean as in Montague Square." A lesson there. The crossing took ten days. Then another ten days were needed in London, with the tailors, preparing his wardrobe for the coming season—and making considerable depredations on the paternal letter of credit. He arrived in Paris on November 11, and soon found a furnished apartment at 29 rue du Luxembourg (now the rue Cambon), lying between the rue de Rivoli and the Boulevard des

Capucines, very close to that Place Vendôme of his earliest memory. He went to work on his letters to the *Tribune*; the first appeared under the date November 22. Three days later, *Roderick Hudson* was published in book form by J. R. Osgood in Boston. James promptly proposed to the editor of the *Galaxy* a new novel for serialization in its pages. He was at work.

"Do not allow yourself to be 'put off' by the superficial and external aspect of Paris," James later said to a young friend setting off on a first visit there. "Or rather (for the *true* superficial and external aspect of Paris has a considerable fascination) by what I may call the superficial and external aspect *of* the superficial and external aspect of Paris." Or as he couched it in the first of his *Tribune* pieces, "the problem of existence is solved more comfortably here than elsewhere. . . . So far as a man lives in his senses and his tastes, he certainly lives as well here as he can imagine doing." Paris was a place of luxury, pleasure, beautiful surfaces, sensuous enjoyment. Brother William in his letters will call it "the modern Babylon." There is a kind of admixture of Puritan reservation in James's evident pleasure in Parisian existence—the food, the shops, the theaters, the new Opera house, the ornate monument designed by Charles Garnier during Napoleon III's Second Empire, just now opened, after the fall of Napoleon and of the empire. "You will have heard from my people that I am safely housed in this glittering capital, & that I take to it very kindly," he wrote to his old friend Lizzie Boott on December 31, adding: "Such is the immoral truth: it suits me to a T." Quincy Street morals hover in the background as he gratefully takes possession of the old world.

It's somewhat surprising that the Paris James discovered in 1875 was so prosperous and comfortable. France had only just emerged from the maximum trauma of a century in which it endured several. The seemingly solid, wealthy, well-administered Second Empire, which had created the legend—and to a great extent the reality—of Paris as the city of light, *la ville-lumière*, and of *la vie parisienne* as the most desirable life, which had rebuilt Paris in often sumptuous style through the vast urban projects of the Baron Haussmann, which had seemed destined to last for many generations, collapsed in the absurdly unnecessary Franco-Prussian War of 1870, to which the French army marched off cockily, only to prove ill-trained and appallingly commanded, to encounter tremendous losses and then utter defeat, the remnants of its army surrounded in the eastern town of Metz, the emperor himself taken prisoner by the Prussians. Bismarck had triumphed, and in the process unified Germany as a potent political and military power.

The collapse of the empire led to the founding of a republic—the Third Republic, following those initiated during the first French Revolution, in 1792, and the short-lived Second Republic of 1848, soon terminated by Napoleon III's coup d'état. But then—as the Prussians laid siege to Paris, as the government left the capital for the provinces and negotiated an armistice, with the capitulation of Paris—came the seizure of power by the radical Paris Commune, which rejected the terms of the armistice and in dire circumstances of siege and famine sought to remake society. The official government, now established at Versailles, deployed its army far more effectively against its proletarian compatriots than against the Prussians; the Communards were suppressed in the bloodiest class warfare France has ever known, forever remembered as *la semaine sanglante*, the bloody week. When peace finally was arranged, much of central Paris, including the Tuileries Palace and the Hôtel de Ville, lay in smoking ruins, torched by the desperate Communards, and the column of the Place Vendôme, symbol of imperial grandeur, had been toppled and demolished. The "recent devastations," noted Karl Baedeker's guidebook for 1872, have left a "sadly mutilated metropolis." France appeared not only humiliated but prostrated by the heavy heel of the Hun, and the imposition of reparations of 200 million francs, payment required before the occupying forces would withdraw. It has often been a source of astonishment to historians that the fledgling republic, under the presidency of that long-enduring political performer Adolphe Thiers, was able to finance the repayment of the indemnity with remarkable speed, to liberate the territory by July 1873, and to begin reconstruction of Paris. Real France, *la France profonde*, was rich in resources.

James in his December 28 *Tribune* letter indeed marvels at "the amazing elasticity of France. Beaten and humiliated on a scale without precedent, despoiled, dishonoured, bled to death financially—all this but yesterday—Paris is today in outward aspect as radiant, as prosperous, as instinct with her own peculiar genius as if her sky had never known a cloud." But for all its outward glory, the France James encountered in 1875 was far from secure politically; indeed it was full of tensions, intrigue, and the threat of another upheaval. Thiers had fallen in the spring of 1873, and was replaced by Marshal MacMahon, chief of the army and responsible for the savage repression of the Commune—and a monarchist. France came breathtakingly close to a restoration of the monarchy toppled in 1848, in fact to a restoration of the line of old Bourbon kings dethroned by the Revolution of 1830. The chronic quarrels between the Bourbon Legitimists, partisans of the Comte de Chambord, who was supposed to ascend the throne as Henri V, and the Orléanists, the younger branch of the royal family that had ruled under the "citizen king" King Louis-Philippe from 1830 to 1848, were patched up in a rough compromise. The Bourbon Henri V would ascend the throne, and then, since he had no heir, after his death it would be the turn of the Orléanist Comte de Paris.

Unimaginable as it may seem to us today, France probably would have become a monarchy in 1873 or 1874 had it not been for the intransigence of Chambord, who was a prime example of the adage that the Bourbons learned nothing and forgot nothing. He insisted on taking the country back to the white flag of the Bourbons, fleur-de-lys in its center, in place of the *tricolore* that most French had long known as the glorious national flag, the one that had led its armies to far-flung conquest under the first Napoleon. "I will not allow the standard of Henri IV, François Ier, and Jeanne d'Arc to be snatched from my hands," Chambord declared in a sentence that led further and further back into the past. Only in France could compromise have foundered on the color and symbolism of a flag. Chambord returned to exile. The vote that assured France would remain a republic came on January 30, 1875—the so-called Wallon (after statesman Henri Alexandre Wallon) Amendment—and it carried . . . by one vote.

James had stumbled into the prolonged birth-pangs of republican France—a time that would be determinative for decades to come in the development of the political culture of the Third Republic. Just following his arrival in Paris, the process of electing a senate for the fledgling republic got underway: a senate devised by conservatives to be a counterweight to the Chamber of Deputies, elected in a manner that was supposed to ensure its conservatism. In search of material for his *Tribune* letters (though he was not supposed to cover politics—that was another correspondent's job), James went out to Versailles, to observe the election process, with keen interest. In the event, Republicans and Legitimists made an unholy alliance to defeat the Orléanists and Bonapartists—with the result that the Senate emerged with an unexpectedly solid republican majority. James, cosmopolitan expatriate and Europhile though he might be, was firmly American in his response: the republic now was governed by republicans, and—so long as they remained moderate and responsible—that was a good thing.

He told his *Tribune* readers, in his third letter, "By hook and by crook, through thick and thin, by something that seemed at times like a clumsy accident, the Republic has been weaned from babyhood and set on its feet." On February 20 and March 5 came the crucial elections for the new Chambre des Députés, and the return of a large republican majority—frightening conservatives, provoking a plunge in stock prices: "It may be affirmed," says James, "that the situation is as serious as it has been for many a day. But it is serious in a good and healthy sense. The Republic is now for the first time in Republican hands, and it remains to be seen what they will make of it." There was in fact here the makings of a confrontation and crisis, which would come on May 16, 1877—after James had left Paris—when MacMahon tested his powers against the Assembly—and lost, then resigned two years later. That crisis would quickly come to be celebrated as a national holiday, the day the republic overcame its enemies, and laid to rest—forever, as it turned out—the possibility of a restored monarchy.

So James encountered a Paris of political ferment and dissension. The society he began to make his way in—American expatriates and some French, including the *Nation*'s political correspondent, Auguste Laugel—was largely composed of Orléanist monarchists. "I see none but ardent monarchists and hear everything vile said about the Republic but I incline to believe in it, nevertheless," he wrote to his sister Alice on February 22, 1876. He reacted with an American liberalism, of a sort that Quincy Street, and his old companion Oliver Wendell

Holmes, would have approved. Also, with a certain sang-froid: he was after all in a city that had a few years before known violent insurgency and bloodshed, and there was dire talk of recurrence if the conservatives didn't have their way. Before his time in Paris was up, the United States would undergo its own, rather lesser, political trauma in the disputed Tilden-Hayes election of November 1876, which led to the compromise that saw Hayes become president, and the southern states authorized to liquidate the post–Civil War Reconstruction practiced by the Radical Republicans. But the French situation was potentially more explosive, and James met it with equanimity.

He organized daily life swiftly, in order to get on with his writing. "If you were to see me," he wrote to his father a week after his arrival, "I think you would pronounce me well off: a snug little *troisième* with the eastern sun, two bedrooms, a parlor, an antechamber and a kitchen. Furniture clean and pretty, house irreproachable, and a gem of a *portier*, who waits upon me." He insisted it was all for very little money—that he was being far more economical than in New York. A month later, he was chilly but still cheerful: "The cold in itself is not so bad (it has been snowing these three days), but the draughts thro' windows and doors, the ineffectual fires and the black darkness. But I sit muffled in rugs, cardigans and strange cloth shoes and I get on." He got on, not only with his *Tribune* letters, but also with the new novel. Already on December 1 he was able to write to F. P. Church, editor of the *Galaxy*: "I propose to take it for granted, as soon as I can, that you will be ready to publish, on receipt of them, the opening chapters of a novel. I have got at work upon one sooner than I expected, and particularly desire it to come out without delay. The title of the thing is *The American*."

James may have been taking too much for granted. Church's reply did not come. James then was rescued by his good friend William Dean Howells, editor of the *Atlantic Monthly*—which had serialized *Roderick Hudson*. His new novel had to wait a bit, but it began its serial publication in June 1876. Since we tend to think of James as a novelist who perfected artistic form, we may need to remind ourselves that he followed the journeyman practice of his day, beginning the serial publication of a novel long before he had finished writing it. When he came to write his preface to the novel, years later—for the "New York Edition" of his works—James recalled the anxiety of meeting his deadlines, the "habit of apprehension" that gradually became "the habit of confidence that one would pull through." The original idea of *The American* had been with him for some time. Paris brought what he called its "resurrection." Paris, he wrote in the preface, "ever so promptly offered me, and with an immediate directness at which I now marvel (since I had come back there, after earlier visitations, but a few weeks before), everything that was needed to make my conception concrete." That preface indeed makes of Paris the condition of the novel's "objectivity," its "particular cluster of circumstances" that depended on the Parisian setting that was now his daily experience.

Life in Paris was hence first of all work, getting on with the daily production of copy. He had chosen Paris, after all, as the best professional context, the place to spend his life as a writer. Sociability was a problem, though. "I shall eat my Xmas dinner in a lonely restaurant and think wistfully of you, & your turkey & cranberries," he wrote to Alice on December 24. And then to his mother on January 11 of the new year: "Xmas & New Year have come & gone, but I had—alas!—no Xmas & no New Year. I passed the festive season in solitary *recueillement*. Nothing happens to me worth relating; & I see no one of consequence. I do a good deal of work, which is the principal thing; but outside of this my days are a blank." Evenings too, apparently: "No one in fact appears to receive of an evening; the only time people are visible is in the afternoon." James was very much alone. The man who later on would encounter the greatest social success in London was, like many a foreigner, finding French society hard to enter. The theater became an habitual evening resource, and also something he could write about—probably too often—in his *Tribune* letters.

By late January he was able to write to his mother: "I have taken a desperate plunge into the American world, and have lately been to two balls and a dinner party . . ." On the whole, he found the American expatriate encampment in Paris detestable, but also unavoidable. Alice Mason (divorced from Senator Charles Sumner), Mrs. Charles Strong (née Eleanor Fearing, who had sought refuge in Paris from domestic scandal in Newport), and other American hostesses sent invitations.

He saw Edward Lee Childe (great nephew of General Robert E. Lee), whom he found dull, and his French wife, Blanche de Triquéti, whom he liked—he would visit them the following summer in their château in the Loiret. Then there was Henrietta Reubell, whom he found ugly but frank, intelligent, and agreeable. "If I wanted to desire to marry an ugly Parisian-American, with money and *toutes les élégances*," he wrote to William in the spring, "Miss R would be a very good objective. But I don't—*j'en suis à 1000 lieues*." This marital hypothesis immediately negated is particularly striking in context, since James a moment later introduced the figure of Pavel Vasilievich Zhukovsky—or Paul Joukovsky as he was called in France and by James—the young Russian aesthete, "very sweet and *distingué*," who would be a major figure in his Parisian stay.

There were some French, too, including Auguste Laugel and his wife who introduced him into Orléanist circles—including a ball given by the Duc d'Aumale, one of the sons of King Louis-Philippe (dethroned by the Revolution of 1848) and brother to the Orléanist pretender to the throne, the Comte de Paris. He met Duc Albert de Broglie—the leading conservative statesman of the moment, chief of the Center-Right—and the historian and philosopher Ernest Renan; he entered the salon of the old Marquise de Blocqueville, daughter of the Napoleonic Marshal Davout and "a literary dowager." One senses in some of these letters to Cambridge that James wants to "do" French society in a suitably novelistic style. He continues in this letter to William to describe Madame de Blocqueville as "a great invalid, very corpulent, never leaves the house and has her head swathed in long veils and laces *à la sultane*—but with the remains of beauty." He was impressed by old Madame Jules Mohl, born Mary Clark, "a little old woman of ninety with her hair in her eyes, precisely like a Skye terrier," who evoked an early Romantic Paris, in which she had kept a salon to rival that of her celebrated friend Madame Récamier, mistress to the writer and diplomat Chateaubriand. "Unfortunately, she appears somewhat to have lost her memory," James adds.

Then there was William's friend, Charles Sanders Peirce. It is odd to think of James dining at least weekly—often several times weekly—with Peirce, the founder of pragmatism, the inventor of semiotics, the brilliant and thorny astronomer and physicist who was in Paris on business for the U.S. Coast and Geodetic Survey. He had been sent to Paris to work out some problems in gravimetrics in order to produce more precise measurements of land masses and the shape of the earth. He was using the fine instruments of the Paris Observatory to test American measurements. Peirce's wife, Zina, had recently left him to return to America, and Peirce suffered a depressive breakdown. The Peirces would reunite only briefly, then divorce—but not before Peirce had taken up with Juliette Pourtalai, creating a scandal from which his career never recovered: though he married Juliette, news that they had cohabited before marriage caused his dismissal from Johns Hopkins University. Zina's departure may well have been caused by her husband's infidelity: it would not have been the first, and Paris offered obvious opportunities. William, one imagines, knew the elements of all this: later on, in any event, Peirce became something of a moral pariah in Cambridge. But in writing to Henry he emphasized especially that Peirce was like a "nettle" that must be grasped firmly. "I confess I like him very much in spite of his peculiarities, for he is a man of genius and there's always something in that to compel one's sympathy."

On his own in Paris, Peirce spent large amounts on dandyish clothing, fine wines, and high living—apparently money advanced to him by the Survey for business expenses: his accounts were a mess. His pleas to the Survey for more funds were in vain because he repeatedly failed to provide a return address—even telegrams from the Superintendent failed to reach him. And he was hopelessly lonely, seemingly shunned by his French colleagues, with no one but his secretary to talk to for days on end. "He is busy swinging pendulums at the Observatory and thinks himself indifferently treated by the Paris scientists," Henry wrote to William. "We meet every two or three days to dine together; but tho' we get on very well, our sympathy is economical rather than intellectual." Though James was beginning to receive invitations, he was lonely, too ("I know the Théâtre-Français by heart!" he will eventually confess to William, admitting to many an unbooked evening spent at the theater). So these two lonely American men of genius would meet over dinner in Paris. Their dialogue, unrecorded, ought to be reinvented in a play by Tom Stoppard. Peirce wrote William that Henry, while "a splendid fellow," didn't have a "philosophic" turn of mind, didn't like to "turn over questions." But Peirce read *Roderick Hudson* and declared himself an "extreme admirer" of the novel. Yet his reading of his dinner companion seems to have ended there. Years later, he queried William on his brother's subsequent career as a novelist, asking if he had fulfilled his ambitions. William in return sent him *The Golden Bowl*, with the admonition: "I hope you will be able to finish it!" William in fact detested this novel, as he did most of his brother's late production. Henry, on his side, noted in his journal a few years after the Parisian meetings: "I saw a good deal of Charles Pierce [sic?] that winter—as to whom his being a man of genius reconciled me to much that was intolerable in him."

Councils of the Gods

James had more interesting conquests to make. There was first of all the great Ivan Sergeyevich Turgenev. Admiration for the Russian novelist, whose *Sportsman's Diary* (1852) called eloquently for the abolition of serfdom, was a longstanding family affair in Quincy Street. In 1874, Henry James, Sr., wrote an unabashedly friendly—one might say a very American—fan letter to Turgenev, including this flourish: "should you ever cross the ocean, you must not fail to come to Cambridge, and sit with us on the piazza in the evening, while you tell us between the fumes of your pipe what the most exercised and penetrating genius of the old world discerns, either of promise or menace for humanity in the civilization of the new." One would indeed like to imagine this evening, with the New England wooden porch, the "piazza" (in a usage that still endures, though just barely) metamorphosed into something closer to the Italian original. To which Turgenev replied, in a letter from Karlsbad: "let me assure you, that it would make me the greatest pleasure not 'to smoke my pipe under your verandah'—I don't use tobacco—but to enjoy a quiet and pleasant conversation with the intelligent men and women of your society."

James, Sr., refers in his letter to a "tribute" recently published by his son Henry: the first of his essays on the Russian novelist, published in *North American Review* in 1874. Henry, Jr., sent it to its subject, receiving in return an amiable reply, and an invitation to call when in Paris. He in fact wrote to Turgenev almost immediately after arriving in Paris. The reply was quickly forthcoming:

> My dear Sir,
> I will be happy indeed to make your acquaintance and shall expect you Monday between 11 and 1 at my house. I hope you will find time and place convenient and beg you to accept the expression of my best feelings.
> Yours very truly,
> Iv. Tourgenieff

James enclosed this precious communication in a letter to William, and called on Turgenev on November 22, promptly at 11:00.

Turgenev lived in Paris—from which he made yearly trips back to Russia—with the actress and singer Pauline Viardot and her husband. Turgenev had fallen in love with Pauline during her concert tour in Russia, some thirty years back, and was reputed to be the father of one of her children. She, as well as the hostile reaction to his novel *Fathers and Sons* (1862) in Russia, had determined his expatriation. In Paris, the *ménage à trois* was ruled despotically by Pauline, who set the rules of visits, and imposed a 9:30 p.m. curfew. When some months later James managed, through the good offices of Paul Zhukovsky, to dine out with Turgenev and the Princess Ourousov at a restaurant near the Opéra-Comique, the Russian novelist had to leave early, to meet the curfew. James would come to recognize that Turgenev was enslaved to the Viardots, without a will of his own. He was nonetheless to James "the immortal"—and the complaints about restrictions on access to him set by the Viardots may reveal most of all a certain jealousy.

James came away from his visits to Turgenev always with a sense of high admiration for the novelist and the man. His tone is one of adoration. There is what you would call in psychoanalytic terms a transference onto the older man, who takes a place of paternal authority to James, a source of wisdom and guidance. From their first meeting, he recorded that "he is a magnificent creature, and much handsomer than his portraits. . . . He seemed very simple and kind etc; his face and shoulders are hugely broad, his stature very high, and his whole aspect and temperament of a larger and manlier kind than I have ever yet encountered in a scribbler." At the year's close, James wrote to Lizzie Boott: "he is a true, ideal genius." A month later, he wrote to Howells that Turgenev is "everything that one could desire—robust, sympathetic, modest, simple, profound, intelligent, naïf—in fine, angelic." Then to William: "he is an *amour d'homme.*" And James went on to recount proudly that Turgenev talked to him for the whole of a rainy afternoon about his novelistic practices, the ways in which he went about creating a fictional character. Then one Sunday evening he was invited to join Turgenev and the Viardots in charades. He responded with both chagrin and affection to the sight of the great man crawling around on the floor covered in shawls, acting without talent but with enthusiasm.

Here, then, was a famous novelist—a novelist with a worldwide reputation—who was kindly avuncular to James, discussed craft with him, promised to read his work, and, according to Paul Zhukovsky's report, spoke of his young admirer with a tender appreciation: "*qui alla jusqu'à l'attendrissement.*" There is an element of idealization—as in all transferences—in the young man's worshipful attitude toward the Russian twice his age. The word "adorable" recurs with somewhat startling frequency. James elects Turgenev as exemplar of what, at this point in his career, he conceives the novel to be. In the 1874 essay, he notes (in discussion of *Spring Torrents*) that Turgenev "almost invariably appeals at the outset to our distinctively *moral* curiosity, our sympathy with character." And in his final piece on Turgenev, in 1896, James returns to praise of "that sign of the born novelist which resides in a respect unconditioned for the freedom and vitality, the absoluteness when summoned, of the creatures he invokes." This capacity to "invoke" character entire, in all its freedom and vitality, becomes a major Jamesian touchstone for the kind of novelist he wants to be.

Parallels have been drawn between the Russian and the American, novelists of two countries of large vistas and yet-unfolded possibilities. "American readers of Turgénieff have been struck with certain points of resemblance between American and Russian life," James wrote in 1874. "The resemblance is generally superficial; but it does not seem to us altogether fanciful to say that Russian young girls . . . have to our sense a touch of the faintly acrid perfume of the New England temperament—a hint of Puritan angularity." Such women "mainly represent strength of will—the power to resist, to wait, to attain." These strong young women, especially in their American incarnation, will become a Jamesian theme. Even more to the point, the sense of loss and renunciation characteristic of Turgenev's hapless noblemen is not unlike the emotional and psychological world of such a Jamesian "man of imagination" as Lambert Strether, on his unfulfilled mission to Paris in *The Ambassadors*. Christopher Newman's renunciation of vengeance at the end of the novel James was now writing, *The American*, bears comparison to Lavretsky's in Turgenev's *Home of the Gentry* (1859).

Turgenev himself apparently wrote little while in Paris, held hostage to Viardot sociabilities; he devoted himself to writing on his regular visits to his Russian estates. At the time James met him, he was engaged in the protracted composition—over six years—of his final novel, *Virgin Soil*, published early in 1877. James's critics have paid curiously little attention to the close affinities between *Virgin Soil* and the novel James would undertake eight years later, *The Princess Casamassima*. Turgenev writes of Russian revolutionaries—populists, nihilists, anarchists—and their futile struggle to change a land both needing radical transformation and seemingly impervious to it. Turgenev is both sympathetic and severe in his treatment of the revolutionaries. His protagonist, Neshdanov, is of illegitimate noble birth, son of Prince G. and his daughter's governess. Neshdanov is committed to "going to the people," all the while attracted to the aesthetic and to upper-class sensibilities. He is attracted to a woman, another aristocrat turned revolutionist—but wavering in that commitment as well. The final solution to the contradictions of his existence and allegiances can only come in suicide. James's novel has all these elements, indeed its situation and plot are in many ways very close imitations of Turgenev's, and Hyacinth Robinson, would-be revolutionist in love with the Princess, shares Neshdanov's divided commitments. *The Princess Casmassima*, James's one attempt to do a socially and politically committed novel, and something of an anomaly in his work, stands among other things as a tribute to Turgenev and his sense of the possible uses of fiction.

James's future visits to Paris would always—until the Russian's death in 1883—include a call on Turgenev. Yet Turgenev's most important service to James may have been introducing the young novelist to a man he would admire far less: Gustave Flaubert. Turgenev offered James introductions to Flaubert and to George Sand—but the latter was not often in Paris; she would die the next summer, and James never met her. On December 12, 1875, however, he took James to the Faubourg Saint-Honoré, up five flights of stairs to the apartment where Flaubert—when he was in Paris rather than his permanent home in Normandy—received his friends on Sunday afternoons. Flaubert had recently left a grander apartment, in order to raise money to bail out the bankrupt husband of his niece Caroline Commanville, the nearest thing he had to a child; he would sell a farm in Normandy that summer, and describe himself as "ruined." The financial debacle put him into a state of depression in which he could do little writing—though James was not, I think, at the time aware of this.

James found Flaubert "a great, stout, handsome, simple, kindly, elderly fellow. . . . He looks like some weather beaten old military man." He presided over his gathering of literary *confrères*, James later recalled, in a "long colloquial dressing-gown," his at-home "uniform really of freedom of talk." On that first visit, James met as well: the novelist Edmond de Goncourt, the publisher Georges Charpentier, the young poet Catulle Mendès, and the leading younger novelist Émile Zola—at age thirty-five, James's nearly exact contemporary. Guy de Maupassant and Alphonse Daudet would figure in subsequent Sundays. No wonder he soon wrote to his friend Thomas Sargent Perry—in a letter mainly in French—"*Tu vois que je suis dans les conseils des dieux—que je suis lancé en plein Olympe.*" He has entered the councils of the gods; he is up on Mount Olympus. Here he was with the French confraternity at its best.

Later in life, recollection of these afternoons in the Faubourg Saint-Honoré would become "all such a golden blur of old-time Flaubertism and Goncourtism!" as he wrote to Edmund Gosse in 1912 when evoking "a fantastic tale, irreproducible here" that Maupassant told him about Swinburne, concerning "the relations between two Englishmen, each other, and their monkey!"—a story that James never does quite tell in his subsequent exchange with Gosse, but which he evokes indirectly, and at length, and which apparently concerned the suicide of "the resentful and impassioned beast," from homoerotic jealousy. If by 1912 he recalled these days with mellow indulgence, at the time his reactions were more mixed. He found Flaubert himself more compelling than his novels, which at this point in his life he admired only grudgingly, and really only in the single example of *Madame Bovary*. He was exhilarated by the free and easy range of their talk—though also bemused by it, possibly a bit shocked beneath his urbanity. He found that writers valued in Quincy Street—Victor Cherbuliez, Gustave Droz, Octave Feuillet—simply didn't exist for Flaubert's circle. Were Flaubert & Cie. right, or was this just the French spirit of *coterie*, the insistence that everyone be of a "school"? He complained of the French tendency to explore narrow and eventually blind alleys.

To Howells he wrote: "They are all charming talkers—though as editor of the austere *Atlantic* it would startle you to hear some of their projected subjects. The other day Edmond de Goncourt (the best of them) said he had been lately working very well on his novel—he had got upon an episode that greatly interested him, and into which he was going very far. *Flaubert*: "What is it?" *E. de G.*: "A whore-house *de province*." This sounds like preparation for *La Fille Elisa*, published in 1877, which James duly reviewed in the *Nation*, noting that "even readers who have flattered themselves that they knew the French mind tolerably well find that it has some surprisingly unpleasant corners. . . . M. de Goncourt's fault is not that he is serious or historical or scientific or instructive, but that he is intolerably unclean." It's not easy to know how to take James's "shocked" reactions. He writes in an essay published in *Lippincott's Magazine* in 1877 that French literature can resemble "little vases, skilfully moulded and chiselled, into which unclean things have been dropped." Many of his public reactions to the "immoralities" of French literature sound similarly prissy. In contrast, his brother William was, for instance, far more willing to find Baudelaire and *Les Fleurs du mal* interesting, innocent, and unfairly prosecuted by the Second Empire. William commented on Baudelaire in a letter to the *Nation* in October 1875, and in December he wrote to Henry: "B. is really in his fleurs du mal original & in a certain sense elevated, & on the whole I can bear no rancor against him, altho at times he writes like a person half awake & groping for words. The most amusing thing about it all is the impression one gets of the innocence of a generation in wh. the fleurs du mal should have made a *scandal*. It is a mild & spiritualistic book to day." Henry exonerates Baudelaire of the charge of immorality but nonetheless writes, in his own contribution to the *Nation* in April 1876: "He tried to make fine verses on ignoble subjects, and in our opinion he signally failed."

One senses that James is more than a little stimulated by the presence of sexuality in private conversation, whereas in public he must exercise a certain censoriousness. He will over time work out his own compromise-formation, in which repressed sexuality very much marks the fragile cover holding it down. He reports to William that Turgenev has told him that Flaubert's problem was "that he has never known a decent woman—or even a woman who was a little interesting." This rather too conveniently explains what's wrong with Emma Bovary, for instance. Turgenev appears to assume that Flaubert's only women were whores, "*des courtisanes et des rien-du-tout*." Apparently he did not at the time know about Flaubert's protracted affair with Louise Colet—long since over—though from the way Flaubert treated Louise Colet one may doubt that Turgenev's opinion would have been much altered. In any event, James uses Turgenev's comment to see Flaubert as "almost tragic," all intellect and no passion. "So much talent, and so much naiveté and honesty, and yet so much dryness and coldness." The imputation of naiveté is a fairly audacious move on the part of the thirty-two-year-old American provincial toward the fifty-five-year-old French literary lion. It is perhaps James's way of reasserting Quincy Street values in the Faubourg Saint-Honoré.

In a letter to Alice two weeks later, he claimed that it made him sick to hear Turgenev seriously discussing Daudet's recently published novel *Jack* with Flaubert, so unworthy a subject does that novel seem to James. At this point in the letter, James draws a dash—and jumps to the query: "Of course you have read *Daniel Deronda*, and I hope you have enjoyed it a tenth as much as I." He goes on to mention the defects of this final novel of George Eliot's, but then adds: "But I enjoyed it more than anything of hers—or any other novelist's almost—I have ever read. Partly for reading it in this beastly Paris, and realizing the superiority of English culture and the English mind to the French. The English richness of George Eliot beggars everything else, everywhere, that one might compare with her."

This is curious, and characteristic: conversation in the Paris literary Olympus suddenly produces a reaction, in the form of a declaration of allegiance to George Eliot and *Daniel Deronda*. Eliot's remarkably ambitious novel—it would be her last—had just begun its serial publication in *Blackwood's Magazine*. James offered an assessment of its early chapters in the *Nation* on February 24, noting in particular (picking up a phrase from the novel itself) Eliot's "sense of the universal": "It strikes us sometimes perhaps as rather conscious and over-cultivated; but it gives us the feeling that the threads of the narrative, as we gather them into our hands, are not of the usual commercial measurement, but long electric wires capable of transmitting messages from mysterious regions." Though James would later criticize the completed book rather severely, he also seemed to believe it—quite rightly, in my view—one of the summits of the novel. References to *Daniel Deronda* will punctuate James's correspondence over the coming months—the novel is a kind of touchstone, a reference to a richness of concern with the place of character and ethical choice, in the novel as in life, that he holds up against what French culture presents him—which is all too sadly lacking in "the messages from mysterious regions." One might say he uses Eliot as an antidote to the French: an assertion of his need to find a way to profit from the lesson of Flaubert and his circle without entirely giving in to their view of humanity, and of what the novel is, and is for.

There was a memorable weekday afternoon, also, when James found Flaubert alone. In his account to his father, James balances his increasing personal affection for Flaubert with the rather uppity judgment: "I think I easily—more than easily—see all round him intellectually." They talked of poetry, and of Flaubert's late friend Théophile Gautier, whom Flaubert found the quintessential French poet—irreproducible in any other language. He read James some of Gautier's poems, his voice sonorous, melancholic, making them seem on the spot "the most beautiful things in the world." James would long remember and evoke this afternoon as a moment of privileged communion with the older writer. And we shall want to come back to James's relation to Flaubert since it lies at the heart of his reaction to French modernism and his own maturing understanding of the forms and uses of fiction.

Meanwhile, there were the letters to the *Tribune* to get on with. James was ruefully aware that he wasn't quite producing what Whitelaw Reid, publisher of the *Tribune*, had in mind—though with characteristic pride he later described himself as having been sacked by the *Tribune* for producing letters that were too good, not vulgar enough. What was wanted, he sensed, was something a bit gossipy, about Parisian life and fashion and personalities, and the amusing misadventures of Americans in French society—the kind of stuff that provides the cultural confrontation dramatized in high style in James's novel of 1887, *The Reverberator*. Instead, James gives his readers a good deal on French politics, even more descriptions of Parisian places, including a day-trip to Chartres cathedral, reports on the theater, music, and art.

The new Opéra proved a worthy subject for some pages in James's first letter. The Palais Garnier, as it later became known from the name of its architect, Charles Garnier, thoroughly incarnated, as James recognized, the wealth, glory, and pretension of the Second Empire at its apogee. Begun in 1861, the building was not quite finished at the time of Napoleon III's fall, and the fall of the empire with him. It received its finishing touches as France recovered from war and insurrection, and opened on January 1, 1875. To James, the building "resumes in visible, sensible shape what the Empire proposed to itself to be, and it forms a kind of symbol—a very favorable one—of the Empire's legacy to France." He had known that "shining second Empire" as a youthful visitor to Paris; he remembered his view from the balcony of the Hôtel des Trois Empereurs, in the rue de Rivoli, as he looked down at the Palais-Royal and the newly completed wing of the Louvre, with statues of Napoleon's marshals. He was aware of being witness to "a glittering régime," which meant "something that would probably never be meant quite to any such tune again." The empire was self-conscious glory.

But he goes on, in the *Tribune* letter, to hedge a bit his judgment of the Opéra, finding the building "not beautiful" but rather "superbly characteristic . . . it tells the story of the society that produced it. If this, as some people think, is the prime duty of a great building, the Opera is an incomparable success." Surely James is right about the ways in which the Palais Garnier "tells the story" of the empire, of its aspirations to cultural capital, of its massive public expenditure on public works—the Paris we know today is still largely a product of Second Empire urbanism—and its taste for gilt and ornament. "Reasonably viewed," James says of the auditorium of the Opéra, "it is superb and uninteresting. It is nothing but gold—gold upon gold; it has been gilded until it is dark with gold." The whole interior eventually, in James's description, becomes "a trifle vulgar," yet valuable as an assertion of French *gloire*. "If France is down in the world just now, there is something fine in seeing her make her protest, recover her balance, where and how she can."

James reports that during carnival, in March, he went to the masked ball at the Opéra—the first time the new house had been used for this famous affair, which promiscuously mixed social classes, and particularly women of the proper and improper variety, in a momentary world turned upside down. It is a moment brilliantly captured in Edouard Manet's painting of 1873, set in the old Opéra. Karl Baedeker's advice to the traveller may illuminate the image: the balls "present a scene of the most unbridled and boisterous merriment and excitement, and where ladies are of the party should be witnessed by strangers from the boxes only. The female frequenters of the balls always wear masks or dominoes, the men are generally in evening costume." It is a setting in which one may be surprised to find James, even if he does pass it off as the conscientious visit of the reporter on French manners. He did not dance—though the orchestra was conducted by Johann Strauss himself. He must have been like one of those evening-dressed gentlemen in the Manet painting, looking on.

In closing his descriptive discussion of the Opéra, James mentions "the great series of frescoes by M. Baudry," way up on a ceiling barely visible through "the dusky glow of gas and gilding." Praise for Paul Baudry may take the appreciation of the characteristic nature of the

Opéra a bit too far: in our view today, Baudry seems one of the most egregious of the salon artists of the time, who produced work best appreciated as kitsch—the very kind of thing that Manet and the new "painters of modern life" had to react against. Here we come to a crucial issue in understanding James in Paris at a time we now conceive as the very crucible of the modern—in literature, in music, and especially in painting. Flaubert, for instance, had been working through the summer (Caroline's husband's bankruptcy had played havoc with his ability to work that winter) on the unfinished novel published only posthumously, *Bouvard et Pécuchet*. That peculiar novel must, as we shall see, be accounted the most radical work of its time.

James, on the other hand, was now well into writing *The American*, which appears to come straight out of Balzac. At this moment in time, the aging Flaubert—he had only four more years to live—appears to be defining the lineaments of a modernism to come; whereas the young American is still content with more traditional forms. Though that is perhaps not quite right: James over and over again accurately skewers the tired and conventional in literature, most of all in the theater: Alexandre Dumas, Victorien Sardou, and other masters of the well-made but trivial drama; and also Victor Hugo's high-flown political rhetoric: "France occasionally produces individuals who express the national conceit with a transcendent fatuity which is not elsewhere to be matched." What James hasn't yet found is what to put in their place. He would himself become one of the chief modernist pioneers in fiction—but only later, only after negotiating the lessons of Flaubert in original ways, and without ever wholly sacrificing the lessons of Balzac, and George Eliot. James's year in Paris seems to be all about missing things on the spot—but somehow storing them away for later retrieval and reinterpretation.

His comments on painting are instructive in this regard. James had for some time been writing "art criticism." His discussion of painting and sculpture originally falls within his travel writing: reports on what he has seen in Italy and elsewhere, and it tends to remain a kind of descriptive evocation of things viewed rather than something more analytic. He also did occasional reviews of art exhibits. One doesn't sense that he has any principles to support his tastes, his likes and dislikes—

but then, art criticism was only emerging from infancy at the time. In Paris, James wrote about a large number of works of art, mainly in his *Tribune* letters. There was in December the retrospective exhibit of the animal sculptures of Louis Barye, who had just died at age 79. Barye was at this time such a favorite of American collectors that James could not fail to report on the retrospective. In fact, his implication that a taste for Barye could be considered "enterprising" rather than "refined" elicited a letter of protest in the *Tribune*'s columns. The death of Jean-Baptiste Carpeaux led to the display of reproductions of his work all over Paris: "the most modern things in all sculpture." Like much of the French public at the time Carpeaux's *La Danse* was unveiled at the Opéra, for which it was commissioned, James was made somewhat uncomfortable by the "undressed" figures of Carpeaux—as opposed to "the unconsciously naked heroes and heroines of Greek sculpture." They seemed to need covering up. "In this vicious winter weather of Paris, behind their clear glass plates, they make the passer shiver; their poor, lean, individualized bodies are pitifully real."

Then there were several pages of his January 22 letter devoted to Ernest Meissonier's painting *1807*, exhibited before its planned departure for New York, where it had been purchased for the sum of 380,000 francs (about $76,000) by Alexander Stewart, a dry goods merchant then considered the wealthiest man in the United States. This depiction of French victory at the battle of Friedland in 1807—one of Meissonier's many Napoleonic canvases—eventually found its way into the Metropolitan Museum. James runs on in detailed description of the painting—and Meissonier's work is indeed all about detail—but has the good taste to think it hardly worth such a princely sum. He contrasts Meissonier to Millet and Delacroix, touchstones of a more ambitious kind of painting. Another Stewart purchase, Jean-Léon Gérôme's *Chariot Race*, merits a description in James's April 1 letter, but again James shows a properly tempered appreciation for this master of the simulacrum. More reviews of exhibits follow, with comments on such as Gabriel Decamps and Prosper Marilhat—early "Orientalists"—and Giovanni Boldini, in whom James recognizes a new talent.

Then in May came the annual Salon, to which James devoted two full letters in the *Tribune* (this was no doubt becoming rather too

high-toned for what was supposed to be a gossip column). With the Salon, James obviously had to work with what was there, and we should
not fault him for going on about artists now largely forgotten. The Sa-
lons of these years are after all largely remembered for the artists they excluded, rather than for the thousands of paintings—there were 2,095 in
1876—hung, row over row, in the Palais de l'Industrie. James is often
witty and arch in describing what he finds: "there is an immense Jeanne
d'Arc by M. Monchablon, bounding over agglomerated corpses, brandishing her sword and heroically screaming . . ." He dutifully describes Joseph-Noël Sylvestre's *Locusta Trying the Effects of Poisons
Before Nero*—one of those immense academic history paintings that
were trying to make up for the lifelessness of the genre through their
blood-curdling content—while recognizing that "M. Sylvestre is not a
painter who sets you dreaming about his future." What he selects as
the most popular painting in the Salon is Edouard Detaille's *En
Reconnaissance*—one of that painter's many canvases on the Franco-
Prussian War, five years back. It is a work "of which nothing but good
is to be said." Then there are a number of descriptions of work in
portraiture, by such as Jules Bastien-Lepage, Carolus Duran, William
Bouguereau, Alexandre Cabanel, Paul Baudry. James is properly
appreciative—and after all these were artists who were beginning to
figure in the collections of rich American industrialists, readers of the
Tribune—yet also without real enthusiasm. His taste for Delacroix and
Millet, and especially his hours spent looking at Italian masters, keep
him from overpraising this Salon art.

   The problem—problem, that is, for us—is that James also attended
two other exhibits, one just before and the other just after the official
Salon. The first was the show at Durand-Ruel's of the Independents—
those artists who following their first exhibit, two years earlier, had
been dubbed, on the basis of Claude Monet's *Impression: soleil levant*,
the "impressionists." This was, then, the second of the notorious Impressionist exhibits—exhibits that in our perspective changed the
course of art irrevocably, exhibits that we look back to with a certain
reverence, as a glimpse into the very crucible of the modern. And
James simply missed the point, completely. The "effect" of the exhibit,
he wrote, "was to make me think better than ever of all the good old

rules which decree that beauty is beauty and ugliness ugliness, and warn us off from the sophistications of satiety." He went on: "The young contributors to the exhibition of which I speak are partisans of unadorned reality and absolute foes to arrangement, embellishment, selection, to the artist's allowing himself, as he has hitherto, since art began, found his best account in doing, to be preoccupied with the ideal of the beautiful." Then, in a sentence that resonates curiously against his brother's elaboration of Pragmatism, he accused them of considering the beautiful as Positivists do the supernatural, "a metaphysical notion, which can only get one into a muddle and is to be severely let alone."

James understands that these painters are interested in "the actual" (Zola at the time often referred to them as *actualistes*), "to give a vivid impression of how a thing happens to look, at a particular moment." Here he finds similarities to the English Pre-Raphaelites; "but this little band is on all grounds less interesting than the group out of which Millais and Holman Hunt rose into fame. None of its members show signs of possessing first-rate talent, and indeed the 'Impressionist' doctrines strike me as incompatible, in an artist's mind, with the existence of first-rate talent." Such is James's report on his encounter with Monet, Renoir, Degas, Morisot.

James's misestimation of the new art of his time is striking. We think of James as an artistic innovator, an experimenter in techniques of seeing and telling, one whose own manner came in many ways to resemble that of an impressionist, even a *pointilliste*. Something of what motivates his judgments comes forward as he continues his parallel to the Pre-Raphaelites. While breaking the canons of beauty and going in for "hard truth and stern fact," the English artists tried to make up for their innovations "by an exquisite, patient, virtuous manipulation—by being above all things laborious. But the Impressionists, who, I think, are more consistent, abjure virtue altogether, and declare that a subject which has been crudely chosen shall be loosely treated." That odd word "manipulation"—which I think needs to be read with an etymological emphasis: the patient, careful work of the hand—may give a clue to what's wrong with impressionism in James's eye of 1876. The problem has to do with representation. That is, it has to do with the use of signs, written or pictorial, that stand for and give a picture of the world. How one understands representation will turn out to be a deep source of misunderstanding not only between James and the impressionists, but as well between James and Flaubert, and I'll come back to it.

James in June also visited the Salon des Refusés—the exhibit of those refused entry to the Salon—but gave it only a few lines, since he found it a "melancholy collection," and singled out for praise only the American landscapist James Fairman. James would eventually, belatedly, come to revise these views: in 1904, he will speak of the Hill-Stead collection in Farmington, Connecticut, as containing "wondrous examples of Manet, Degas, of Claude Monet, of Whistler, of other rare recent hands . . . it was like the sudden trill of the nightingale." But to appreciate these masters in 1904 was hardly avant-garde. Virginia Woolf notably tells us that James visited the Post-Impressionist Exhibition held at the Grafton Galleries, London, in 1912—including the work of Gauguin, Seurat, Cézanne, Matisse, Rouault, Picasso— and that curator and critic (and painter) Roger Fry took him to the basement for tea, over which James expressed "the disturbed hesitations which Matisse and Picasso aroused in him," while Fry attempted to explain "that Cézanne and Flaubert were, in a manner of speaking, after the same thing." Woolf and Fry cut to the quick here: Cézanne and Flaubert are indeed in many ways "after the same thing," preoccupied by a renewed attention to perspectivism, and James is troubled by both of them—yet surely also, well before 1912, deeply immersed in his own perspectival experiments that owe much to the troubling predecessors he originally rejected.

James's musical tastes in 1876 were no more adventurous than his painterly ones. In late spring, the Salle Ventadour presented a brilliant short season of Italian opera, including Verdi's *Aïda* and his *Requiem*. *Aïda* was then five years old—it premiered at the Cairo Opera in 1871—and James heard it with Verdi's favorite singers: the soprano Rosine Stoltz, mezzo Maria Waldmann, baritone Paolo Medini, and tenor Angelo Masini. It was a "feast of vocalism," according to James, but he professed not to have "enjoyed very profusely the somewhat obstreperous (from the Italian point of view exotic) music of *Aïda*."

"Obstreperous" may be a good word for the brassy and plangent score of the opera, but it may also suggest James's liking for a more familiar, more traditional kind of music. He liked the *Requiem* better, "the more so that Signor Verdi himself stood there, conducting the orchestra with a certain passionate manner." The *Requiem* was quite recent work, composed for the funeral, in 1874, of novelist and poet Alessandro Manzoni—himself a kind of Italian national monument by the time of his death. James makes no mention of Manzoni, yet he must have known his great historical novel *I Promessi Sposi* (*The Betrothed*), given his extended forays into Italian culture. The Paris evening on which Manzoni, Verdi, and James connected—if only in our retrospective imagination—deserves a passing salute.

James was also subjected to musical soirées, at the Viardots and elsewhere. Madame Viardot's "musical parties are rigidly musical and to me, therefore, rigidly boresome, especially as she herself sings very little," he wrote to his father. "I stood the other night on my legs for three hours (from 11 to 2) in a suffocating room, listening to an interminable fiddling, with the only consolation that Gustave Doré, standing beside me, seemed as bored as myself." Some months later, in the fall, at Paul Zhukovsky's, from 9 to 2 a.m., "A young French pianist of great talent played to a small Russian circle a lot of selections from Wagner's Bayreuth operas. I was bored, but the rest were in ecstasy." This exclusive soirée followed the summer that saw the inauguration of Wagner's Bayreuth Festspielhaus, and Zhukovsky, later to become Wagner's favorite set designer, had been one of the passionate pilgrims to that place of worship. The "Bayreuth operas" must have been the four operas of *The Ring*, given its first full performance at Bayreuth in 1876, which at the time represented the absolute avant-garde of European music, and a place of artistic pilgrimage both intense and fashionable. James seems to have greeted *The Ring* with indifference.

James's reports from Paris were punctuated by news of deaths of the famous—collectively, a substantial representation of an earlier generation tied to romanticism. He noted the death of Comtesse Marie d'Agoult—who had notoriously, scandalously eloped with Franz Liszt decades before, and then become famous, under the pen name Daniel Stern, with her history of the Revolution of 1848—and Louise Colet, whose loves included the philosopher Victor Cousin, the poet Alfred de Musset, and, especially, Flaubert. Then there was the funeral of Jules Michelet, the great romantic historian—who had died the year before, but was exhumed from his grave in Hyères to be more suitably interred in Paris—to fears that the funeral would (as funerals so often had in the past) become the occasion of political disturbances, even an uprising. But the event went off without incident. In February came the death of Frédéric Lemaître, the extraordinary actor who made melodrama into a grand art, brought it onto the legitimate stage with his performances of Alexandre Dumas (the elder) and Victor Hugo's "romantic drama" and created a kind of legend of himself—one that may be most familiar to us from Marcel Carné's film, *Les Enfants du paradis*. James revealed his own allegiance to a certain melodramatic romantic theatricality, such as he appreciated in Balzac, in his tribute to Lemaître: "The theater of our own day, with its relish for small, realistic effects, produces no more actors of those heroic proportions. . . . Frédéric Lemaître, as we see him in his *légende*, is like a huge, fantastic shadow, a moving silhouette, projected duskily against the wall from a glowing fire. The fire is the 'romantic' movement of 1830." When, close to two decades later, James made his ill-fated attempt to become a playwright, one of his problems was that he was obliged to work for a London stage of small and vulgar effects rather than the romantic theater. The Jamesian nostalgia for romanticism corresponds to a continuing need, in his imagination, for the grandiose and significant gesture.

The literary death recorded at greatest length in James's *Tribune* letters was that of George Sand, whom he had hoped to meet through Flaubert. James's tribute to her is generous, if nuanced by the sense that her love life is not a matter for Anglo-Saxon approval. But he is impressed by her professionalism—he recalls her lover Prosper Mérimée's appalled reaction when she arose from bed early in the morning to light the fire herself, and get on with her writing. "She was an *improvisatrice*, raised to a very high power; she told stories as a nightingale sings. No novelist answers so well to the childish formula of 'making up as you go along.'" This is tempered praise, especially when you add to it his stricture that her novels lack certain qualities that "the realistic novel of the last thirty or forty years" has made indispensable. Her novels "are not exact nor probable; they contain few living figures; they produce a limited amount of illusion." For all that, he salutes her, in words he quotes from Renan, as "the Aeolian harp of our time." A certain romantic image of the writer again predominates. James returned to Sand in an essay for the *Galaxy* a year later, to affirm that she "has the advantage that she has portrayed a *passion*," as more virtuous Anglo-Saxon novelists have not. He continued: "few persons would resort to English prose fiction for any information concerning the ardent forces of the heart—for any ideas upon them. It is George Sand's merit that she has given us ideas upon them." Curiously, it is precisely that which makes the Anglo-Saxon reader most uncomfortable that James declares to be Sand's main claim on our attention. Those "ardent forces of the heart," however disguised or closeted, matter to him.

His visits to Flaubert's Sunday afternoons continued, until Flaubert returned to his Norman home in Croisset, near Rouen, in May. But one senses his growing restiveness at a circle that prizes only its own works, won't speak of others—and where no one reads English fiction, not even George Eliot. He wrote to Thomas Sergeant Perry that he has heard Zola characterize Gustave Droz—one of those Quincy Street favorites—as *merde à la vanille*, sweetened shit, one might say. Then he added: "I send you by post Zola's own last—*merde au naturel*. Simply hideous." "Zola's last" is the novel *Son Excellence Eugène Rougon*, published in February, which James mentions also in his *Tribune* letter of May 13, noting that it has had a success "owing partly to its cleverness, partly to the fact that it is a presentation, through a transparent veil, of actual persons, and chiefly, I suspect, to its brutal indecency." Zola's novel on the political caste of the Second Empire no doubt is based on a number of real figures—Eugène Rouher, the Duc de Morny—from Napoleon III's reign. It is indeed brutal, not for "indecency," but for the deeply cynical picture of politics it gives. One senses that Zola himself is depressed by his subject in *Son Excellence Eugène Rougon*, and it does not seem to me one of his most successful novels, despite the rather sensational heroine, Clorinda Balbi (fictional version of the Countess Castiglione), who sleeps her way to the very top, into the emperor's bed. James explains Zola to his American readers as "a 'pupil' of Gustave Flaubert" and "the most thoroughgoing of the little band of the out-and-out realists. Unfortunately the real, for him, means exclusively the unclean, and he utters his crudities with an air of bravado which makes them doubly intolerable."

This is prissy and priggish. Since the published judgment is backed up by the "simply hideous" in his private letter to Perry, one has to take it as James's genuine reaction, not simply a concession to American Puritanism. Zola shocks him—but he was of course not alone in this reaction at the time, and for long after: in 1888, Zola's English publisher was fined, imprisoned, and enjoined from printing further of the novelist's works. A few weeks after the letter to Perry, James recounted to Howells his last visit to Flaubert—on Flaubert's last Sunday in Paris—and the circle's talk of Zola's "catastrophe": the suspension during its serial publication of a new novel, on account of protests from provincial subscribers against its indecency. The novel in question was *L'Assommoir*, which began its serial publication on April 13, in the weekly *Le Bien Public*; after its suspension it would eventually be picked up and continued by *La République des Lettres*. As Flaubert and friends predicted, the scandal surrounding it only assured its immense success: it was the novel that made Zola the highest-profile writer of the time. On his way down the five flights from Flaubert's apartment, James met Zola coming up the staircase, "looking very pale and sombre, and I saluted him with the flourish natural to a contributor who has just been invited to make his novel last longer yet." Howells, that is, had invited James to make *The American* of a length to run for twelve installments in the *Atlantic*. James senses himself launched as a professional writer, greeting Zola as *confrère*—though *The American* and *L'Assommoir* scarcely appear to belong to the same universe.

James would later come to appreciate *L'Assommoir* as one of Zola's three masterpieces—with *Germinal* and *La Débâcle* as the other two. (And he would report with a certain tenderness that he, aged thirteen, was himself part of the crowd in a scene described at length in *Son Excellence Eugène Rougon*, the christening of the Imperial Prince: he had, as it were, figured in a Zola novel.) But appreciation of Zola took time, and took work. Four years after the encounter on Flaubert's staircase, James complained about the "monstrous uncleanness" of *Nana* in a review of that novel, while at the same time conceding that the English novel is constricted by its need to be wholesome "for virgins and boys": "Half of life is a sealed book to young unmarried ladies, and how can a novel be worth anything that deals only with half of life?" In his long later essay on Zola, in 1903, he attempted to raise the problem of Zola's "indecency" to a higher plane of debate, arguing that Zola lacked the discriminating principle of taste; that with such a subject as the alcohol-driven proletarians of *L'Assommoir*, this made no difference; but that it otherwise limited Zola's reach and penetration. James ultimately sees Zola as a powerful but limited novelist, restricted to the gross, the crowd, the physiological, incapable of exploring complexity of human motive and character. There is a good deal of truth in James's strictures, so long as you accept his definition of what novels are supposed to be and accomplish. One can't help feeling, though, that his elaboration of discrimination and taste are reared on the basis of a Quincy Street reaction to open discourse of whores and gutters. As James matures into his later fiction, which often is obsessed with sexuality and exploitative sexual relations, he has to hide such subjects in order to come upon them obliquely, spyingly. They are closeted, the door only barely ajar.

Paul Zhukovsky

By April, James's letters breathe a deep contentment with his life, while nonetheless suggesting some lingering loneliness. To Howells he wrote, "What shall I tell you? My windows are open, the spring is becoming serious, and the soft hum of this good old Paris comes into my sunny rooms, whence, thro' an open door, I see my porter, the virtuous Adrien, making up my bed in an alcove of voluminous blue chintz. I like Paris, I like alcoves, I like even porters—abhorred race as they generally are. In these simple likings my life flows gently on. I see a good many people, but no one intimately." Through opened windows, he later recalled, came "the particular light Parisian click of the small cab-horse on the clear asphalt," itself part of "the great Paris harmony." As the spring went on, evening entertainment improved somewhat. On May 29 he wrote his father that he was going to a "grand fête at the Ministry of Public Instruction . . . where half the artiste [*sic*] of the opera and the Comédie Française are to recite and sing." And to his increasing Parisian sociability was added a number of visiting Americans, including Francis Boott and his daughter Lizzie, aspiring painter whom her father had brought to Paris to study in the studio of Thomas Couture, a leading academic painter, best known for his vast and rather artificial *Les Romains de la décadence*—taken to be a discreet satire of manners and morals under the Second Empire—and for a time the teacher of Édouard Manet. Somewhere in the background of James's Paris there was always the American set, added to and subtracted from by comings and goings. American wealth, and the seemingly inveterate attraction Paris has held for Americans over the ages, assured a constant renewal of the set. James gives an amusing and considerably satiric portrayal of some representatives of the set in his novel *The Reverberator*. The Bootts were soon "in Paradise," in a delightful villa with a large garden, "with Ernest Longfellow and lady as fellow-seraphs." James adopted the aphorism attributed to the Bostonian Thomas Appleton: "Good Americans, when they die, go to Paris."

The arrival of the Bootts prompted James to arrange "a modest repast," a dinner party to which he invited Paul Zhukovsky, who found Boott "*extrêmement sympathique*," looking like a Titian; and the dinner revealed that Lizzie, among her other "unsuspected accomplishments," had "a complete mastery of the French tongue." The friendship with Zhukovsky was by this point becoming something real and important in James's life. He first mentioned Pavel Vasilievich Zhukovsky (he always used the French transliteration: Paul Joukovsky) in a letter to William on April 25. He had met him through the family of Madame Nikolai Turgenev (distant relative to Ivan), which he described as "of a literally more than Bostonian virtue. They are an oasis of purity and goodness in the midst of this Parisian Babylon." He had just, as I mentioned earlier, been talking about Henrietta Reubell, the Parisianized American with a fortune who would make a very good choice if he wanted to marry—"But I don't—*j'en suis à 1000 lieues*." Then came the mention of Zhukovsky: "He was brought up at court as an orphan by the present Empress (wife of Nicholas), his father having been tutor of the present Emperor; so you see that I don't love beneath my station." The announcement of his friendship for Zhukovsky has a warmth, sustained throughout his letters from Paris, that makes William dutifully ask to have the young Russian's portrait.

Zhukovsky clearly bathed in a certain glamour. He had been the pet of the Russian court, where his father, Vasilij Andreevich Zhukovsky—an important poet and translator, and a friend of Goethe's—had tutored the Tsarevich; he had lived in Venetian palaces; he had a large Paris studio and apartment full of Italian objets d'art and "drawings (awful) by Goethe," James noted in a letter to his mother. James went on to call him "one of the flowers of civilization." Although Zhukovsky, aged thirty-one, had two paintings accepted in the Salon of 1876, James judges—on what grounds he does not say—that he "will never be anything but a rather curious and delicate dilettante." He was also, as an avant-garde aesthete should be, a passionate Wagnerian, and spent the summer of 1876 in Bayreuth, for the premiere of *The Ring*. Two weeks later James reiterated to Alice that Zhukovsky, "for whom I entertain a most tender affection," is "one of the pure flowers of civilization and Ivan Sergéitch says of him—'*C'est l'épicurien le plus naïf que j'aie recontré.*' (I. S. likes him extremely.)." James continued in his letter to Alice (to whom he often reported his more intimate concerns) that his new Russian friend is "the most—or one of the most—refined specimens of human nature that I have ever known," then describes him as characterized by "a considerable *dévergondage* of imagination and an extreme purity of life . . . he is much to my taste and we have sworn an eternal friendship."

Debauchery of the imagination along with purity of life? One could question both of these terms, and why James chooses them to describe this aesthete and bachelor. Is this how he wishes Zhukovsky to be, and to remain? One should probably not overinterpret James's word "love" in the letter to William: it ostensibly represents the kind of idealized male friendship that was taken for granted in their culture. Yet the way Zhukovsky is presented—after the strange business about Henrietta Reubell as a good marriage match, "If I wanted to desire to marry" (strange phrase), which he emphatically doesn't, a decision then glossed by a slide into French (*"j'en suis à 1000 lieues"*), then the presentation of the Nikolai Turgenev milieu, where he met Zhukovsky, as of a Boston virtue—does make one wonder. One James biographer, Sheldon Novick, insists that James and Zhukovsky were lovers. His evidence, though, is truly non-existent, and his use of passages from the novel *Confidence*, published in 1879, that ostensibly describe a heterosexual love as reflections of James's feeling about his male friend, offers an abuse of interpretation.

Still, one senses that there is real passion here, and that "love" for Zhukovsky hovers in a more-than-platonic realm—that the erotic, however censored, is very much part of it, consummated or not. James is so good at covering his tracks—not only in relation to Zhukovsky: throughout his life—that it becomes impossible, barring further evidence, to catch him in the act. Since he is generally so careful to cover his tracks—as he will do, later, in his close relation to Constance Fenimore Woolson—one might suppose that talking about Zhukovsky as much as he does is a negative sign of a physical erotic relationship. If they had been lovers, Zhukovsky's name would probably have been more severely censored from James's correspondence. Yet perhaps his own understandings of his feelings about Zhukovsky were unclear enough at this point that he saw no need to hide them.

In his retrospective musings to himself in the journal he began to write on a marble-topped table in his room at the Hotel Brunswick, Boston, in November 1881, James looked back on his year in Paris. He noted: "In the spring, at Madame Turgénieff's, I made the acquaintance of Paul Joukovsky. *Non ragionam di lui—ma guarda e passa.*" The line from Dante dismisses Zhukovsky as a subject unworthy of attention—perhaps because too painful. Certainly it appears a strange recording of what seems to have been his closest Parisian friendship, the one in which he had invested the greatest affect. The dismissal comes into clearer focus by way of an incident from the summer of 1880, when James, then in Florence, accepted Zhukovsky's invitation to join him in Naples. He spent three days with him at Posilippo, a place of great beauty on the bay of Naples.

James found his friend—Herr von Joukowsky to the Germans—wholly absorbed into the Wagner entourage, a famously "immoral" group that flaunted its liberation from conventional behavior. The visit was not a success. James refused Zhukovsky's proposal to introduce him to Wagner, pretexting that "Wagner speaks no French and I no German." (Wagner did speak some French, from his extended stays in Paris.) He explained in a letter to Alice that Zhukovsky has decided to go live at Bayreuth "*afin de prendre part au grand oeuvre*"—specifically, to paint sets for Wagner's operas. James shows no sympathy for the great work, and declares that Zhukovsky's plan will "probably last about six months." He is "the same impracticable and indeed ridiculous mixture of Nihilism and bric à brac as before." James judges: "He is always under somebody's influence: first (since I have known him) under Turgénieff's, then under the Princess Ourousoff's, whom he now detests, and who despises him, then under H.J.Jr. (!!) then under that of a certain disagreeable Onéguin (the original of Turgenieff's Neshdanoff, in *Virgin Soil*), now under that of Wagner, and apparently in the near future under that of Mme W., who is the daughter of the Abbé Liszt and Daniel Stern (Mme d'Agoult) and the divorced wife of von Bülow, the pianist." To Grace Norton he wrote of the "manners and customs" of Zhukovsky's set: "They are about as opposed to those of Cambridge as anything could well be—but to describe them would carry me too far."

The letter to Alice has the spite and the slight hysteria of a disillusioned lover. James's predictions about Zhukovsky's lack of sustained commitment to Wagner proved wholly unfounded: the Russian continued an intimate of the composer (who chose to describe him as his son by his first marriage) and designed the sets for Wagner's final opera, *Parsifal*, which premiered in Bayreuth in 1882. His set for the Grail Temple—modelled after the cathedral of Siena, which he and Wagner had visited together in that summer of 1880—was such a marvel it endured at Bayreuth until 1934, and the Metropolitan Opera set still today clearly takes its inspiration from the design. After the *Parsifal* triumph, Wagner wanted Zhukovsky to do scenic sketches for all his earlier operas, to establish a canonical Bayreuth presentation. This project was never undertaken: Wagner died in February 1883. Zhukovsky made the last drawings of the *Meister*, and was with him at the end.

It is impossible to say exactly what led James to leave Posilippo after only three days, and to go off, alone, to Sorrento. It may have been jealousy that Zhukovsky no longer was under the "influence" of "H.J.Jr. (!!)." But we do know from Cosima Wagner's *Diaries* that Zhukovsky now had living with him a young Neapolitan man—"sturdy, thickset, simple and proud," in Cosima's words—sometimes described as a servant, sometimes as an adopted son. There was no doubt in the Wagners' minds that Zhukovsky and Peppino were lovers: Cosima reports a conversation on the subject, in which Richard said to her: "It is something for which I have understanding, but no inclination. In any case, with all relationships, what matters most is what we ourselves put into them. It is all illusion." Wagner sounds strangely Jamesian at this point. And James would curiously create in *The Sacred Fount* an image of the storyteller who ends up comparing himself to mad King Ludwig of Bavaria watching *Parsifal* in private performance: "the exclusive king with his Wagner opera."

One can only speculate, but to me it seems likely that the overt homosexual relationship with Peppino revealed to James something about his own feelings for Zhukovsky that he did not want to recognize. Surely it is significant that James makes no mention of the presence of Peppino at Posilippo, either in his letters or in his notebooks. While James makes much of the Wagnerian influence on Zhukovsky, the liaison with Peppino seems a more plausible cause of James's discomfort and early departure. We seem in any event to have come upon a crucial moment in James's affective life during the Paris stay, one that he later feels the need both to recall and to deny. *Non ragionam di lui*— the Dantean original says *di lor*, the plural: them; James changes it to the singular: him—*ma guarda e passa*. The line comes in Virgil's response to the pilgrim Dante's query about the crowd wailing at the gates of hell: the crowd of the "neutrals," those who lived worthless lives, worthy neither of praise nor of blame.

> Fama di loro il mondo esser non lassa;
> 　misericordia e giustizia li sdegna:
> 　non ragionam di lor, ma guarda e passa.　(*Inferno* III, 49–51)

("The world suffers no report of them to live. Pity and justice despise them. Let us not talk of them; but look thou and pass.") This is a harsh dismissal of someone once loved and prized.

That James was "in love" with Zhukovsky in Paris in 1876 seems clear enough, and in the retrospect of his later, more openly homo-erotic letters to young friends (see chapter 6), it also seems clear enough that James was at least by his late maturity fairly comfortable with his sexual attractions. At the time of his meeting with Zhukovsky, the cate-gory of "the homosexual"—as some recent studies have tended to demonstrate—had not fully emerged, though it would have by the 1890s. James's sexual attraction to another male lies on some contin-uum with close male friendship—a continuum that would be jeopard-ized by the increasing stigmatization of homosexuality. The parallels and contrasts to brother William are instructive: William suffered from nearly clinical depression during the 1860s and early 1870s, and his self-doubts about his sanity and his capacity for living seem possibly connected to his masturbation guilt. He would find a "solution" in marriage, after a long and tortured courtship: a marriage from which he often sought escape but which he simultaneously figured as his sal-vation. He became a preacher of vigorous "manhood"—a quality he found conspicuously lacking in his brother.

Henry, whom his mother (who had a quarrelsome relation with William) tended to refer to as "the angel"—a term then taken up by Al-ice James—never of course sought the solution of marriage, and never subscribed to the American cult of masculinity. He mostly found it hideous, of a piece with all that he detested in his native land, incar-nated at the end of the century by the jingoism of the Spanish-American War and then by President Theodore Roosevelt, "the mere monstrous embodiment of unprecedented and resounding noise." Roosevelt was, like William James, one of those who conquered the "sissiness" of their youth—and perhaps repressed a certain homoerotic disposition—in vigorous "manly" pursuits. Henry's expatriation spared him from that kind of solution, though at the time of the encounter at Posilippo he seems unable to accept an uncloseted homosexuality. His reaction to Zhukovsky and Peppino still contains elements of Cam-bridge. And it is not clear—can probably never be clear—how far a later relaxation of attitude led to any active participation in gay sex.

The Zhukovsky episode may most of all plead in favor of a "Jame-sian" approach to sexuality and the emotions: an understanding that we are faced with an arena of shaded and conflicting desires. James's original desires in regard to Zhukovsky may have been somewhat inchoate, and the encounter at Posilippo may have clarified them in ways that needed to be both censured and censored. But as time goes on, he is more and more explicitly fascinated by what lies under the bar of censorship—as in the intense voyeurism of *The Sacred Fount*, for instance. If he is unable to enact his homoerotic desires, he certainly turns them effectively to the sexed search to know—of the sort that Freud (in his discussion of the obsessional "Rat Man" and the homoerotic Leonardo da Vinci) called "epistemophilia." William would later call Freud "a dirty fellow." Henry might have been more sympathetic to the psychoanalyst's attempts to get at the latent signification of everyday behavior. And even his dismissal of Zhukovsky in the 1881 journal entry is subject to revision: James was back in occasional friendly correspondence with Zhukovsky a couple of decades later.

Revisions

Back to Paris, 1876, as spring changed to summer: James began to swelter in the July heat, and to plan, like any Parisian, an escape to the seashore. The beach was coming into fashion: the paintings of Eugène Boudin, and then of Manet, Monet, and others, record the discovery of the seaside and of bathing by the French bourgeoisie. In late July, James packed and took a steamer down the Seine, to Rouen and then Honfleur and Le Havre. He came to rest in Etretat, a place that would be famous in impressionist painting—especially Monet's many evocations of its famous cliffs—though he makes no mention of its consecration by artists he didn't appreciate. From Etretat he addressed his last letter to the *Tribune*. He was reduced to description of the picturesque sites of the coast, and the French going about the serious business of bathing.

His work for the *Tribune* was at an end, largely through his own fault. James on July 25 wrote to Whitelaw Reid requesting a raise in his pay per letter, from $20 to $30. Reid's reply was not what he wanted:

Reid proposed that rather than more money, there be fewer and shorter letters, and these more "newsy." Alleging that the presidential campaign in the United States left less room for foreign news, Reid added: "we have feared that your letters were sometimes on topics too remote from popular interests to please more than a select few of our readers" (a reproach to Jamesian writing that would be heard again, is heard still). Reid closed diplomatically: "You must not imagine that any of us have failed to appreciate the admirable work you have done for us. The difficulty has sometimes been not that it was too good, but that it was magazine rather than newspaper work."

James's reaction suggests the arrogance of the wounded: "I know the sort of letter you mean—it is doubtless the proper sort of thing for the *Tribune* to have. But I can't produce it—I don't know how and I couldn't learn how. . . . I am too finical a writer and I should be constantly becoming more 'literary' than is desirable. . . . If my letters have been 'too good' I am honestly afraid that they are the poorest I can do, especially for the money!" To his father he wrote a couple of weeks later: "I think I mentioned in my last that Whitelaw Reid had stopped off my letters to the *Tribune*—practically at last—by demanding that they should be of a flimsier sort. I thought in all conscience they had been flimsy enough. I am a little sorry to stop, but much glad. I can use the material more remuneratively otherwise." It seems clear that James did nothing to rescue the failing collaboration with the *Tribune*, and one senses that injured pride is accompanied at relief at the lifting of the burden of the letters.

Etretat brought the company of Mr. and Mrs. Edward Boit, of Boston (and Rome), who would later be the subject of a grand portrait by John Singer Sargent, plus glimpses of Jacques Offenbach (whose operettas James never appreciated) sitting quietly of an evening in the Casino, and the actress Mlle X (probably Céline Chaumont) in "a bathing dress in which, as regards the trousers, even what I have called the minimum has been appreciably scanted," doing a somersault off the diving board into the waves. Toward the end of August, he paid a promised visit to the Edward Lee Childes in their country place near Montargis, in the Loiret, which turned out to be "a little moated 15th century palace, which clamors for you to come and paint it," he wrote to Lizzie Boott, "a chateau with walls 3 feet thick, turrets & winding staircases." As "pretty as a *décor d'opéra*," he described it to his mother. The Childes were perfect hosts. There were excursions. He accompanied Mrs. Childe in her charity visits to the local peasants, which were like something out of one of George Sand's rustic novels. A visit to the local *curé* produced a figure from Balzac. Then he moved on to Biarritz and Bayonne, where the Childes went to stay with friends in the Casa Caradoc—which James would call the most splendid house he'd ever been in. They all made an expedition across the border to San Sebastián, to see a bullfight. James confessed to enjoying the bullfight more than he ought: "It is beastly, of course, it is redeemed by an extreme picturesqueness and by a good deal of gallantry and grace on the part of the *espada*." One wonders at this image of Henry James as Ernest Hemingway.

Back in Paris, James was deeply annoyed to find that his old rooms at 29 rue du Luxembourg had been let to someone else, despite what he thought was his understanding that he was to have them again. After a fruitless search for another place, and some days in "a small dusky hotel of the Rive Gauche," he finally settled on "an inferior apartment in the same house," and set to finishing *The American*: "the tale was taken up afresh by the charming light click and clatter, that sound as of the thin, quick, quite feminine surface breathing of Paris, the shortest of rhythms for so huge an organism." Despite these loving retrospective lines addressed to Paris (in the preface to *The American*), the Paris experiment was failing, and not simply on grounds of his lodgings. After many months of presenting himself as content—"I feel quite Parisianized—I have taken root," he wrote to Arthur Sedgwick on July 6—he suddenly began to paint a revisionary picture. From Etretat at the end of July, he wrote to William of "a long-encroaching weariness and satiety with the French mind and its utterance." He went on: "I have done with 'em, forever, and am turning English all over." He explains: "I have got nothing important out of Paris nor am likely to. My life there makes a much more succulent figure in your letters, as my mention of its thin ingredients, comes back to me, than in my own consciousness. A good deal of Boulevard and third rate Americanism: few retributive relations otherwise."

He was ready to liquidate the choice of Paris as the place of his writerly life. It can't have been easy to admit that Paris was not the solution he had envisioned: Quincy Street took decisions of this sort seriously, and James was ever conscious of how slow he had been in finding his way in the world. In the complex of reasons that made him decide to end the Parisian experiment, "the councils of the gods" to which he had so proudly announced his admission was certainly one of the most important. Already at the end of May he wrote to Howells, again in the revisionary mode: "I have seen almost nothing of the literary fraternity, and there are fifty reasons why I should not become intimate with them. I don't like their wares, and they don't like any others; and besides, they are not *accueillants* [welcoming]. Tourguéneff is worth the whole heap of them, and yet he himself swallows them down in a manner that excites my extreme wonder." Just after these lines, James claims to have broken off the writing of his letter to pay a last visit to Flaubert—about to return to Normandy—and found himself reconfirmed in the view that Flaubert himself was a fine old fellow. (This would in fact prove to be the last time he saw Flaubert, who did not return to Paris until the next January, and who died in 1880.) And it was on leaving Flaubert's that he saluted the censored Zola on the staircase. The image of Olympus, the confraternity of the literary set, seems to have been tarnished. Is he denying the pleasure he took in Flaubert's circle because he is writing to puritanical Cambridge and to the editor of Boston's leading cultural magazine? There may be some of that: he may be giving vent to his own more Cambridge reactions to the easy cynicism of the French literati. Nonetheless, his conclusion that Paris was not the hoped-for nurturing context for his own development as novelist was serious enough that he chose to act on it.

As the years passed, James's attitudes toward the French literary confraternity began to settle and mellow. As he matures, there is a relaxation in his judgments, a more catholic appreciation of their strengths. To Howells in 1884—on the occasion of a new visit to Paris—he wrote: "They do the only kind of work, today, that I respect; and in spite of their ferocious pessimism and their handling of unclean things, they are at least serious and honest." Then much later on—in essays on Flaubert and Zola in particular—he revised further, evoking with nostalgia the apartment in the Faubourg Saint-Honoré "where on Sunday afternoons, at the very top of an endless flight of stairs, were to be encountered in a cloud of conversation and smoke most of the novelists of the general Balzac tradition." He recalls those gathered as a "rich and eager *cénacle*" of "the more finely distinguished" minds of the time. "They exchanged free confidences on current work, on plans and ambitions, in a manner full of interest for one never previously privileged to see artistic conviction, artistic passion (at least on the literary ground) so systematic and so articulate." This handsomely pays tribute to what must have been an extraordinary experience for a young writer. Yet in the spring of 1876, his disillusion with the Flaubert circle—as a group to which he might belong, where he might make his mark—is evidently real.

In some measure James no doubt simply encountered the hermetic nature of French culture and society that many an outsider before and since has run up against. As he was to say later, precisely in presenting Flaubert's circle, the French are "the people in the world one may have to go more of the way to meet than to meet any other . . ." Yet he had gone a long way; he had the requisite command both of the French language and of French culture, and he had been admitted to the most exclusive literary circle in France. Nonetheless, he felt excluded and lonely. It is worth noting that very soon after he settled in London he became a great social success, sought after by hostesses, an inveterate diner-out, a member of fashionable clubs. But not in Paris. There, as he later noted in his journal, he was doomed to be an "eternal outsider."

In fact, it may have been James's very cosmopolitanism that doomed him to outsider status. Recall that he was reading Eliot's *Daniel Deronda* while carrying on relations with Flaubert, Goncourt, and Zola—and lamenting that they didn't read English, and no doubt wouldn't appreciate Eliot if they could. Nor, probably, Henry James. Though two of his short stories appeared in French translation (at least one pirated, it seems) in the *Revue des Deux Mondes* during his Paris stay, and Turgenev read *Roderick Hudson*, James sensed that his work did not and could not quite take its place in the realist and naturalist canon approved and promoted by Flaubert and his disciples. And no doubt he was right. He implicitly levelled at the French writers an accusation of parochialism (*"affreusement bornés,"* he called them in a letter to Perry), and it may be fair to say that parochialism has long been a trait of French culture. Convinced, with some justification, that Paris is the capital of letters and intellectual culture, the French tend to resist imports. They tend to see themselves rather in the business of cultural exportation, if not what one might call cultural imperialism. The problem may hark back to the Enlightenment, when a cosmopolitan France was truly the capital of civilization, and came to believe that its ideas were universals, a problem compounded by the French Revolution and the sense that France had a *mission civilisatrice*, in the exportation of universals of the Rights of Man to the rest of the globe.

James in any event was now ready to terminate the Paris experiment— prematurely, given that originally he had intended to stay for several years, perhaps forever. "I remember how Paris had, in a hundred ways, come to displease me," he later wrote to himself in his journal; "I couldn't get out of the detestable *American* Paris. Then I hated the Boulevards, the horrible monotony of the new quarters." He disliked the brand-new Hausmannized Paris that was becoming a favorite of the new "painters of modern life," in part because those wide boulevards opened up vistas, made the city visible in a new way. Then, James claimed in the journal, it was a word from his older brother that made the difference: "I think a letter from William had a good deal to do with it, in which he said, 'Why don't you [try London]?—that must be the place.' A single word from outside often moves one (moves *me* at least) more than the same word infinitely multiplied as a simple voice from within." So that the "permission" to liquidate the Paris venture came from the somewhat censorious older brother—or was at least attributed to him. If William tells him it's all right to give up on Paris, it must be. He crossed the Channel on December 10, 1876, and took up lodgings in Piccadilly, London. His arrival there more or less coincided with publication, in the *Atlantic*, of a major essay on George Eliot: "*Daniel Deronda*: A Conversation"—as if in declaration of allegiance to what the French ignored, or were incapable of understanding.

The 1875 edition of *Bradshaw's Illustrated Guide Through Paris and Its Environs* reaches for a moment of uncharacteristically poetic prose: "There is a certain charm in the very aspect of Paris, in her boulevards, her gardens, her public promenades, which produces a fascination upon the senses . . ." This cliché of Paris, as the fascinating seductress of Anglo-Americans, was in part what James wanted for the setting of the novel he began writing in December 1875, soon after his arrival. "Great and gilded the whole trap set, in fine, for his wary freshness and into which it would blunder upon its fate," James wrote of his hero, Christopher Newman, in the preface to *The American*. The "great and gilded" trap was provided by Paris itself. James, in the retrospect of his preface, recounts how his arrival in Paris "ever so promptly" resurrected from "the deep well of unconscious cerebration" the idea for his novel, offering him "everything that was needed to make my conception concrete." The concreteness, what he also calls the "objectivity," is in Paris itself: "I saw from one day to another my particular cluster of circumstances, with the life of the city playing up in it like a flashing fountain in a marble basin." The "splendour" of Paris was crucial to his story: "it was important for the effect of my friend's discomfiture that it should take place on a high and lighted stage." It is indeed very much Paris as a kind of icon in the American imagination—Paris as *la ville lumière*—that James wanted for the adventure of his American self-made man in search of something other, something more: a woman, and an alternative to American money-grubbing culture. Newman's adventure will begin "in the great gilded Salon Carré of the Louvre."

"Gilded," one notes, is a word James can't seem not to use about Paris. The Salon Carré of the Louvre—grouping its chiefest treasures of painting—and the contiguous Galerie d'Apollon, "that bridge over to Style" in which he "inhaled little by little, that is again and again, a general sense of *glory*" constituted James's introduction to style, art, culture, even literature. In *A Small Boy and Others*, James devotes a whole chapter, and a particularly moving one, to his trips during his family's 1855 stay in Paris across the river to the Left Bank, then up the rue de Seine to the rue de Tournon and the Luxembourg Palace, which displayed the art of his own century—where he in particular discovered the historical canvases of Paul Delaroche, while William tried making sketches from Delacroix—and then his visits to the Louvre, first with his tutor and then on his own. These visits were "educative, formative, fertilising" in a way no other education was. Amidst the presences of the wondrous romantic paintings came a kind of sense of future vocation: "It came of itself, this almost awful apprehension in all the presences, under our courier's protection and in my brother's company—it came just there and so; there was an alarm in it somehow as well as bliss. . . . The beginning in short was with Géricault and David, but it went on and on and slowly spread . . ."

Paris returns nearly thirty years later as the setting of *The Ambassadors*, the place where the emissary from New England with a name from Balzac, Louis Lambert Strether, will belatedly discover the missed stuff of life. Strether's famous outburst to little Bilham at the sculptor Gloriani's garden party—"Live all you can!"—seems very much to embrace the sexual as part of "to live," indeed as an essential part, and one that James has deliberately associated with Paris, since "the *likely* place had the great merit of sparing me preparations." Paris is here part of Strether's experience and his problem, since "almost any acceptance of Paris might give one's authority away"—that is, one's moral authority as ambassador from the land of puritan blacks and whites. The passage from which I just quoted famously continues: "It hung before him this morning, the vast bright Babylon, like some huge iridescent object, a jewel brilliant and hard, in which parts were not to be discriminated nor differences comfortably marked. It twinkled and trembled and melted together, and what seemed all surface one moment seemed all depth the next." The relation of the aesthetic of that seductive, feminine Paris to the ethical lies at the heart of Strether's perceptual problem, and his eventual betrayal of his ambassadorial function.

But if Strether's Paris is, like Newman's, a gilded trap, it is alluring and sinister in a slightly different way, since Strether's adventure is less a happening, a set of events—such as Newman's betrayal by the Bellegardes, and his loss of Claire de Cintré—than a perceptual experience. What has occurred in between the two novels is James's discovery of and commitment to an extreme perspectivalism. It is not things and persons and happenings that matter so much as the way they are perceived by a certain consciousness. James no doubt from his earliest fiction often created a zone of shadow around central characters, so that one can never quite see into their motives. In the early tale *Mme de Mauves*—published the year before he arrived in Paris—we, like the protagonist Longmore, can never entirely penetrate the opacity of the unhappy title character. But that opacity is not in the earlier fiction subject to the play of different interpretative possibilities that comes with the fiction of the 1890s. There, it's much more like a cubist painting: seeing a figure from several different perspectives that can never quite be reconciled into one harmonious whole.

The adventure of consciousness is pursued in James's fiction of the 1890s, in particular, with a nearly epistemological fervor, a constant questioning of how we can know what we claim to know, a doubting of our bases of knowing. And when he emerges into the masterpieces of his final phase—*The Ambassadors, The Wings of the Dove, The Golden Bowl*—it is with a constant preoccupation with angle of vision, point of observation, and center of consciousness. One has the sense that the lesson of Flaubert—and of Maupassant and Zola, and of the impressionist painters—repressed in 1875–76 stages a return. If James misses so much that is taking place in the crucible of modernism, in Paris when he lives there, the missing seems to have been merely conscious, and merely of the moment. Somehow James was storing these experiences of what it means to be modern in art deep in what he called, in regard to *The American*, the processes of "unconscious cerebration." They were marking experiences after all, and destined to re-emerge into consciousness.

Figure 1. Young Henry James, c. 1863–64. By permission of the
Houghton Library, Harvard University.

Figure 2. The Paris Opera House. Photo credit: Adoc-photos/Art Resource, NY. "*[T]he Empire's legacy to France . . . it tells the story of the society that produced it*" (pages 26–27).

Figure 3. Edouard Manet, *Bal masqué à l'Opéra* [Masked Ball at the Opera] (1873). Gift of Mrs. Horace Havemeyer in memory of her mother-in-law, Louisine W. Havemeyer. Image © 2006 Board of Trustees, National Gallery of Art, Washington. "*[A] scene of the most unbridled and boisterous merriment and excitement*" (page 27).

Figure 4. Edouard Detaille, *En reconnaissance* (1876). *A work "of which nothing but good is to be said"* (page 30).

Figure 5. Claude Monet, *Impression, soleil levant* [Impression, Sunrise] (1873). Photo credit: Erich Lessing/Art Resource, NY. *"[P]artisans of unadorned reality and absolute foes to arrangement, embellishment, selection . . ."* (page 31).

Figure 6. Emile Zola, c. 1875. Photo credit: Adoc-photos/Art Resource, NY.

Figure 7. Pavel Zhukovsky (Paul Joukovsky), c. 1875. By permission of the Houghton Library, Harvard University. *Probably the photo that Henry sent his brother William* (page 39).

Figure 8. Claude Monet, *Falaise d'Etretat*, 1883 (oil on canvas), © Private Collection/The Bridgeman Art Library. (*See page 44.*)

Figure 9. Henry James, early 1880s(?). By permission of the Houghton Library, Harvard University.

Figure 10. Gustave Caillebotte, *Man on Balcony, Boulevard Haussmann* (1880). Photo credit: Erich Lessing/Art Resource, NY. *James disliked the brand-new Hausmannized Paris that was becoming a favorite of the new "painters of modern life"* (page 49).

Figure 11. Jean-Léon Gérôme, *Rachel* (1821–58) (oil on canvas), ©
Musée de la Vie Romantique, Paris, France/Lauros/Giraudon/
The Bridgeman Art Library. "[T]*he pale Rachel invested with the antique*
attributes of tragedy" (page 82).

Figure 12. Edouard Manet, *Nana* (1877). Photo credit: Bildarchiv Preussischer Kulturbesitz/Art Resource, NY. (*See page* 95.)

Figure 13. Gustave Flaubert.

Figure 14. Paul Cézanne, *Houses on the Hill* (1900–1906), oil on canvas. Collection of the McNay Art Museum, bequest of Marion Koogler McNay. *Nearly analogous to James's reticences in his late work* (page 149).

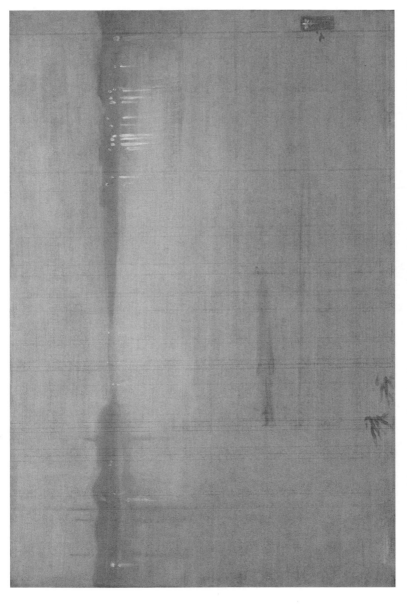

Figure 15. James Abbott McNeill Whistler, *Nocturne in Blue & Silver: Cremorne Lights* (1872). Photo credit: Tate Gallery, London/Art Resource, NY. "Mr. Whistler's experiments have no relation whatever to life; they have only a relation to painting" (page 149).

Figure 16. Zola's funeral cortège. (See page 156.)

Figure 17. Hendrik Andersen, *The Angel of Life (Eternal Life)*. Museo
Hendrik C. Andersen, Rome; courtesy of Ministero per i Beni e le
Attività Culturali. *"I could howl—howl with anguish—over your
continued* parti-pris . . ." (page 173).

Figure 18. Edith Wharton's Chariot of Fire. Photograph of Edith Wharton, Henry James, Teddy Wharton, and the Whartons' chauffeur in the Panhard motorcar. Courtesy of the Lilly Library, Indiana University, Bloomington, Ind., William Royall Taylor Collection. (*See page 206.*)

2. The Dream of an Intenser Experience

It was December 1, 1875—three weeks after his arrival in Paris—that James wrote to F. P. Church, editor of the *Galaxy*, that he had begun writing a new novel called *The American*, and that he proposed to "take for granted" that Church would begin publication of it in nine monthly serials just as soon as he received copy for the first installment. This was perhaps a bit audacious, at least over-optimistic: Church did not reply. James's proposal to the *Galaxy*—where he had often published— was in part a calculation that William Dean Howells's *Atlantic*, where *Roderick Hudson* was just ending its run, wouldn't want a new Henry James just yet. And James needed cash. He needed $150 a month, the terms on which he proposed the novel to Church. In January, he had a letter from his mother accusing him of extravagance and thoughtlessness in his expenditures from the letter of credit provided by his father. So he couldn't draw on that any more, and most of his royalties went directly to Quincy Street, to liquidate the debts incurred to his parents. It was a typical James Family double-binding operation: on the one hand, paternal largesse and encouragement to pursue a writerly vocation, on the other hand the maternal censure for lack of thrift. James's reaction, now as later, was to be nearly Balzacian: to drive his pen faster, to multiply his projects, fictional and critical, and to approach publishers as though there were no question about the viability of his work.

When Church finally replied on February 18, acknowledging having received the first installment of the *The American* but hedging on date and terms of publication, James responded at once that it was of "the very greatest importance to me that the publication of my novel should begin immediately," and that he must have $150 per installment. If Church couldn't meet those terms and begin publication by May, he was to send the manuscript back to Henry James, Sr., in Quincy Street. Then Howells came to the rescue, proposing directly to Church to take over the novel, at the price James had proposed. The *Atlantic* began serialization in June 1876. With Howells's proposal that the novel be extended beyond the nine installments originally envisioned, James eventually wrote twelve monthly installments. He was safely ensconced in London by the time it was finished. The total take came to $1,350. It was solid financial ground, of sorts. And the novel, while it had a somewhat mixed reception from American reviewers, has been judged by generations of readers since as marking a major step into artistic maturity. The mature James himself described the novel as "redolent of good intentions baffled by a treacherous vehicle," and undertook to produce a major revision, correcting "the old catastrophes and accidents, the old wounds and mutilations and disfigurements."

It was some thirty years after writing *The American* that James reread the novel in order to revise it. He had decided that all his early fiction needed revision before publication in the collection of his selected works by Scribner's—what became known as the "New York Edition" of his works. The rereading led James to a bemused perception. Where he thought he had been writing a realist account of Christopher Newman's encounter with the French, in truth he "had been plotting archromance without knowing it" and in retrospect the novel "yields me no interest and no reward comparable to the fond perception of this truth." In a definition that would have been acceptable to the group that gathered for Flaubert's Sunday afternoons, James wrote that "the real represents to my perception the things we cannot possibly *not* know, sooner or later, in one way or another." In contrast, "The romantic stands, on the other hand, for the things that, with all the facilities in the world, all the wealth and all the courage and all the wit and all the adventure, we never *can* directly know; the things that can reach us only through the beautiful circuit and subterfuge of our thought and our desire" (1063).

James was in his early sixties when he wrote this retrospect on his early novel. He was by then an artistic if not greatly a commercial success, even something of a cult figure to younger writers, as well as a prized dinner guest during the London social season. We might take his judgment that *The American* is more the product of the circuit and subterfuge of thought and desire than truly an encounter with the real as both a rueful perception that he had not met the French realists on their own ground even in his novel dedicated to Paris, and also an indulgent recognition that his own forms of imagination always contained an admixture of the romantic. What is romantic to James is the potential, hidden within reality, of a heightened drama: the drama of "common and covert" dangers that "'look like nothing' and that can be but inwardly and occultly dealt with, which involve the sharpest hazards to life and honour and the highest instant decisions and intrepidities of action" (1063–64). It's no coincidence that two sentences later James evokes *Madame Bovary*, to note that despite the heroine's romantic temper "nothing less resembles a romance than the record of her adventures." *The American*, he seems to be saying, is more like a Balzac novel. Its "pursuit of life itself" will offer "the dream of an intenser experience" (1063).

Most readers of *The American* sense that for better or worse the novel veers abruptly onto a different course about two-thirds of the way through, at the moment Christopher Newman is betrayed by the Bellegardes, who withdraw their consent to his marriage with the beautiful young widow Claire de Cintré, daughter of the dowager Marquise de Bellegarde and sister to the arch-snob Urbain de Bellegarde. Here, in James's later judgment, was the most unrealistic element of his novel: real-life impoverished French aristocrats would have jumped at the chance to bring Newman's American millions into the family, and not have minded in the least his common origins and unsophisticated manners. It is at this moment of reversal on the part of the Bellegardes that what has up to this point been largely social comedy—broad, amused, generally good-natured—suddenly produces the emotional conditions and the vocabulary of melodrama, unleashing a new and heightened drama for which the reader has scarcely been prepared. The very stakes of the novel suddenly seem changed.

The change comes at the start of chapter 18 (of the 26 in the novel), when Newman makes his way into the Hôtel de Bellegarde: "He felt, as soon as he entered the room, that he was in the presence of something evil; he was startled and pained, as he would have been by a threatening cry in the stillness of the night." Evil has come onstage, overt and menacing. We seem to have encountered a persistent Jamesian mode that we might label as "moral melodrama": a mode that may be kept in abeyance for long stretches in his fiction, held at bay by the play of social satire and urbane wit, but that most often makes its latent presence felt by the time the climax is reached. What makes *The American* different from James's later fiction is, first of all, the abruptness with which the melodramatic mode erupts in the text. In much of the later fiction, one feels its latent, brooding presence from the start. Then, the melodrama here is going to be more specific and more traditional: overtly blood-curdling acts.

"There is some foul play," says Newman in chapter 18 (318). By the time of his final meeting with Claire de Cintré at the Bellegardes' château at Fleurières, evil has assumed fully melodramatic shape. "They have bullied you, I say; they have tortured you," Newman cries out; and Claire replies, "There's a curse upon the house; I don't know what—I don't know why—don't ask me. . . . I wanted to escape from it. . . . But I can't—it has overtaken and come back to me. . . . Why are there things I can't ask about—that I am afraid to know?" (351–53). When Claire announces her decision to "entomb" herself as a Carmelite nun, the scene unleashes all the staginess of theatrical melodrama: "The idea struck Newman as too dark and horrible for belief, and made him feel as he would have done if she had told him that she was going to mutilate her beautiful face, or drink some potion that would make her mad. He clasped his hands and began to tremble, visibly. . . . 'You—you a nun!' he exclaimed; 'you with your beauty defaced—you behind locks and bars! Never, never, if I can prevent it!' And he sprang to his feet with a violent laugh" (355–56).

Violence in fact emerges as the new mode of the novel when, two chapters later, the old English servant of the Bellegarde family, plain

Mrs. Bread, reveals that Newman's hypothesis of "foul play" is fully justified. She fills in the past history of the old Marquis de Bellegarde's
murder by his wife, assisted by son Urbain. The felt presence of evil has
now been overtly specified, backed up by a dark deed, which itself is
documented by the deathbed note of accusation against his wife written by the old marquis and passed on to Newman by Mrs. Bread. A
novel that began in urbanity and the play of worldly wit, with our introduction to Newman seated on a divan in the gilded Salon Carré of the
Louvre, making his first discovery of the aesthetic, seems to have
veered into the gothic.

Looking back at the twist he gave to his novel, James recognized the
"deflexion" of his fiction from realism to romance. He considered what
the novel might have been if he had he treated the Bellegardes "in the
light of comedy and of irony." This would have given a fiction controlled by "our general sense of 'the way things happen'" rather than
the "disconnected and uncontrolled experience" of romance. Yet that
novel, he continues, would not have been *The American* as he originally conceived it. From its very inception, his novel was committed to
the idea of a "wrong" done to Newman, with his subsequently gaining
access to knowledge of the Bellegardes' evil nature and past dark deeds,
thus holding them in his power. This leads James to a parenthetical reflection on power as the defining characteristic of romance: "It is as difficult, I said above, to trace the dividing-line between the real and the
romantic as to plant a milestone between north and south; but I am not
sure an infallible sign of the latter is not this rank vegetation of the
'power' of bad people that good get into, or vice versa. It is so rarely,
alas, into our power that anyone gets!" (1067).

The reflection on power cuts close to the heart of the matter in
James's fiction: it raises questions about moral attitude as well as fictional presentation. Note that James sees realism as faithful to "our
general sense of 'the way things happen,'" and he sees his own lapse
from realism in the implausibility of the Bellegardes behaving as such
stagey villains—the much greater plausibility of their deciding to milk
Newman for all he is worth. By stating the problem in terms of plausibility, James may avoid facing up to what many readers have felt to be
the real problem: the change of tone and mode in his novel, its swerve

toward the gothic, the sudden melodramatization of experience. James may be shifting too much of the problem onto the Bellegardes' behavior, and not accepting it as the novelist's.

But the novel in fact has not done "turning" with the introduction of the Bellegardes' betrayal, Mrs. Bread's dark revelation, and Newman's gaining of power over the villains. The gothic romance itself is transformed by Newman's final renunciation of revenge, his decision not to make use of the damning documentary evidence put in his possession. As James retrospectively describes his original vision of Newman's final decision, "he would simply turn, at the supreme moment, away, the bitterness of his personal loss yielding to the very force of his aversion. All he would have at the end would be therefore just the moral convenience, indeed the moral necessity, of his practical, but quite unappreciated, magnanimity; and one's last view of him would be that of a strong man indifferent to his strength and too wrapped in fine, too wrapped above all in *other* and intenser, reflexions for the assertion of his 'rights'" (1055). If with the betrayal of Newman by the Bellegardes melodrama is unleashed in the novel, in its final pages that melodrama is transmuted into the intensity of moral choice, the assertion that the real and crucial melodrama is interior, that it resides in the dramas of consciousness. In this manner, *The American* prefigures James's latest fiction, perhaps most of all *The Golden Bowl*, a novel that turns on the temptation to melodrama and its renunciation, as Maggie Verver sets aside the forms of behavior "usually open to innocence outraged and generosity betrayed," and chooses instead to repair the breaking of her marriage, her trust, and her belief in the possibility of human relations, all the while experiencing that temptation to melodramatic behavior as an intensely heightened form of moral consciousness. The end of *The American* turns toward this "melodrama of consciousness" characteristic of James's final and greatest work.

I have dwelt on the "turns" of *The American* because I think we can see in them a kind of allegory of James's hesitations and uncertain choices, in 1875–76, of different paths open to the novelist, of different kinds of novels one might write. It's as if he were testing, uncertainly and in a kind of serial form, the definition of what would be his own kind of novel. Writing in Paris a novel about an American's experience of Paris, suspended between visits to Flaubert's group of "realists" and the monthly installments of George Eliot's *Daniel Deronda*, he is searching for his way. That search is recorded also in the many essays James devoted to the novelists he sensed had the most to teach him: Balzac, Turgenev, Eliot, Flaubert, Zola. The year in Paris resulted not only in *The American* but also in the volume of essays published in 1878 under the title *French Poets and Novelists*. And he continued to write about them almost obsessively.

In the course of a later essay, "Gustave Flaubert" (published in 1902 as preface to a translation of *Madame Bovary*), James evokes the English novel of Jane Austen—and also Fielding and Pater—as "instinctive and charming," and then goes on to say: "For signal examples of what composition, distribution, arrangement can do, of how they intensify the life of a work of art, we have to go elsewhere; and the value of Flaubert for us is that he admirably points the moral." "Elsewhere" was always Paris, and despite his disillusionment with his Parisian existence, he never altered his view that on the whole the English and American novel had not really come of age, that it was still too much an entertainment for middle-class maidens, compromised by autocensorship and a lack of self-consciousness concerning the novel as an artistic form—propositions forcefully argued in his essay "The Art of Fiction," a reply to the insipid program for the English novel advanced by Walter Besant. Recall that on his revisiting Paris in 1884, he wrote to Howells, concerning Daudet, Goncourt, and Zola: "There is nothing more interesting to me now than the effort and experiment of this little group, with its truly infernal intelligence of art, form, manner— its intense artistic life. They do the only kind of work, today, that I respect; and in spite of their ferocious pessimism and their handling of unclean things, they are at least serious and honest."

James is most interested in those novelists who can teach him something about the novel, and some twenty years after Flaubert's death he has finally granted the lion of the Faubourg Saint-Honoré exemplary status along with Balzac. His most important critical reflections in fact fall under the rubrics "The Lesson of Balzac"—the title of the major lecture presented in several cities during his extended American tour, published in 1905—and what we might call the "case" of Flaubert conceived as "more interesting . . . as a failure however qualified than as a success however explained." It is in dialogue with these two French novelists that we find James working out his critical positions and even his vocabulary for talking about fiction. It surprises many readers that despite his admiration for Flaubert's consummate artistry and his heroic effort to establish the novel as a serious artistic genre, and despite his awareness of Balzac's artistic lapses, vulgarity, implausibilities, romantic and other claptrap, James over the years remains faithful to a perception that Balzac provides the best lesson for those who wish to recover the "wasted heritage" of the novel, whereas Flaubert, although he remains ever "the novelist's novelist," is somehow limited and limiting, a writer whose view of life is too exclusively behavioristic, and who does not develop the full potential of the novel. Over time, James comes to appreciate Flaubert's novels more fully, and to understand better their project. But he never revises the hierarchy that makes Balzac the greater of the two—because more pertinent to the Jamesian novel.

We can best enter into James's dialogue with these two masters by citing two passages, the first in praise of Balzac's respect for the "liberty of the subject," the second criticizing Flaubert's limiting narrative vision. On Balzac:

There is never in Balzac that damning interference which consists of the painter's not seeing, not possessing, his image; not having fixed his creature and his creature's conditions. "Balzac aime sa Valérie," says Taine, in his great essay—so much the finest thing ever written on our author—speaking of the way in which the awful little Madame Marneffe of "Les Parents Pauvres" is drawn, and of the long rope, for her acting herself out, that her creator's participation in her reality assures her. He has been contrasting her, as it happens, with Thackeray's Becky Sharp or rather with Thackeray's attitude toward Becky, and the marked jealousy of her freedom that Thackeray exhibits from the first. I remember reading at the time of the publication of Taine's study—though it was long, long ago—a phrase in an English review of the volume which seemed to my limited perception, even in extreme youth, to de-

serve the highest prize ever bestowed on critical stupidity undis-
guised. If Balzac loved his Valérie, said this commentator, that
only showed Balzac's extraordinary taste; the truth being really,
throughout, that it was just through this love of each seized identity, and of the sharpest and liveliest identities most, that Madame
Marneffe's creator was able to marshal his array at all. The love, as
we call it, the joy in their communicated and exhibited movement, in their standing on their feet and going of themselves and
acting out their characters, was what rendered possible the saturation I speak of. . . . It all comes back, in fine, to that respect for the
liberty of the subject which I should be willing to name as *the*
great sign of the painter of the first order.

As is so often the case in James's critical essays, we have a judgment
that is at once technical and somehow moral. A "respect for the liberty
of the subject"—which is expressed in the novelist's giving his created
life "the long rope" for acting itself out—creates a fiction in which
readers are not limited by the judgmental interference of the novelist,
where they can exercise their own freedom of discrimination. James
praises Turgenev in similar terms: "No one has more of that sign of the
born novelist which resides in a respect unconditioned for the freedom
and vitality, the absoluteness when summoned, of the creatures he invokes." The novel should give a sense of indetermination rather than
manipulation—and this is not only a precept for art but very much an
ethical precept as well. In James, the manipulators of others tend to be
morally stigmatized, and to impose fatal rigidities on life.

That Balzacian respect for the "liberty of the subject" also makes its
way into James's evaluations of George Eliot, the novelist of high English moral seriousness whom he uses in 1876—as he is reading *Daniel
Deronda* in monthly installments—as a standard against which to
judge the limitations of Flaubert and his circle. Reviewing Henry
Cross's *Life of George Eliot* in the *Atlantic* in 1885, James came upon a
journal entry of the novelist's—from the time she was writing *The Mill
on the Floss*—that read: "We have just finished reading aloud Père
Goriot, a hateful book." James finds the comment on "Balzac's masterpiece" important, "significant of so many things that the few words are,

in the whole *Life*, those I should have been most sorry to lose." He uses
Eliot's comment to suggest her failure to give life its "long rope": "it il-
luminates the author's general attitude with regard to the novel, which,
for her, was not primarily a picture of life, capable of deriving a high
value from its form, but a moralised fable, the last word of a philosophy
endeavouring to teach by example." He continues, trying to suggest
that his high estimation of Eliot is tempered by "the absence of free
aesthetic life": her characters and situations arise "from her moral consciousness, and are only indirectly the products of observation" (1003).
He approves of Eliot's philosophical and moral concerns, what he calls
"her preoccupation with the universe," and her capacity to combine
"her love of general truth and love of the special case." But he adds:
"All the same, that little sign of all that Balzac failed to suggest to her
showed at what perils the special case got itself considered."

Some critics, he notes, hold that the "special case" virtually disap-
pears from Eliot's later work, from *Middlemarch* and *Daniel Deronda*:

> Such critics assure us that Gwendolen and Grandcourt, Deronda
> and Myra [*sic*], are not concrete images, but disembodied types,
> pale abstractions, signs and symbols of a "great lesson." I give up
> Deronda and Myra to the objector, But Grandcourt and Gwen-
> dolen seem to me to have a kind of superior reality; to be, in a
> high degree, what one demands of a figure in a novel, planted on
> their legs and complete. (1004)

James largely reiterates here his judgment of 1876: if the parts of
Daniel Deronda concerning Deronda and Mirah (Eliot's spelling)
have too much of the abstract and the didactic, Gwendolen Harleth
and Grandcourt are largely realized as dramatic characters. His long
piece on *Daniel Deronda*, published in the *Nation* in 1878, takes the
form of a "conversation" among two women and a man, no doubt in
an effort to do justice to James's divided sense of Eliot's accomplish-
ment in her final novel. Constantius, the male character—a book
reviewer—pays handsome tribute to the novel, and especially Gwendolen's story. But he also notes of Eliot: "Instead of feeling life itself, it
is 'views' upon life that she tries to feel." Here precisely is Eliot's failure
to appreciate the way Balzac—in the words of Theodora in the

conversation—"gets down upon all fours to crawl through *Le Père Goriot* or *Les Parents Pauvres*" (983). Is James recalling Turgenev on all fours in Viardot charades? In any event, Balzac is ever and again the test of represented life in the novel.

Flaubert is not guilty of Thackeray's censorious comments on and overt interferences with his characters, nor of Eliot's tendency to the abstract and didactic. But James sees Flaubert as "absolutely and exclusively condemned to irony"—an attitude and form of writing that betrays his "comparatively meagre human consciousness." As a result, one may feel that he, too, violates the "liberty of the subject," showing human agents only in a straitened, controlled, and simplified form. In the following passage, James discusses the central consciousnesses of *Madame Bovary* and *L'Education sentimentale*, Emma Bovary and Frédéric Moreau, who largely convey Flaubert's imagined worlds to us:

> Why did Flaubert choose, as special conduits of the life he proposed to depict, such inferior and in the case of Frédéric such abject human specimens? . . . He wished in each case to make a picture of experience—middling experience, it is true—and of the world close to him; but if he imagined nothing better for his purpose than such a heroine and such a hero, both such limited reflectors and registers, we are forced to believe it to have been by a defect of his mind. And that sign of weakness remains even if it be objected that the images in question were addressed to his purpose better than others would have been: the purpose itself then shows as inferior. (326–27)

For James, choice of a narrative point of view that is inherently limiting and restrictive of the experience it is called upon to record constitutes a major "defect" of novelistic technique. To the objection that Flaubert may have *wished* to present such an impoverished point of view, he replies in advance that the defect must then be one in the novelistic project itself: it betrays a misconception of what the novel is and is for. Emma Bovary's deficiency as a character, for instance, derives from "the poverty of her consciousness for the typical function," defined as the lack of sufficient "points of contact" between her and the world (328).

We are close to the heart of the matter of James's dissent from Flaubert and his *kind* of novel. Consider, as contrast, James's image of Balzac's "contacts" with the world: "He could so extend his existence partly because he vibrated to so many kinds of contact and curiosity. To vibrate intellectually was his motive, but it magnified, all the while, it multiplied his experience" (123). Despite his pretentious claims of knowledge beyond his means, then, Balzac manages to give the effect of having understood the lives of others and having given them a large stage for their enactments. In this manner, where we feel an impoverishment of life in Flaubert, we everywhere sense Balzac's "spiritual presence in his work." In a summary statement, James claims: "What it comes back to, in other words, is the intensity with which we live—and his intensity is recorded for us on every page of his work" (127). In opposition to this intensity stands Flaubert's detached spectatorship.

In the essay on Flaubert and the minor novelist Charles de Bernard that he published in the *Galaxy* during his Parisian year—in January 1876—then reprinted in *French Poets and Novelists,* James writes: "Flaubert's theory as a novelist, briefly expressed, is to begin on the outside. Human life, he says, is before all things a spectacle, a thing to be looked at, seen, apprehended, enjoyed with the eyes. What our eyes show us is all that we are sure of; so with this we will, at any rate, begin." This is accurate enough as a shorthand characterization of Flaubert's— and most—realism. James goes on to claim that Flaubert may admit that life includes as well something else "beneath and behind," but estimates that "on the whole, we will leave it to take care of itself." Balzac, in contrast, was a novelist always probing behind and beneath the surface, seeking the hidden drama and the occult truth. And James will make the question of what he dubs "going behind" a major issue of narrative technique, repeatedly discussed in his prefaces.

James's unease with Flaubert comes through with particular force in his stricture on the "moral" error of presenting Frédéric Moreau's beloved (but never possessed) Madame Arnoux exclusively through his limited consciousness. This is again from the 1902 essay:

What *was* compromising—and the great point is that it remained so, that nothing has an equal weight against it—is the unconsciousness of error in respect to the opportunity that would have counted as his finest. We feel not so much that Flaubert misses it, for that we could bear; but that he doesn't *know* he misses it is what stamps the blunder. We do not pretend to say how he might have shown us Madame Arnoux better—that was his own affair. What is ours is that he really thought he was showing her as well as he could, or as she might be shown; at which we veil our face. For once that he had a conception quite apart, apart I mean from the array of his other conceptions and more delicate than any, he "went," as we say, and spoiled it. (330–31)

This is very strange, since James by 1902 was pre-eminently a perspectival novelist, someone interested the limitations and uncertainties imposed upon observation. One would think that he might find much to praise in Flaubert's careful restriction of Madame Arnoux to what Frédéric sees and believes, to the point that we never can tell what she is "objectively" like.

What James seems to mean here is not that Flaubert has been unfaithful to some real-life model for Madame Arnoux, or even unfaithful to some "type" of the virtuous woman, but rather that he has not made good on the conception that presides at the creation of this character. You can't imagine a Madame Arnoux and then not do her justice in terms of your representation of her, James seems to be saying; you have to give her the long rope to act herself out. To be unaware of or unconcerned with the full potential of one's created fictive lives seems to James some sort of moral error. He sees in Flaubert a kind of artistic impoverishment or even totalitarianism that reveals a lack of respect for life, and for the capacities of fiction to represent life. James's strictures turn to the ethical because what is at stake for him is the commitment and project of the novel itself, as representation, as cognitive instrument in the study of life.

Readers who prize Flaubert will find James to be off the mark in his judgment. The limited view of Madame Arnoux presented in *L'Education sentimentale*, and indeed the antinovelistic mediocrity of "experience" in general recorded in that novel, are very much the subject of Flaubert's fiction, what it is all about. But if we want to contradict

James's judgment of Flaubert, we should recognize that in his own terms he is right: he has detected that *L'Education sentimentale* is, in some radical and disquieting manner, an antinovel that undermines the very bases of the Balzacian and the Jamesian novel. Much of his rejection of Flaubert seems motivated by an alarmed perception that Flaubertian practice would deconstruct James's own writing.

One could continue the discussion with the "cases" of Maupassant— "for M. de Maupassant himself precisely presents all the symptoms of a 'case' in the most striking way," writes James in 1888—and Zola: "We become conscious, for our profit, of a *case*," James says of Zola in 1903, one that may be summarized as "the most extraordinary *imitation* of observation that we possess," in contrast to the real observation offered by Balzac. The remark takes us back to a passage in "The Lesson of Balzac" where James discusses "representation" as "the most fundamental and general sign of the novel," labelling Zola's performance "an extraordinary show of representation imitated," whereas with Balzac, whatever "his faults of pedantry, ponderosity, pretentiousness, bad taste and charmless form," we sense that "his spirit has somehow paid for its knowledge" (130). Zola too much sacrificed to "the idea," the didactic theme each novel must document and demonstrate, whereas Balzac engages "the palpable, proveable world before him, by the study of which ideas would inevitably find themselves thrown up" (127). I noted in the last chapter that a notion of representation also underlies James's strictures on impressionist painting. Representation, in paintings and in novels, ought to involve the use of signs to make the world comprehensible as well as visible. An attention to impressions alone, to surfaces, never gets to the heart of the matter, never makes full use of the possibilities of representation—issues that we will find at the heart of James's next novel to deal with a Parisian milieu, *The Tragic Muse*.

Why James continues to declare his allegiance to the lesson of Balzac while recognizing the superior artistry of Flaubert, Maupassant, and Zola comes through if we juxtapose two comments, written some twenty-seven years apart, on an incident in one of Balzac's novels. The first comes from the essay published in the *Galaxy* in December 1875, just following James's arrival in Paris, which largely praises Balzac the realist but displays a certain distrust of his "visionary" streak. James par-

ticularly demurs here from Balzac's portraits of women of the aristocracy, which he labels "a laborious and extravagant failure," noting
archly: "These ladies altogether miss the mark." His decisive example
concerns an incident in *Illusions perdues* (*Lost Illusions*) where the
Faubourg Saint-Germain aristocrat, Madame d'Espard, who is entertaining her provincial cousin Madame de Bargeton at the Opéra, discovers that Madame de Bargeton's protégé, who calls himself Lucien
de Rubempré, and who is ludicrously decked out, really is one Lucien
Chardon, son of a village apothecary. After scolding her cousin on
such an acquaintance, she sweeps out of the Opéra box and goes
home. "The caste of Vere de Vere in this case certainly quite forgot its
repose," comments James. In the essay of 1902, James returns to this
incident, as if in implicit reparation for his earlier strictures:

> The whole episode, in "Les Illusions perdues," of Madame de
> Bargeton's "chucking" Lucien de Rubempré, on reaching Paris
> with him, under pressure of Madame d'Espard's shockability as to
> his coat and trousers and other such matters, is either a magnifi-
> cent lurid document or the baseless fabric of a vision. The great
> wonder is that, as I rejoice to put it, we can never really discover
> which, and that we feel as we read that we can't, and that we suffer
> at the hands of no other author this particular helplessness of im-
> mersion. It is *done*—we are always thrown back on that; we can't
> get out of it; all we can do is to say that the true itself can't be more
> than done and that if the false in this way equals it we must give
> up looking for the difference. Alone among novelists Balzac has
> the secret of an insistence that somehow makes the difference
> nought. He warms his facts into life—as witness the certainty that
> the episode I just cited has absolutely as much of that property as if
> perfect matching had been achieved. If the great ladies in ques-
> tion *didn't* behave, wouldn't, couldn't have behaved, like a pair of
> nervous snobs, why so much the worse, we say to ourselves, for the
> great ladies in question. We *know* them so—they owe their being
> to our so seeing them; whereas we never can tell ourselves how we
> should otherwise have known them or what quantity of being they
> would on a different footing have been able to put forth.

James's relaxation of attitude toward Balzac's excessive dramatization appears to signal a greater understanding of his own needs and wants in "representation." It's not so much "perfect matching" that is needed; rather it's a capacity for the "document" to figure the "vision." Representation is less concerned with the details of the real than with what it signifies and connotes, less attached to the surface of things than to what may be suggested and concealed, behind and beneath. This later Jamesian version of Balzac is someone in whom the "directly historic" and the "romantic" are never wholly distinguishable and in whom the representation of reality is ever subject to "those smashes of the window-pane of the real that reactions sometimes produce even in the stubborn" (113). Windows, and looking in and out of them, are always important in James, as in all realists: the window frames the visual presentation of reality. Zola, for instance, famously compares the prose of the realist or naturalist to a "transparent screen." The need James recognizes occasionally to smash the "window-pane of the real" seems to claim the pertinence of a heightened, hyperbolic, more visionary sort of vision.

As James puts it three years later in "The Lesson of Balzac": "Balzac's great glory is that he pretended hardest" (134). Some part of that pretending may resemble the play of the imagination suggested in a well-known image from the preface to *The American*: "The balloon of experience is in fact of course tied to the earth, and under that necessity we swing, thanks to a rope of remarkable length, in the more or less commodious car of the imagination." We might set beside this passage one from the 1902 essay on Flaubert, where James has been describing *L'Education sentimentale* as "a sort of epic of the usual," and goes on to say: "it affects us as an epic without air, without wings to lift it; reminds us in fact more than anything else of a huge balloon, all of silk pieces strongly sewn together and patiently blown up, but that absolutely refuses to leave the ground" (328). In this juxtaposition of the balloon lifting the commodious car of the imagination and the laboriously stitched balloon that refuses to leave the earth we may detect a representation of James's somewhat paradoxical choices from models of "the novelistic." On the one hand there are his repeated declarations that the art of the novel can best be learned from Flaubert, Maupassant, and Zola, the only serious technicians and theorists of the genre. On the other hand, there are the repeated declarations of allegiance to Balzac, who despite his lapses remains the "father of us all" (120). Turgenev, too, inspires James to evoke in contrast a Flaubert who "imparted something to his works (it was as if he had covered them with metallic plates) which made them sink rather than sail." The work of Flaubert and his followers does not appear to swing in the commodious car of the imagination; it is too tightly bound to experience, to the earth. The turn of *The American* toward melodrama and the gothic may be like one of Balzac's "smashes of the window-pane" of the real. And James will criticize himself for having in this youthful novel "cut the cable" tethering the balloon to earth. If *The American* is too much romance, and too close to Balzac, nonetheless James takes a certain satisfaction in its refusal to fit fully under the realist label. The turn of *The American* represents in somewhat crude form a quest for something more, something behind and beneath, that James would always want to include in his fiction—that would in fact seem definitional to the reach of fiction as he understood it.

The American itself—not simply the later preface—often reads as a kind of drama pitting the restrictions and limitations of a strict realism against the claims of a greater freedom, staginess, and vision. When we first meet Newman, in that Salon Carré of the Louvre that from boyhood was James's locus of the high cultural imagination, we are told that this American man of business faces a "new kind of arithmetic" in the aesthetic. And the result appears to be, not arrogance or dismissiveness, but "a vague self-mistrust" (34). So that if Newman is definitely, identifiably an American, and one who makes all sorts of mistakes in his aesthetic valuations, he nonetheless carries the promise of learning and change. "Decision, salubrity, jocosity, prosperity, seem to hover within his call; he is evidently a practical man, but the idea, in his case, has undefined and mysterious boundaries, which invite the imagination to bestir itself on his behalf " (36). We may see in Newman the potential to be a better "register and reflector" of experience than such as Emma Bovary and Frédéric Moreau. In James's view, Flaubert's figures don't invite the reader's imagination to bestir itself *on their behalf*.

Newman, on the other hand, interests because his new "self-mistrust" promises a drama of exploration and possible illumination, and because his perspective on the world seems to offer the reader an interesting optics of reading, an imaginative potential, maybe a vision.

Viewing paintings—and buying copies of them—provides an initial step in Newman's opening to a fuller and freer appreciation of life and culture. His liberal response to the Louvre is set in contrast to the suspicious bafflement of Tom Tristram, the expatriate ensconced in the American colony in Paris, and then in contrast to the "moral *malaise*" of the Unitarian minister Benjamin Babcock, of weak digestion, to whom European ways seem "unscrupulous and impure." Babcock's dietary manias, strenuous conscience, and moral perplexities, and his attempts to infuse Newman with more "spiritual starch," reminded some contemporary readers of William James (including William himself). And Babcock provides an American foil to Newman's more relaxed yet finally more imaginative tourism, the "singular inward tremor" he experiences before the relics of European history. James is interested, here as in all his fiction, in the kind of moral consciousness he prized in George Eliot, but he makes it clear from the outset that there is a narrow version of morality and conscience that is limiting, imprisoning, and all-too-American. In fact, too Quincy Street.

The limitations of the unfortunate Mr. Babcock set up a more unexpected discovery for the reader: the discovery that the world of the French aristocrats represented by the Bellegarde family is also limited, narrow, and set in opposition to the practice of freedom. Their nature is suggested first in a very Balzacian description of their hôtel in "the Faubourg Saint-Germain whose houses present to the outer world a face as impassive and as suggestive of the concentration of privacy within as the blank walls of Eastern seraglios" (79). As in Balzac, the description of the surfaces of the external world also "throws up ideas." "The house to which he had been directed had a dark, dusty, painted portal, which swung open in answer to his ring. It admitted him into a wide, gravelled court, surrounded on three sides with closed windows, and with a doorway facing the street, approached by three steps and surmounted by a tin canopy. The place was all in the shade; it answered to Newman's conception of a convent." This of course foreshadows Claire de Cintré's eventual decision to immure herself in a convent; it suggests that the "document" provided by description will produce the "fabric of vision," an intensified kind of dramatic experience. Then, the presentation of the members of the Bellegarde clan insists on their unfreedom, their determination by inherited identities and rigid manners. Madame de Bellegarde's countenance, for instance, "with its formal gaze, and its circumscribed smile, suggested a document signed and sealed; a thing of parchment, ink, and ruled lines (180)—which makes her a text that gives no free play to the imagination, and foreshadows revelation of the damning document written by her dying husband. Claire, on the other hand, invites interest because she suggests the potential of a movement out of this world of fixity into one of freedom. Following Newman's marriage proposal, "She had the air of a woman who had stepped across the frontier of friendship and, looking around her, finds the region vast" (172).

As someone who claimed to know the Théâtre-Français by heart, and was intent to give his novels a kind of scenic intensity—even before he made his ill-fated attempt to write for the London stage—James creates in the clash of Newman and the Bellegardes a kind of theatrical dramatization first comic and later melodramatic. Claire de Cintré's possible liberation from the immobile, stultifying world of the Bellegardes is played out as a conflict of fixity versus freedom. The subplot that features her brother, Valentin, makes the stakes of this drama all the more explicit. Valentin admires Newman's freedom, he dreams of starting a new life in America, he derogates from his family's aristocratic reserve. But his liaison with Noémie Nioche, while it may seem a gesture of freedom, in fact follows the most conventional of scripts—with Noémie only too happy to play the role of theatrical adventuress—and it ends in the murderous convention of the duel. "Your duel itself is a scene," Newman tells Valentin, "that's all it is! It's a wretched theatrical affair" (309). As he sits by the dying Valentin's bedside following the duel, Newman is given a book to while away the hours. It turns out to be Choderlos de Laclos' *Les liaisons dangereuses*, the supreme dramatization of the cruelty that can be wrung from conventions, in games played with and on other people.

The American as it unfolds becomes more and more overtly theatrical. Newman is obliged to play his role as American while also observing the social comedy of the milieu he seeks both to enter and to rescue Claire from. Visits and receptions at the Bellegardes, for instance, come with well-marked entrances and exits, bits of dramatic dialogue, various *apartés*, strong curtain lines. Newman, the narrator tells us, "sat by without speaking, looking at the entrances and the exits, the greetings and the chatterings, of Madame de Cintré's visitors. He felt as if he were at the play, and as if his own speaking would be an interruption; sometimes, he wished he had a book to follow the dialogue; he half expected to see a woman in a white cap and pink ribbons come and offer him one for two francs" (147). James in this manner both calls attention to the theatricality of his novel, and disarms criticism of it, gives himself license to be "stagey," in Balzac's way. But as in Balzac, it turns out that social comedy is not the whole of reality—that there is a "beneath and behind" waiting to break through the façade of manners, to turn the novel toward a more overt melodrama.

There are a few intimations of the hidden presence of this other drama. For instance, when Tom Tristram reacts with heavy irony to what he sees as his wife's overly dramatic claim that the Bellegardes want to marry Claire off to "some dissipated little duke." Tristram faults his wife's vision:

"She has seen the lovely Claire on her knees, with loosened tresses and streaming eyes, and the rest of them standing over her with spikes and goads and red-hot irons, ready to come down on her if she refuses the tipsy duke. The simple truth is that they have made a fuss about her milliner's bill or refused her an opera-box."

Newman looked from Tristram to his wife with a certain mistrust in each direction. "Do you really mean," he asked of Mrs. Tristram, "that your friend is being forced into an unhappy marriage?"

"I think it extremely probable. Those people are very capable of that sort of thing."

"It is like something in a play," said Newman; "that dark old house over there looks as if wicked things had been done in it, and might be done again." (121)

The scene of Claire on her knees threatened with a red-hot iron in fact comes directly from one of Balzac's novellas, *La Duchesse de Langeais*, and it suggests that, for all Tom Tristram's ironic tone, we should be prepared for something dark and gothic.

In fact, forced marriage will be confirmed as not merely hypothetical but a real crux in Claire's history when Valentin tells Newman about her first marriage: "It was a chapter for a novel," says Valentin, describing how his sister met the elderly M. de Cintré only a month before the wedding, and turned white; then, the eve of the wedding, "swooned away" (154). This kind of reference (and there are a number of others) to plays and novels prepares Newman's prophetic flight of fancy in which he suggests—as will often be the case in James's fiction—how the future is to be written. He is in conversation with Mrs. Tristram about the Marquise de Bellegarde, Claire's mother, and the Marquis Urbain, her brother:

> "Well," said Newman, "she is wicked, she is an old sinner."
> "What is her crime?" asked Mrs. Tristram.
> "I shouldn't wonder if she had murdered some one—all from a sense of duty, of course."
> "How can you be so dreadful?" sighed Mrs. Tristram.
> "I am not dreadful. I am speaking of her favourably."
> "Pray what will you say when you want to be severe?"
> "I shall keep my severity for someone else—for the marquis. There's a man I can't swallow, mix the drink as I will."
> "And what has *he* done?"
> "I can't quite make out; it is something dreadfully bad, something mean and underhand, and not redeemed by audacity, as his mother's misdemeanours may have been. If he has never committed murder, he has at least turned his back and looked the other way while someone else was committing it." (225–26)

Newman's play of humor here may be a way of being wittily ironic about your melodramatic cake while eating it too—in the sense that the wicked deeds he imagines will turn out to have occurred in pretty much the form he fantasizes. His imagination generates the coming turn of the novel toward the gothic. The novel is now going to demonstrate that Newman has not over-read the Bellegardes' clues, that they are indeed as bad as they appear.

What comes to pass, then, is what I have called the "turn" of the novel. Despite foreshadowings, the transport into a world of overt evil, constraint, and the power of the wicked is abrupt. A melodramatic predicament and a nightmare atmosphere take over—and they are then authenticated by a true crime recounted by old Mrs. Bread, documented by the former Marquis' deathbed note. Then follows Claire's choice of claustration in the convent, and Newman's plotting of revenge. The social drama of the novel, with its comic encounter of American freedom with French fixity, reaches a kind of impasse—and then is blown apart by the irruption of melodrama. It is something like one of those "smashes of the window-pane" that James detected in Balzac. *The American* in my view represents a kind of hesitation on James's part about the kind of novel he wishes to write, and a desire to have it more than one way at once, to write a comic novel of manners that mutates into a gothic romance, complete with a family murder and a lurid document to use for revenge.

Since the novel was published serially, the kind of "turn" it would make may not have been wholly clear to James as he published the first installments. Yet its advent may have been in his mind from the start. If we often think of James as primarily a novelist of manners, I believe the melodramatic intensification and clarification of the moral stakes of actions and choices also is crucial and nearly omnipresent in his imagination. The social drama must live up to the demands of the penetrating imagination; under the pressure of crisis, it will release its latent melodrama. Be it the crisis of *The Ambassadors*, "a sharp fantastic crisis that had popped up as if in a dream"; or of *The Wings of the Dove*, the "Venice all of evil" unleashed by Lord Mark's visit to Milly Theale; or Fanny Assingham's smashing of the golden bowl, leaving its pieces to Maggie and the Prince; or the burning of Poynton; or any other of James's strong climaxes—we enter a realm where the stakes have been raised, where at issue are questions of good and evil, life and death. We don't in the later novels feel such a climax as a "turn" in which the novel changes course because in these novels the weight of the melodramatic, or perhaps more accurately its latent presence held at bay, is

there from the outset. These novels don't need the explicit foreshadowings provided in *The American*: the way in which experience is
recorded by consciousness, and the prose that renders the adventure of
consciousness, unceasingly tells us that we will need to reach an overt
encounter with what has been repressed.

Yet—and this should make us hesitate to describe *The American* as
immature work—the novel "turns" again before it is done, in Newman's renunciation of his possible revenge, in his burning of the documentary evidence of the Bellegardes' crime, in his becoming "a strong
man indifferent to his strength and too wrapped in fine, too wrapped
above all in *other* and intenser, reflexions for the assertion of his
'rights.'" The melodrama at the last turns inward, becomes the melodrama of the moral consciousness. And in fact, if we believe the preface, this final re-turn of the novel was present from the outset, was indeed James's original idea for the novel. James describes in the preface
how the idea of the novel came to him while seated in an American
horse-car—much as Newman's original conversion from money making to his European venture comes to him while riding in a New York
hack—and that it consisted in the idea of "the situation, in another
country and an aristocratic society, of some robust but insidiously be-
guiled and betrayed, some cruelly wronged, compatriot." The interest
of the story, says James, was from the outset what the American would
do in such a situation:

> He would behave in the most interesting manner—it would all
> depend on that: stricken, smarting, sore, he would arrive at his just
> vindication and then would fail of all triumphantly and all vul-
> garly enjoying it. . . . He wouldn't "forgive"—that would have, in
> the case, no application; he would simply turn, at the supreme
> moment, away, the bitterness of his personal loss yielding to the
> very force of his aversion. All he would have at the end would be
> therefore just the moral convenience, indeed the moral necessity,
> of his practical, but quite unappreciated, magnanimity; and one's
> last view of him would be that of a strong man indifferent to his
> strength and too wrapped in fine, too wrapped above all in *other*
> and intenser, reflexions for the assertion of his "rights." This last

point was of the essence and constituted in fact the subject: there
would be no subject at all, obviously,—or simply the commonest
of the common,—if my gentleman should enjoy his advantage.

On this account, the very germ of the novel was Newman's reaction to
his wrong: not the nature of that wrong but "the interesting face presented by him to any damnable trick," that is, a situation of having
been wronged that makes it possible for Newman to turn, at the
supreme moment, away. For James to get to where he wanted to be at
the end—to Newman's particular predicament and decision—the
novel had to veer from what seemed to be its original course and tone.

James in his preface ascribes the "romantic" element of the novel to
the way it has the Bellegardes behave: the more plausible social comedy would have them seizing upon Newman and his fortune with
alacrity. Yet of course that plot wouldn't have led to those "*other* and intenser" reflections of Newman at the end—wouldn't, it seems, have
given a melodrama of consciousness. But blaming it all on the Bellegardes' behavior may be something of a cover-up on James's part. What
his preface seems to recognize as a kind of youthful waywardness may
be a constant element in his imagination, and one that he is not entirely unaware of. James remains something of a romantic, concerned
with intensified experience and occult moral drama. The way he treats
"the romantic" in his preface suggests at once a recognition of this element in himself, and a repression of the recognition.

It's interesting that those "*other* and intenser" reflections never are
specified. James's italicizing of "*other*" only adds to its mystery. The
very end of the novel doesn't fill in the content. Newman burns the in-
criminating document, then appears to regret doing so when Mrs. Tristram suggests he has merely behaved as the Bellegardes foresaw he
would; he turns to the fireplace, to find the document is consumed.
But just what is going on in his intensified consciousness remains mysterious; it is the intensity of dreams. The preface repeats a key word
characterizing Newman at the end: in rejecting overt danger (caravans
and tigers, pistols and knives), James declares that "the panting pursuit
of danger is the pursuit of life itself, in which danger awaits us possibly
at every step and faces us at every turn," and thus romance becomes

"the dream of an intenser experience" (1063). All James's fiction will be concerned with this "intenser experience" and the ways in which the pursuit of life leads to it, reveals its presence and importance "beneath and behind" the everyday real.

The critique of romance in the preface to *The American* isn't, then, quite the act of self-criticism it appears to be. It's just as much an attempt to account for the continuing romantic strain in James's fiction, and his desire to achieve a perfected melodrama of consciousness, one where social incident that "looks like nothing" releases "*other* and intenser reflections." The very next preface in the New York Edition, that to *The Portrait of a Lady*, continues James's effort to define his own manner, in its description of that novel's climactic scene, the vigil in which Isabel Archer recognizes the truth of her marriage to Gilbert Osmond, the truth of all the wretchedness her life has become: "It is a representation simply of her motionlessly *seeing*, and an attempt withal to make the mere still lucidity of her act as 'interesting' as the surprise of a caravan or the identification of a pirate." One senses here James's confidence that with *The Portrait of a Lady* he has achieved that fusion of the romantic and the real in the melodrama of consciousness that he always sought. The "surprise of a caravan" and "the identification of a pirate" have been transmuted into the movements of consciousness reflecting on its own choices and possibilities. This is what *The American* turns toward. The earlier novel uses Paris and derivatives of French literature to distance itself from Flaubert's realism, and to reaffirm its allegiance to Balzac's romantic realism. At the same time, it may suggest that James hasn't finished with the lessons of the Paris avant-garde, that they will be back.

When *The American* finished its serial run in the *Atlantic* and shortly thereafter appeared as a volume, James had moved to London, and settled in to stay. Though he found London ugly, gloomy, uncomfortable compared to Paris, the English lower classes sordid and the food unspeakable compared to French cuisine, James was decided in his judgment that England was the place for him. The intellectual parochialism of the French—which many a visitor since James has discovered—must ultimately, I think, be held responsible for his choice. Flaubert's circle received him graciously, but made no place for him. Even if they had read him they would not have made a place for the Jamesian novel of 1876. Had Flaubert, Zola, and Maupassant been alive to read the novels James would publish in 1903–5, they might have felt differently—had they bothered to read outside their own parish.

London for all its faults proved more cosmopolitan than Paris: more open to a world outside itself. To some extent, the very lack of an artistic tradition of the novel may have been a liberation for James. His own cosmopolitanism liked to pick and choose among different inheritances. Still, he complains often about the restriction, the lack of self-consciousness and artistic aspiration of the English novel. He continues to read the French novelists, and more and more speaks of them with respect. Residence in London doesn't of course preclude trips across the Channel—very frequent ones. And then, as James's fame grew and his social circle expanded, he became a magnet for French visitors to England. He was—and this is no doubt something he strove for—unclassifiable, worldly, creative, like the dandy, of his own style and mode of being.

Style and mode of being were performed in London by a person always identified as American who continued to find—who more and more found—in French fiction, theater, and manners the wellspring of his own sensibility. The lessons of Flaubert and his circle, as well as the lesson of Balzac absorbed so early in life, would become more important as the Parisian residency grew more remote. He would learn to meet the French on his own terms.

3. What a Droll Thing to Represent

Settled in London, James repeatedly escaped to the Continent: to Italy and Switzerland and France. Most often his trips included a stay—of weeks, sometimes months—in Paris. Sometimes he gave as excuse for his trips the need to get away from the London social season. Especially in his correspondence with Cambridge, one senses cover-ups of his deepest motives of certain excursions—to see Paul Zhukovsky in Posilippo, for instance, to share a villa with Constance Fenimore Woolson, his American novelist friend, in Bellosguardo, outside Florence. "Europe" after all was freedom: from the James family, from Cambridge provincialities, from American puritanical attitudes. Much has been made of his secrecy about the relationship with Fenimore Woolson, but if she was most probably in love with him, I think he took no sexual interest in her. The point is rather that any intimate friendship implied a protective shielding from publicity for James. Many of his novels and tales dramatize his loathing of—as well as his excitement at—publicity and exposure. One of the most effective of these is the short novel *The Reverberator*—the title is that of the American tabloid newspaper that prints the heroine's indiscreet revelations, to an American journalist acquaintance, about the French family of her fiancé, with reverberating effects. It explains in advance why James would destroy so much correspondence and other intimate material, including everything he could lay his hands on from Fenimore Woolson's papers, in Venice, following her suicide in January 1894.

James published *The Reverberator* in June 1888, a very productive year. Then he went back to a project undertaken as a short fiction but now reconceived as a full-length novel, *The Tragic Muse*. After mailing the first two installments of the new work for publication in the *Atlantic*, now edited by Thomas Bailey Aldrich, James crossed the Channel again early in October. This time he bypassed Paris: he had an important piece of research to carry out there, but it concerned a later chapter of the new novel, and as a now well-exercised writer of serial fiction, he could afford to wait a bit. Instead, he went straight to Geneva, to be with Fenimore Woolson—though in a neighboring rather than the same hotel. There he carried on with *The Tragic Muse*. It is a novel that has never become central to the James "canon," never been much attended to by critics, perhaps because it doesn't fall into the usual categories for talking about James's life and fiction. To my mind, it is a greatly entertaining and interesting confrontation of issues and situations that mattered profoundly to James: art, the theater, sex, power, and the various uses of "representation."

Like *The American*, *The Tragic Muse* opens with viewing art works in Paris. This time it is not the collections of the Louvre but rather the new works of the annual Salon of painting and sculpture, and the foreign viewers are not American but English: Lady Agnes Dormer, impecunious widow of an MP, and her children Nick, Grace, and Biddy. Lady Agnes and Grace are substantially worn out by "the horrors" of the Salon, whereas Nick and his younger sister, Biddy, happily venture further in quest of interesting sights. "Do you really think it's necessary to the child's development?" Lady Agnes asks Nick. "What we've been through this morning in this place, and what you've paraded before our eyes—the murders, the tortures, all kinds of disease and indecency." To which Nick replies: "Ah dear mother, don't do the British matron!"

"Doing" in this sense is of key importance in the novel: "doing" as playing a role, enacting a part, giving a representative version of some way of being. Nick's recognition that Lady Agnes is performing the part of the British matron in Paris gives him a certain freedom from the set role he might be in, while allowing the narration of this first chapter to give an amusingly stagey version of cross-Channel cultural clash. In particular, the set roles played by Lady Agnes and the elder daughter,

Grace, allow Nick and Biddy to emerge as somewhat free spirits, ready—like Christopher Newman—to respond to the aesthetic. Lady Agnes, we learn, "hated talking about art" (23), which suggests that the issues engaged by the novel will have to do, even more than with art, with talk about art, especially in the figure of the Oscar Wildean aesthete Gabriel Nash, who soon appears on the scene. In contrast, there is the handsome and wealthy widow, Julia Dallow, whom Nick is supposed to marry in furtherance of a career in politics. Nick suggests that where art is concerned, Julia "has no taste at all." To which his mother replies: "That's better, I think" (20).

Gabriel Nash speaks in epigrammatic generalizations, as befits an imitation of Oscar Wilde. His extravagant paradoxes allow James to maintain the theatricality of the novel, the sense that a number of the characters are engaged in "performances," while excusing the author from responsibility for the resulting staginess. The outrageous Nash indeed becomes the arch-plotter of the novel, the person who appears to arrange some of its most dramatic moments. And when he in the second chapter announces that he thinks the Théâtre-Français a finer institution than the House of Commons, he states the essence of one of the key conflicts of the novel. On the one hand stands Nick Dormer's life as Member for Harsh—the place in the House of Commons he achieves with Julia's support—and on the other the life of the theater as incarnated by Miriam Rooth: two competing forms of "representation." James is very much aware that these two different senses of representation, ordinarily considered to have nothing to do with one another, in fact bear a close comparative scrutiny. The novel will in essence pit political representation against artistic representation throughout. Nick will resign his seat in the House in order to become a painter, in the process losing Julia, and impoverishing his mother and sisters as well as himself since he loses also the legacy long promised by Mr. Carteret, former MP and friend of Nick's father, who believes that the pencil and the brush "are not the weapons of a gentleman" (337). The quality of representation involved in political candidacy and political office on the one hand and in artistic imaging of the world on the other is debated throughout James's novel, and eventually worked through to a compromise rather than a reconciliation.

But the question of representation is made far more complex by the

figure of the actress, Miriam Rooth—one of James's most remarkable
creations, I think. Miriam has been "discovered" by Nick's friend Peter Sherringham, brother of Julia Dallow, a rising young diplomat who
is enamoured of the theater but never quite sure what place he can afford to give an actress in his life. Miriam has been compared to the
nineteenth-century French tragediennes Rachel and Sarah Bernhardt.
I think she also owes much to a character in George Eliot's *Daniel
Deronda*—a novel of great importance to James, and during the time
he read it, in Paris in 1876, part of his dialogue with French writers—
that is, Mirah Lapidoth. Like Mirah (and Rachel and Sarah Bernhardt), Miriam is Jewish ("More than half a Jewess" [49]), which
contributes, in James's presentation, to her artistic temperament and
also to her marginal, bohemian, almost unclassifiable social status.
George Eliot's Mirah is saved from the stage—figured as a kind of
prostitution—because her beautiful singing voice is too weak for the
theater; she is restricted to private performance in the drawing room.
The actress of that novel, the Princess of Halm-Eberstein—Daniel
Deronda's mother—verges on immorality precisely because of the
multiform, kaleidoscopic mutability of her nature, the instability that
accompanies theatricality. Mirah figures in a novel largely complicit
with an English puritan antitheatrical prejudice, whereas Miriam is
the creation of a novelist himself deeply enamoured of the Parisian
stage.

On his way back to London in December, 1888—after the time with
Fenimore Woolson in Geneva, then three weeks at Monte Carlo—
James spent a month in Paris, in the course of which he went backstage at the Comédie Française to visit the renowned actress Julia
Bartet in her *loge*. Here he gained material that he used in chapter 21
of *The Tragic Muse*, where Miriam and Peter Sherringham meet the
fictional actress Mademoiselle Voisin in the *foyer* of the theater, under
the aegis of the painter Jean-Léon Gérôme's "fine portrait of the pale
Rachel invested with the antique attributes of tragedy" (229). The
scene provides one of several encounters of Miriam and Peter, her admirer, would-be protector, aspiring lover, who is himself in thrall to the
theater yet deeply mistrustful of people of the theater. In the course of
this scene, Miriam says to Peter: "How you hate us!" (228)—echoed

when Julia Dallow tells Nick that she hates art. Peter's response is to propose marriage—but only if Miriam will give up the stage. "You shall be anything you like except this," Peter tells her (233), in a kind of self-cancelling statement. For what fascinates him about Miriam is her mutability, her capacity to play different lives and represent a spectrum of emotions—yet this is also what makes him deeply suspicious of her. The life of the actress seems deeply duplicitous and dubious to Peter. The idea of being husband to an actress disgusts him—whereas Miriam's capacity to play the role of ambassador's wife could legitimate the kind of *mésalliance* he contemplates.

What Miriam understands far better than the irresolute Peter is that what he wants of her would negate her very nature—and that nature consists in her "negative capability," to use Keats's term, her ability to always be other. She has no essential "nature"; she is always imaginatively assuming some other person's character. Such mutability is related to the talk, in this scene, about actresses and their lovers and keepers—seen as an inevitable part of the life of the stage, part of a world of "immoral" behavior that belongs to the theater, and to France, whereas England is supposed to be represented by the solid political values of Julia Dallow and Lady Agnes. Peter, promised to a successful diplomatic career yet smitten with the theater, can't quite choose between worlds—but in essence has his choice made for him by the determinants of his background. Near the dénouement of the novel, on the way to his posting abroad, he stops to witness Miriam's triumph on the London stage, then plays out a long and dramatic posttheater scene with her, only to return to the same proposal: that she leave the stage in order to become his wife.

Here Miriam breaks out:

> "You're dishonest, you're ungrateful, you're false!" Miriam flashed. "It was the theatre brought you here—if it hadn't been for the theatre I never would have looked at you. It was in the name of the theatre you first made love to me; it's to the theatre you owe every advantage that, so far as I'm concerned, you possess." (434)

Miriam goes on in the scene to rub Peter's nose in the scandal of theatrical self-display:

"Yes, we show it for money, those of us who have anything decent to show, and some no doubt who haven't, which is the real scandal." (439)

"We show it for money": Miriam both theatrically and candidly puts Peter before what he does not want to face—the artifice and venality of the actress, whose only immorality lies in not having anything decent to show. The suggestions of indecent exposure in the unspecified "it" are no doubt part of Miriam's message: actresses are not suited to the world of conventional virtues that Peter inhabits.

Miriam's brave declaration here echoes the words of her acting teacher Madame Carré early in the novel. When Miriam's mother objects: "I shouldn't like to see her represent a very bad woman—a *really* bad one," (89), Madame Carré ripostes that the English are confused about the relations of morality and artistic talent. "To be too respectable to go where things are done best is in my opinion to be very vicious indeed; and to do them badly in order to preserve your virtue is to fall into a grossness more shocking than any other. To do them well is virtue enough, and not to make a mess of it the only respectability." From Madame Carré comes this uncompromising message—similar to the message of Gabriel Nash, but more convincing from this expert and veteran practitioner—about the morality of art well practiced, professionally conceived, studied, worked at. The English notion of "respectability"—to which Mrs. Rooth subscribes because she is of dubious respectability herself, but which eminently characterizes Lady Agnes and Julia Dallow—simply has no applicability where art is concerned. And to use respectability as an excuse to do things poorly, and to refuse to go learn where things are practiced best, is a betrayal of art.

Madame Carré's message echoes James's own comment in a review, "The London Theatres," that ran in the *Galaxy* in 1877: "The only immorality I know on the stage is the production of an ill-made play." James repeatedly contrasted the English to the French theater, stressing always the higher degree of civilization represented by the perfection of acting—and of training in acting—represented by the Théâtre-Français. And even the "well-made plays" of the popular Boulevard theaters of Paris present a far more professional sense of dramatic art than the best-known English stage idols, such as Henry Irving. The London stage is held hostage to an audience of respectable British middle-class suburbanites, an audience that "suggests domestic virtue and comfortable homes; it looks as if it had come to the play in its own carriage, after a dinner of beef and pudding." The London playgoers are no doubt "much more the sort of people to spend a quiet evening with than the clever, cynical, democratic multitude that surges nightly out of the brilliant Boulevards into those temples of the drama in which MM. Dumas, *fils*, and Sardou are the high priests. But you might spend your evening with them better almost anywhere than at the theatre." That French audience can be ill-mannered, but "has the critical and the artistic sense, when the occasion appeals to them; it can judge and discriminate. It has the sense of form and of manner; it heeds and cares how things are done, even when it cares little for the things themselves." (102) This Paris-London contrast resonates as well with James's reply to such literary pundits as Walter Besant, who would keep the English novel in a kind of infancy by their insistence it protect the morals of virgins. The "moral timidity" of the English novel has come over time to include "an unreasoning instinct of avoidance," in particular "a mistrust of any but the most guarded treatment of the great relation between men and women." English novelists who refused to look to France for its lessons in the art of fiction, who saw French fiction as merely "shocking," were guilty of the "vicious" error proclaimed by Madame Carré.

The novel provides us, then, with sets of oppositions: the power of art versus the power of politics, or more simply art versus life, and moral respectability versus the negative capability of art—which may mean abandoning moral conventions in favor of sympathy with the devil, which for the artist may precisely *be* morality. These oppositions extend across the Channel: the conflicts of the novel pit England against France, both using the clichés of English respectability, stolidity, and philistinism versus French immorality, theatricality, and aestheticism, and complicating them by Nick's move, within the English context, from politics to art, and Peter's inability, within the French context, to rid himself of English "morality" and let himself go in his love for

Miriam. These oppositions are repeatedly stated by Gabriel Nash as epigrammatic paradoxes. And the paradoxes multiply in the structure of the book, when Miriam appears to fall in love with Nick instead of Peter, then later when the alienated Julia appears to return to Nick by way of the request to have her portrait painted. James notes in his preface to *The Tragic Muse* that he began in his thinking with two separate "cases": the political and the theatrical, then decided to join them in one novel. He manages the two together by a structure of "chiasmus": that is, one that looks like an X, but where the extremities of the X start to trade places.

James seems to suggest in the preface that Miriam is ready to do for Nick what she clearly isn't ready to do for Peter—become his lover without a marriage proposal; James appears to say that the conventions of the English novel prevented him from representing such a liaison. It's not clear to me that James is at all points in his preface the best re-reader of his own novel—he seems to delineate areas of his drama that are more potential than realized. It's hard to say, because the sexuality of *The Tragic Muse* is both very intense, very present, and heavily concealed. There is a sexual drama by innuendo throughout the book, especially in Peter's courtship of Miriam, where the paradox of an actress means that he cannot respectably marry her, yet to be respectable and have her must marry her. Miriam is fascinated by the actress Mlle Voisin's lovers—particularly the "way a woman like that receives one of the old ones"—but this is a domain of knowledge into which Peter can't allow himself to follow her lead. "What do you want of me then?" Miriam inquires of Peter here. It's not clear that Peter ever can answer that, since what he wants is so heavily overlain by self-censorship.

During the time between his election to Parliament and his resignation of his seat, Nick is pushed by his mother toward marriage with Julia—a marriage that would offer him the solution of a number of nineteenth-century fictional heroines obliged to provide not only for themselves but as well for their indigent families through marrying well; Gwendolen Harleth in her choice of Grandcourt, in Eliot's *Daniel Deronda*, is one the best examples. Lady Agnes urges that Nick prolong his visit to Julia at Harsh:

"Aren't you her member, and can't her member pass a day with her, and she a great proprietor?"

Nick turned round at this with an odd expression. "*Her* member—am I hers?"

Lady Agnes had a pause—she had need of all her tact. "Well, if the place is hers and you represent the place—!" she began. But she went no further, for Nick had interrupted her with a laugh.

"What a droll thing to 'represent,' when one thinks of it! And what does *it* represent, poor stupid little borough with its strong, though I admit clean, smell of meal and its curiously fat-faced inhabitants?" (159–60)

Hmm. The disguised sexual banter here suggests that Julia has taken over Nick's phallus: she owns his "member." Nick, one could say, merely is the phallus, while she *has* the phallus: she has the place, he merely represents it. The phallus—and this often seems to be the case in James—may be the signifier of meaning but it is not in the place of meaning as power.

Does James know what he is doing here? Possibly not, but there is in fact much sexual innuendo in James, and a certain fascination with hidden bodily parts: see, for instance, his letters to the young sculptor Henrik Andersen, from which I quote in chapter 6. This is a novelist capable of naming a principal character Fanny Assingham, after all. Reading this kind of sexual innuendo into an exchange between mother and son may be perverse, but the novel is quite explicitly about forms of "perversity" in the conduct of life, as it is also explicitly about representation and sexual power. The problem with loving an actress, Peter discovers as he watches Miriam perform for Madame Carré—as if he were the official sponsor and keeper of Miriam that he is only financially—lies in that negative capability developed to the point where there is no "real woman" under the act:

It came over him suddenly that so far from there being any question of her having the histrionic temperament she simply had it in such perfection that she was always acting; that her existence was a series of parts assumed for the moment, each changed for the

next, before the perpetual mirror of some curiosity or admiration
or wonder—some spectatorship that she perceived or imagined in
the people about her. Interested as he had ever been in the profession of which she was potentially an ornament, this idea startled
him by its novelty and even lent, on the spot, a formidable, a really
appalling character to Miriam Rooth. It struck him abruptly that a
woman whose only being was to "make believe," to make believe
she had any and every being you might like and that would serve a
purpose and produce a certain effect, and whose identity resided
in the continuity of her personations, so that she had no moral privacy, as he phrased it to himself, but lived in a high wind of exhibition, of figuration—such a woman was a kind of monster in
whom of necessity there would be nothing to "be fond" of, because there would be nothing to take hold of. He felt for a moment how simple he had been not to have achieved before this
analysis of the actress. The girl's very face made it vivid to him
now—the discovery that she positively had no countenance of her
own, but only the countenance of the occasion, a sequence, a
variety—capable possibly of becoming immense—of representative movements. . . . The expression that came nearest belonging
to her, as it were, was the one that came nearest being a blank . . .
(126)

Peter discovers here an age-old critique of the actress: that she is capable of constant variety and change, donning and doffing masks at will,
and therefore is no one on her own. Peter's would-be Frenchness
reaches its limits in love for Miriam: it encounters the panic fear that
there is nothing to love, that she is a blank. As such, she may also be
the frightening incarnation of the feminine whose person offers "nothing to take hold of."

Miriam presents to Peter precisely what Keats meant by "negative
capability": the poet (and Keats's example is Shakespeare: dramatic poetry) is nothing in himself, but always into, and filling, some other
form. It is also the "paradox" commented on in Diderot's *Paradox of
the Actor*, which argues that the actor is most successful in creating a
role precisely when he is the most distant from it, the most capable of

shaping it to the needs and desires of his audience rather than his own. The actor in this sense must be nothing, simply the vehicle through which passion is represented. Jean-Jacques Rousseau, who also reflected on the role of theater and enactment, especially in his *Letter to d'Alembert on the Theatre*, voices the anxiety that such a protean representation of pretended passions is potentially corrupting: it leads not only the actor but the audience to lose its moral compass. Some such suspicion of the capacity to act, to undergo constant metamorphosis, no doubt lay behind the excommunication of actors and actresses by the Roman Catholic Church by the fact of their profession—a condition that endured for several centuries. In Peter's phrase, the actress lacks "moral privacy"—which may be a polite way of saying 'tis pity she's a whore.

Acting is sheer representation, the more effective the more the actress ceases to be herself, to become the vehicle for personating another, for creating the effect of the person she is playing. James's lifelong fascination with the theater takes flight in the creation of Miriam, who moves from humble beginnings to consummate stage artistry. Close to the midpoint of the novel we find Miriam rehearsing scenes from Shakespeare's *King John*—seemingly an odd choice on James's part (though more popular at his time than ours) but interesting as yet another English-French contrast. Miriam begins in the French theater, where the pure art is to be learned. When she moves to London, her great triumph comes in a translated and "idiotized" version of a French romantic drama. (James was a harsh critic of English "adaptations" of French plays.) Then she goes on to more Shakespeare: *Romeo and Juliet*. She virtually realizes a Jamesian dream of ennobling the musty British stage, which he judged too much in thrall to the conventional expectations of its philistine audiences, heavily invested in illusionistic stage-settings, and lacking in the high traditions of declamation and gesture fostered by the French Conservatoire and national theater.

Miriam brings us back to the question of representation in the other plot, Nick's. Nick the newly elected MP is suspected of having a studio in "an out-of-the-way district, the indistinguishable parts of South Kensington" (64). "It was an absurd place to see his constituents unless he wanted to paint their portraits, a kind of 'representation' with which they would scarce have been satisfied; and in fact the only question of portraiture had been when the wives and daughters of several of them expressed a wish for the picture of their handsome young member." This explicitly pits political representation against artistic representation. James evidently wants his readers to juxtapose the two kinds, to see that there is indeed a link—and an opposition—between these two apparently unrelated concepts of "represent." Representation in both cases entails a relation of substitution or standing for: signs or symbols that take the place of "reality." That is, literary and artistic signs and symbols make believe, give a figuration of the real world precisely in a made-up fiction. And political representation involves some person claiming to take the place of many others, to convey their views. One might in this context recall Rousseau's view that representative government—as opposed to direct, participatory democracy—is no better than tyranny. Political representation has the same fatal flaws as theatrical representation. It is a fiction that alienates from direct, personal involvement—in decision making as in emotional life. Rousseau's critique of representation almost seems to hover somewhere in the background of Nick's musings on what it means to "stand for" and represent the borough of Harsh, as it does also in Peter's discovery of the moral proteanism of the actress. Gabriel Nash of course states the unambiguous if paradoxical position: life itself must be art, we must conceive ourselves as fictional creations, self-representation is the only sort that matters.

Nick's dilemma of choice between kinds of representation is complicated not only by Julia and the fortune she brings—and withdraws, along with her consent to marriage, when he resigns from Parliament—but also by Mr. Carteret, the old landed gentleman, friend of his father's and proud former MP, whose ancient estate represents to Nick "the sense of England—a sort of apprehended revelation of his country," and accordingly his inherited responsibilities (187). To be disinherited by Mr. Carteret—as Nick eventually will—is to lose not only a sizable fortune but also a direct and cherished connection to a traditional sovereignty and privilege. But as MP Nick feels himself a "mountebank"—a term used with great frequency in the novel, usually to refer to actors but also, and with greater force, to those who put themselves in false or "humbugging" positions: Peter with Miriam, Nick with Julia.

The out-of-the-way studio in South Kensington will be the setting for a great theatrical scene in which the different sorts of representation come into collision. Gabriel Nash brings Miriam to sit for Nick—to paint her, not as "The Tragic Muse" as originally proposed by Peter, but rather in a casual pose. At the end of a successful morning's work, Miriam has come to lounge in an armchair to view the roughed-in portrait, and Nick has moved round behind the chair and is leaning over its back—when the door opens soundlessly, and Julia Dallow (now Nick's fiancée) appears. "She had taken a step forward, but she had done no more, stopping short at the sight of the strange woman, so divested of visiting-gear that she looked half-undressed, who lounged familiarly in the middle of the room and over whom Nick had been still more familiarly hanging" (270). To Julia's stare, Miriam merely stares back, "motionless and superb." Julia's entrance is a Boulevard-style *coup-de-théâtre*, and the ensuing scene unfolds with high theatricality, both comic and dramatic, since Julia has had "a shock of extreme violence." The scene has been carefully prepared and acts as a fulcrum for the action: it leads directly to Julia's rupture with Nick, his resignation from the House of Commons, and Peter's jealousy. Julia's complaints about his having "women lolling—with all their things off—to be painted" leads to her impassioned outburst: "I hate art." She makes it clear that the only husband she wants is one with the ambition to become prime minister.

Nick passes off the scene with Miriam as wholly art, not eros. Yet it's not clear that he is wholly honest in so describing it. When Peter comes to view the unfinished portrait, he is struck first of all by the power of Nick's painting—"he had no idea Nick moved with that stride" (303)—and then considers that its fineness may constitute a "virtual infidelity" to Julia (322): an infidelity by way of representation, we might say. Gabriel Nash will soon tell Nick that it is he, not Peter, that Miriam really wants—though Nick accuses Gabriel of talking "like an American novel," and it is not wholly clear how much of Miriam's love for Nick is Gabriel's invention. (James in his preface, we saw, thought she was ready to give herself to Nick, but James may be reading more his imagined novel than the one he actually wrote.) In any event, Miriam's possible erotic attachments both to Peter and to Nick never come to fruition. She instead marries the actor Basil

Dashwood—because she needs some man in her life—while Peter never can make up his mind to marry her so long as she remains an actress, nor to marry Nick's sister Biddy till the last page, and Nick remains erotically opaque. In Nick's last scene with Miriam in his studio, it's clear that they both feel some "throb" of unfulfilled passion. But this part of the drama remains occulted.

Gabriel Nash predicts that Julia will eventually come back to Nick: "She'll put up with the palette if you put up with the country-house" (472). And in fact, Biddy will soon come to report that Julia is "dying to sit." So that Nick eventually appears to settle into something of a compromise: an artist, but one who is successful, who makes his way in portraiture. James's choice of portraiture for the resolution of Nick's vocation is interesting. Traditionally, portraiture has not ranked as the highest form of painting, perhaps precisely because it must subordinate artistic freedom to fidelity of representation. It is resolutely a representational enterprise, where resemblance to the object of representation, as well as expressive quality, greatly matters. In portraiture, painterly and novelistic concerns converge: the novelist, too, presents portraits of characters, and James often has recourse to the vocabulary of the painter in an effort to find the right perspective, lighting, and contour for the presentation of a verbally constructed character. James is very much aware that "character" in fiction engages a presentational issue: like the painted person, the literary person is created through illusions of depth, contour, recess, inwardness.

When Nick goes to view "the great portraits of the past" at the National Gallery, James's prose reaches toward a lush evocation:

As he stood before them the perfection of their survival often struck him as the supreme eloquence, the virtue that included all others, thanks to the language of art, the richest and most universal. Empires and systems and conquests had rolled over the globe and every kind of greatness had risen and passed away, but the beauty of the great pictures had known nothing of death or change, and the tragic centuries had only sweetened their freshness. The same faces, the same figures looked out at different worlds, knowing so many secrets the particular world didn't, and when they joined hands they made the indestructible thread on which the pearls of history were strung. (463)

Some of James's most eloquent moments are triggered by painted portraits—perhaps most notably, Milly Theale's "pink dawn of an apotheosis" before the Bronzino portrait that tells of her own fragile mortality, in *The Wings of the Dove*. The art that Nick most prizes here is an art of faces and figures: a representational art of character.

"You'll do things that will hand on your name when my screeching is happily over," Miriam tells Nick in his studio (464). But though Nick's may be the more enduring form of art, it's clear that James also places a very high value on the actress's. James's romance with the theater was life-long; it persisted before, during, and after his attempt to be a playwright. Theater, too, was a medium for the representation of character, character seized in motion. When Miriam says she wishes someone would write a comedy of manners in which she could "do" Julia Dallow, she echoes Nick imploring his mother not to do the British matron—but to do character consciously and artistically is a wholly different thing from its unconscious production. Miriam's theatricality, and her capacity to put herself in the place of the spectator to her own acting, keep before us the theatricality of James's own novel.

One could say that James's fascination with the theater and with theatricality—including the melodramatic Balzacian version—led him from the start of his career to write with the theater in mind. As I noted in *The American*, his fiction tends to remind us overtly of its theatrical qualities, of its enactments and its spectatorships. Later novels—*The Spoils of Poynton* would be a good example, among many others—tend to resolve themselves even more into narrative preparations for dramatic moments played out as scenes. And James would in his prefaces develop a theory of his own "scenic method," which derives in direct line from the Balzacian novel. It was in the logic of his fiction that he should decide to write for the stage in a more literal way. Unfortunately, it was the wrong stage: London rather than Paris, and the five years of effort to be a popular London playwright ended in the disaster of *Guy Domville* in 1895, its author hissed following the premiere. Following this failure, James returned to the novel, but with a yet more conscious understanding of how the novel he wished to write must be dramatic and scenic. "I realize—none too soon—that the *scenic* method is my absolute, my imperative, my *only* salvation," he wrote to himself while working on *What Maisie Knew*, just after the *Guy Domville* fiasco.

The Tragic Muse was written just before James let himself be tempted into his first theater production: a stage adaptation of *The American* (a much impoverished version of the novel, which opened with a provincial tour, then had a respectable run in the West End). It seems almost to predict this next step in his career. And in the later preface to the novel, James insistently evokes theater not only as theme but also as technique in *The Tragic Muse*. Discussing the need for preparations, in the novel as in the drama, James writes: "The first half of a fiction insists ever on figuring to me as the stage or theatre for the second half," which then leads to a discussion of foreshortening as a necessary principle of representation. Noting that his centers of consciousness in this novel include both Nick and Peter but not Miriam, he argues that this makes her an appropriately theatrical figure. She is "an absolutely objective Miriam"—known only through others' views of her—and this makes her central "in virtue of the fact that the whole thing has visibly, from the first, to get itself done in dramatic, or at least scenic conditions—though scenic conditions which are as near an approach to the dramatic as the novel may permit itself."

Now, in the theater there is no "*usurping* consciousness," James tells us; "the consciousness of others is exhibited exactly in the same way as that of the 'hero.'" In his effort to present Miriam the actress in a properly theatrical way, James notes, "I never 'go behind' Miriam." "Going behind" is James's term for entering the mind of a character, espousing that character's perspective, and informing the reader of the processes at work in that consciousness. As a writer interested, like Balzac, in what lies "beneath and behind" the appearances of social life, James is pre-eminently the novelist of "going behind"—into the most subtle and protracted study of the movements of consciousness. Yet his desire to dramatize leads him to the rule that he must limit the number of consciousnesses he will permit himself to enter, in order to have "objective" characters in his fiction who can be known only through others' consciousness of them. It is very often the character with the highest charge of dramatic affect, at the most dramatic moment of the fiction, whose consciousness is in this manner forbidden to the novelist: Milly Theale at the time of her betrayal and her final illness, and death; Charlotte Stant in her anguish of defeat and exile.

There are moments when the male characters of *The Tragic Muse* "go behind" in a more literal sense: go to see an actress, mainly Miriam, backstage. There comes a moment when Miriam in conversation with Peter and Nick and Gabriel Nash expresses a wish to be visited in her dressing room by politically powerful men decorated with "a cordon and a star" (360). Nash points out that in England "gentlemen accoutred with those emblems of their sovereign's esteem didn't so far forget themselves as to stray into the dressing-rooms of actresses." That is the kind of thing that happens in Parisian theaters, and French novels. Miriam "was sorry, for that was the sort of thing she had always figured in a corner—a distinguished man, slightly bald, in his evening dress, with orders, admiring the smallness of a satin shoe and saying witty things." James may be evoking slyly a scene from Zola's *Nana* where Comte Muffat and the Prince, a fictional version of the Prince of Wales, visit the half-naked Nana backstage, or the pendant painting by Manet, *Nana*, which reveals at the very edge of the painting—sliced through, in typical Manet fashion—the evening-dressed old man staring at the actress's satin shoe. This allusion resembles James's somewhat obscure discussion in the preface of what he might have created between Nick and Miriam under different conditions of the novel—presumably French conditions.

This discussion concludes James's meditation on what lies between Nick and Miriam where, as a reader of his own novel, he may find more than many another reader. Miriam is indeed presented so "objectively," so theatrically, that it is difficult to know what she is offering Nick in the way of a liaison; and James's self-censorship obscures even further. It is in fact one of the theatrical, play-like aspects of this novel that Miriam remains somewhat opaque since it is difficult—as Peter noted to his sorrow—to distinguish the actress from the woman, the true emotion from the dramatized emotion. Or rather, with Miriam as we view her—without "going behind"—such questions cannot be posed. As Peter later discovers, "the representation was the deep substance" (306). This means that Miriam, for all the vast differences between them, does resemble Zola's Nana in that she is known in large part through the effects that she creates. *The Tragic Muse* is to a large extent about the "Miriam effect" on the men who encounter her. The discussions of Miriam's lack of a fixed "character," and the decision not to go behind, confirm that this was James's intention. Miriam is like one of the blank canvasses with which Nick begins, a surface on which to paint a gloriously multicolored and lively drama.

The novel that James wrote most purely in the form of a play, *The Awkward Age* (1899), lent itself to a discussion, in the preface, of "going behind" and what it meant, in that novel, to dispense with it entirely, in favor of a completely scenic presentation. When he comes to writing the preface for *The Wings of the Dove* (1902), one of his very greatest novels, he suggests that he has found fullest satisfaction in a technique that uses discriminated centers of consciousness—we may assume that he believes he may go behind each of these centers at the moment it is operative—but precisely makes them viewers of dramatic scenes. He refers to "the secret of the discriminated occasion—that aspect of the subject which we have our noted choice of treating either as picture or scenically, but which is apt, I think, to show its fullest worth in the Scene." In this manner, James proposes to have both his scene and his spectators—and indeed to make his drama most often reside in the inner reaction of these spectators to the spectacle. Following *The Wings of the Dove*, James's final completed novel, *The Golden Bowl* (1904) uses principally two centers of consciousness, the Prince for book 1, the Princess for book 2—though aided by the choral commentators Bob and Fanny Assingham—to register and reflect his high drama of adultery and its repair. The outrageous name James invented for Fanny Assingham—with what degree of conscious intent I can't tell—almost seems a kind of Rabelaisian flagging of the technique of going behind. And if one wanted to tease out the implications for James's sexual interests and orientations, they would all be there.

It's in the preface to *The Golden Bowl* that James reflects on his discovery at the very start of his novelistic career—with *Roderick Hudson*—that showing something by way of someone's "indirect and oblique view" of it is always more interesting than the direct view—since the indirect and oblique view makes not only the action but the interpretation of the action subjects of interest. He again and again has chosen to present narratives "not as my own impersonal account of the affair in hand, but as my account of somebody's impression of it—the terms of this person's access to it and estimate of it contributing thus by some fine little law to intensification of interest." His retrospect leads to the discovery that: "Anything, in short, must always have seemed to me better—better for the process and the effect of representation, my irrepressible ideal—than the mere muffled majesty of irresponsible 'authorship.'" Narrating without point of view—without an attempt to show action reflected in some specific person's consciousness—is "irresponsible." It offers the author as authority, it does not respect that play of perspective on the world that James increasingly defines as the true art of fiction, and the stance that best respects the autonomy of human character.

The Tragic Muse dramatizes and, in its preface, theorizes these presentational issues. It seems to me very much the jumping-off point for James's later development. And I would argue that this later development brought a kind of return of what James repressed during his Paris year of 1875–76: a new understanding of the radical perspectivalism practiced by Flaubert in literature, by the impressionists in painting, for instance. If James at age thirty-two and thirty-three appears to reject some of the key innovations of the European avant-garde—and to reach for older and safer models in Balzac and George Eliot—it seems that by the 1890s (though the moment is hard to date with precision) he has come to an understanding of what he at first missed, or misunderstood, or misestimated.

The question of "representation" was and would remain crucial for James. He is baffled by art that appears to deploy its resources for something other than a portraiture of life. He writes of Whistler, for instance—in the *Galaxy* in 1877—"It may be a narrow point of view, but to be interesting it seems to me that a picture should have some relation to life as well as to painting. Mr. Whistler's experiments have no relation whatever to life; they have only a relation to painting." There is a mixture of the perceptive and obtuse here. Experiments that have "only a relation to painting" is a plausible characterization of much of modern art, in its quest to explore its medium, its formal properties and their potential. But James rejects such experimentation on grounds of its lack of relation to "life." A year later he again judges Whistler: "His manner is very much that of the French 'Impressionists', and, like them, he suggests the rejoinder that a picture is not an impression but an expression—just as a poem or a piece of music is." Over and against impressionism James sets expressionism. This reflects an accurate sense of his own aesthetic in relation to the modern movement just coming into being in Paris. He rejects what he sees as the formal experimentation and fascination with the medium and material of the painted surface he finds in the impressionists and Whistler. He declares his own allegiance to an older, more romantic, more Balzacian belief that painted images and words exist to make manifest, to express, visions of the real, including perceptions and inward states only reached with difficulty, behind and beneath. Like Nick Dormer's portraits, and his own. Like, also, French theater at his best: as James wrote in his most extended discussion of the Comédiens-Français, in 1877, "they solve triumphantly the problem of being at once realistic to the eye and romantic to the imagination." Later, he would discover some of this same marriage of the romantic and the real in Henrik Ibsen, who came very much as a revelation, despite his foreignness: the playwright James had been looking for. Ibsen's characters—especially his young women—resonated fully with James's own portraits.

In the long, late essay on Flaubert (1902), James discusses at length Flaubert's sense of style, his creation of "a blest world in which we know nothing except by style, but in which also everything is saved by it, and in which the image is thus always superior to the thing itself." This doses praise for the beauty of Flaubert's technique with dissent from such a "blest world" in which image is superior to that which it represents. He goes on to say: "Style itself moreover, with all respect to Flaubert, never *totally* beguiles; since even when we are so queerly constituted as to be ninety-nine parts literary we are still a hundredth part something else." That hundredth part appears to represent the claim of life, of what is represented rather than the representation. The hundredth part may make us imperfect as readers, James says, but without it "would we want or get the book at all?" James puts in a plea for the impurity of art, for its use as an illumination of life. That in his view is what the novel in particular exists to provide.

The Tragic Muse turns on these questions. Nick gives up political representation for painting—painting that is at once bold, original, and fully committed to the most traditional form of representation: portraiture, the likeness of people. Paint her as "the Tragic Muse," Peter says to Nick about Miriam (91). If Peter is thinking of such a model as Gérôme's portrayal of Rachel as *La Tragédie*—giving a portrait an allegorical context and significance—that is not what Nick eventually produces in his portrait of Miriam. It is the vivid, expressive informality of the portrait that impresses its viewers. It is portraiture that aims at making external traits expressive of inner characteristics. It uses the language of the face and the body for meaningful statements about "character." Miriam is both an impressive and a problematic instance in that she is too expressive, too various, to be captured as any single meaning.

In the somewhat paradoxical figure of Miriam the actress James figures his somewhat uneasy stance between traditional representation and the modernism represented by French artists and writers. Miriam dedicates her life to representation. She has no character of her own; representation is her "deep substance," as Peter discovers. "Her character," Peter also reflects, "was simply to hold you by the particular spell" (306). Her character is defined here by the bewitching effect she has on her spectators, and this may complicate further her commitment to representation: the effect produced stands for what is claimed to be represented; it is a kind of simulacrum created by the spectator from the representation offered by the actress. That is, its referent really lies more in the spectator's or reader's response than in that which has been represented. This is closer to impressionism than James may realize. The "paradox of the actor" leads us to an aesthetic where the sign is judged less by its actual referent than by its capacity to create the illusion of reference.

James with *The Tragic Muse* stands on the threshold of his exploration of illusions of reference, of any single consciousness's limited vision of the real, and its fantasmatic ways of filling in gaps in order to complete a picture. In the latter half of the 1890s, with such novels and tales as *What Maisie Knew, The Turn of the Screw, The Beast in the Jungle, The Sacred Fount*—and others—James explored a kind of radical perspectivalism, the question of what can one see and—since that is never the whole picture—how one fills in the gaps, in ways that may be tested against others' equally partial perceptions but never against an objective standard. Whether the constructions of such as the governess in *The Turn of the Screw* or the unnamed narrator of *The Sacred Fount* are accurate representations of reality or hallucinatory figurations never can be known. James seems in these fictions to be testing the medium and material of his art—rather in the manner of a Whistler—in preparation for his final three novels, all of which make the adventures of partial and deluded consciousness the stuff of major ethical dramas. Belatedly, begrudgingly, James has learned from the impressionists and from Flaubert, though he has learned in his own way, made his own compromises—and continued to insist that Flaubert and his painterly equivalents failed to comprehend the responsibilities of representation.

James's itinerary from *The Tragic Muse* to his late work, in the early years of the twentieth century, includes this movement into more subjective and partially seen dramas, in a kind of trying-out of what can be learned from the distortions of limited perspective, as in many of Degas' contemporary images of domestic scenes looked at from odd angles, sometimes as if through the keyhole. And then he emerges, in his late work, with a unique personal synthesis or compromise—not without its affinities to Nick Dormer's compromise. It will be an art that combines the use of often radically restricted and baffled perspective with a full-blown scenic method. Partial perspectives lead to and culminate in scenes that remain faithful to James's understanding of Balzacian drama and the romantic element of the Théâtre-Français. It is a peculiar and thoroughly original compromise that gives us the late-Jamesian manner. It's a compromise that allows him to see in distorted perspective and yet to remain committed to the primacy of representation.

The ultimate solution for James thus annexes some of what he learned from Flaubert and his disciples to the lesson of Balzac (and George Eliot). It necessarily differs from the solution that Flaubert himself was working out in the final years of his life, which would come to an end in 1880. Flaubert's solution was more radical—and ultimately, for James, radically unusable.

4. Flaubert's Nerds

When Turgenev brought James to meet Flaubert in December of 1875, the French writer was not at his most productive, and he was more than usually melancholic. To be sure, his literary production mainly took place in his study at Croisset, outside Rouen, in Normandy; his winter stays in Paris were for socializing (and considerable clandestine sex). But he had suffered a number of losses in the past few years—his best friend, Louis Bouilhet, his mother—and the war with Prussia and the ensuing insurgency of the Commune had depressed him further. Then came a blow that plunged the often depressive Flaubert into black melancholy and despair. Ernest Commanville, husband of his niece Caroline—who came closer to being a child than anyone else in Flaubert's life, and to whom he was wholly devoted—went bankrupt. Commanville owned a sawmill at Dieppe; a decline in the price of lumber, no doubt combined with poor management, brought ruin. While Commanville already owed Flaubert income from money the novelist had invested in him, for the sake of his niece Flaubert came to the rescue, selling his one remaining farm, in Deauville, for 200,000 francs. A legal proceeding in bankruptcy was avoided. From his lamentations to his correspondents—"*complètement ruiné*" he writes, again and again—to his bailout of his nephew-in-law, Flaubert behaved like a prudent and honorable Norman bourgeois, which of course he was, though he spent much of his life railing

101

against such persons. "Honor will be preserved, but nothing else," he wrote to his friend Léonie Brainne.

The Commanville débâcle resulted in seriously straitened circumstances that made money a constant worry for Flaubert in his mid-fifties: made visits to Paris more difficult, meant replacing his Paris apartment with a smaller, less expensive fifth-floor walk-up, while also creating the worry that the house at Croisset (which his mother had left to Caroline) might have to be sold. He began to ask friends to find him a paid position as librarian, preferably a sinecure—either a post that didn't really require residence in Paris, or else one that came with lodgings. (In 1879, he would be appointed deputy curator at the Bibliothèque Mazarine, with a stipend of 3,000 francs and no duties.) There was ample reason to be depressed, and to feel the pressure to complete and sell his literary work. He would work though his problems over the next year and a half by way of the composition of the three short fictions published in 1877 under the title *Trois Contes*. Meanwhile, he abandoned for two years— June 1875 to June 1877—work on his long opus, in many ways his most ambitious project, *Bouvard et Pécuchet*. When he picked it up again, the time remaining proved insufficient to bring it to conclusion; it was unfinished when he died on May 8, 1880. James read it when it was published posthumously, less than a year after Flaubert's death.

It was Flaubert's somewhat delusional idea that *Bouvard et Pécuchet* would crown his literary career—it would sum up and give definitive form to his obsessions. Some version of it is present early in his writing projects, under the title *Les Deux cloportes*: literally, the two woodlice; metaphorically, the two creeps, one might say, or the two stooges, since they are regularly the straight men of comedy routines. Given their intellectual preoccupations, perhaps a closer contemporary idiom would style them the two nerds. Nerds they are: two copyists, scriveners (like Bartleby in Melville's tale), who retire, move to the country, and undertake extensive reading projects in order to beautify, transform, and understand their world—projects that inevitably end in grotesque failure. Bouvard and Pécuchet, like Tweedledee and Tweedledum, Laurel and Hardy, Rosenkranz and Guildenstern, or any two Beckett characters, are a quintessentially comic couple. The two of them are barely distinguishable, and in any case the distinctions don't matter. What matters is rather the chance for dialogue provided by having two, the way they feed one another's hapless enterprises and react to their comeuppances. The novel, at least when read in the right mood, is howlingly funny. It offers a kind of generalized housewrecking of major systems of knowledge and belief—agriculture, horticulture, chemistry, history, literature, politics, love, education. Flaubert claimed at one point to have read 1,500 books, ranging over these subjects, in order to compose his novel. It is an encyclopaedic send-up of encyclopaedic ambitions, a "kind of encyclopaedia of modern Stupidity," he wrote to a correspondent in 1872. This makes it, of course, one of the strangest novels ever written.

Flaubert talked about his project with his literary friends, including Turgenev and Taine, who expressed doubts to one another about the wisdom of the project. The Russian novelist in July 1874 sent Flaubert a letter in which he sought to persuade him that such a subject should be treated briefly, in a satire in the manner of Swift or Voltaire. Flaubert's answer is curious and characteristic:

> Despite the immense respect that I have for your critical sense (for in you the Judge is at the level of the Creator, which is saying a lot), I don't agree with you on the way one should take hold of such a subject. If it's treated briefly, concisely and lightly, that will give a more or less witty fantasy, but it will be without reach or verisimilitude; whereas in detailing and developing, I will appear to believe in my story—and one can do something serious and even terrifying. The great danger is monotony and boredom. That's what really frightens me . . .

Something "serious and even terrifying": such is Flaubert's justification for writing his satire (though that is not quite the right word for this unclassifiable work) in the form of a "novel." What are we to make of "terror" as a goal of fiction, especially when it is largely a fiction of ideas? Flaubert is not writing a gothic horror novel or thriller. What are we to make of his call for his novel to be terrifying in its effect?

There may be a clue in his description, from early in his thinking on the project, of the *Dictionnaire des idées reçues*, which it seems clear was to take its place in the second volume of the novel. This

"Dictionary of Conventional Wisdom" or "Dictionary of Clichés," which Flaubert refers to also simply as the *sottisier*—portfolio of stupidities—seems to have been a key element in his encyclopaedic enterprise from the very beginning. To his friend Louis Bouilhet he wrote, back in 1850, that he wanted to arrange this collection of clichés in such a way "that the reader would not know whether or not he was being made a fool of"—*si on se fout de lui, oui ou non*—which would result in a "strange work." That is, the *Dictionnaire* would simply be a collection of citations, of commonplaces, prefaced—as he wrote to Louise Colet in 1852—by "a historical glorification of everything generally approved," completed by an immolation of all men of genius to the cretinous majority. From early on, it appears, he conceived the *Dictionnaire* as a kind of regurgitation (one of his preferred words) of the commonplace, presented as quotations without commentary, resulting in a book that would unsettle the reader, leave him uncertain how to respond. Ultimately, Flaubert suggests, the result of the *Dictionnaire* should be to make it impossible for a reader to say anything at all, for fear of uttering one more cliché. That would truly be a book of terror: one that reduced its reader to silence.

James was predictably not a sympathetic reader of *Bouvard et Pécuchet*—"a work as sad as something perverse and puerile done for a wager," he wrote in 1893. But he was not entirely blind to Flaubert's intentions. In that same 1893 essay on Flaubert's *Correspondance*, in *Macmillan's Magazine*, he noted that the novel was "the intended epos of the blatancy, of the comprehensive *bêtise*, of mankind." He wrote further of Flaubert's search for the perfect specimen of the cliché:

> "Bouvard et Pécuchet" is a museum of such examples, the cream of that "Dictionnaire des Idées Reçues" for which all his life he had taken notes and which eventually resolved itself into the encyclopaedic exactitude and the lugubrious humour of the novel. . . . the finish of his prose was the proof of his profundity. If you pushed far enough into language you found yourself in the embrace of thought. (311–12)

A curious remark that suggests that James in the early 1890s—when he was on the threshold of his most experimental fiction—understood, more than we might have guessed, Flaubert's project in *Bouvard et Pécuchet*. It's not that he ever came to like or to accept the novel, which always seemed to him a mistake deserving only rapid mention before moving on to something else. Yet he did recognize that Flaubert's sustained and radical probe into the verbal cliché and commonplace yields something of high stakes, a commentary on ideologies and mentalities. But this recognition no doubt merely confirmed James's view that *Bouvard et Pécuchet* was deeply subversive of the kind of novel he believed in and wished to write. Some sinister prank is played on the novel in Flaubert's book. James sees as much, and moves to reject it.

If ever the term "deconstruction" deserved an outing, it is with *Bouvard et Pécuchet*. You start from the premise of two copyists, who meet by chance—like two Beckett characters who wander onto an empty stage: "Two men appeared" *[Deux hommes parurent]*, to sit by chance on the same bench. (See Beckett's *Endgame*, where one of the characters asks: "What's to keep us here?" and the other replies: "The dialogue.") Then Bouvard receives an unexpected inheritance from his "uncle," who in his testament recognizes Bouvard as his bastard son, offering one version of the nineteenth-century novel's obsession with fathers and sons, legitimate and illegitimate, and the problematic nature of succession and inheritance (Turgenev and James of course both reflected on the question). The inheritance gives them the means to retire, move to Normandy, buy a house with a farm, and to turn from reading in order simply to copy to reading in order to educate themselves and to master their environment. That is, Bouvard and Pécuchet's big move, in chapter 1 of the novel, is from the mere copying of the written to an instructive reading, one in which they think they can make the written word applicable to and operable in the real world. *Bouvard et Pécuchet* is, like so many (perhaps most) novels the story of an education, a *Bildungsroman*. Here, the education is almost entirely from books, and especially from how-to books, manuals designed to teach the taming of nature and the mastery of life.

When they arrive in Chavignolles, their new domain, they soon decide that the garden is the most immediate task facing them. After various disasters on their farm, including the spontaneous combustion of their entire harvest of wheat, they turn to their kitchen garden. The gardening experience, recounted in chapter 2—part of the novel Flaubert had completed in 1875, before the Commanville bankruptcy interrupted composition—is one of the best and most characteristic episodes in *Bouvard et Pécuchet*, and can stand for the rest of this strange and repetitive book.

They have been having trouble with their fruit trees. They read manuals, but these are contradictory, and too detailed, offering differing recommendations for different fruits. Pécuchet becomes exasperated: *"Où est la règle, alors?"* he exclaims—where is the general rule that would allow you to understand and to master fruit growing? (90) [38]. In the absence of any clear answer, they decide to be more modest in their approach, and simply to prune occasionally. But with a number of dead trees on their hands, the garden looks spotty. They need a plan. "Fortunately," they come upon the work of one Boitard, *L'Architecte des jardins*—an actual work, published in 1852, not Flaubert's invention but rather one of the hundreds of books he read for his project, in a kind of imitation of the itinerary through knowledge that he would have his two nerds enact. It is worth quoting Flaubert's paragraph in summary of the landscape gardening manual, which gives the essential savor of the novel as a whole:

The author divides them [gardens] into an endless number of types. There is, first of all, the melancholic and romantic type, signalled by forget-me-nots, ruins, tombs, and "a shrine to the Virgin, indicating the place where a lord fell under the blade of an assassin." One constructs the terror type with overhanging rocks, splintered trees, burnt-down huts, the exotic type by planting Peruvian candles "to evoke memories for the traveller or the colonist." The meditative type should offer, as at Ermenonville, a temple to philosophy. Obelisks and triumphal arches characterise the majestic type, some moss and grottoes the mysterious type, a lake the dreamy type. There is even the fantastic type, the most beautiful example of which could once upon a time be seen in a Wurtemberg garden—for there one successively encountered a wild boar, a hermit, several sepulchres, and a boat that by itself left the shore and took you to a boudoir, where fountains soaked you when you sat on the sofa. (91–92) [39]

Flaubert is not easy to translate; it is worth having the original to refer to:

> *L'auteur les divise en une infinité de genres. Il y a, d'abord, le genre mélancolique et romantique, qui se signale par des immortelles, des ruines, des tombeaux, et "un ex-voto à la vierge, indiquant la place où un seigneur est tombé sous le fer d'un assassin." On compose le genre terrible avec des rocs suspendus, des arbres fracassés, des cabanes incendiées, le genre exotique en plantant des cierges du Pérou "pour faire naître des souvenirs à un colon ou à un voyageur." Le genre grave doit offrir, comme Ermenonville, un temple à la philosophie. Les obélisques et les arcs de triomphe caractérisent le genre majestueux, de la mousse et des grottes le genre mystérieux, un lac le genre rêveur. Il y a même le genre fantastique, dont le plus beau spécimen se voyait naguère dans un jardin wurtembergeois—car, on y rencontrait succesivement, un sanglier, un ermite, plusieurs sépulchres, et une barque se détachant d'elle-même du rivage, pour vous conduire dans un boudoir, où des jets d'eau vous inondaient, quand on se posait sur le sofa.*

The passage offers a fine example of Flaubert's deadpan humor, his use of the language of others (here the gardening manual) in indirect discourse, presented almost entirely in the words actually used by the manual, yet set in context—one is tempted to say, as of jewelry, *mounted*—in such a manner that the result is comic. It is precisely in the apparently serious credence given to the words of the manual that the humor lies. Stated another way, one could read the passage "straight"—in the spirit of Bouvard and Pécuchet—and it would be perfectly coherent and plausible. Nothing overtly reveals the hand of the ironist. In his late work, Flaubert discovered that beyond irony lies an even more effective technique, which one might call stupidity, a miming of the world's words in such a way that their absurdity becomes apparent.

Here, the types or genres proposed by the *Architecte des jardins* are solemnly presented: "*Il y a*" tends to fix them as unchanging natural categories, and "*on compose*" suggests a prescriptive approach: this is how each of the categories must be done. The voice that speaks through the manual is what Roland Barthes would designate the "Voice of Science": an impersonal and authoritative voice that commands assent. Yet details chosen, such as the requisite shrine to the Madonna on the spot of an assassination, create a kind of doubt about the wisdom conveyed. As the paragraph goes on, the details selected to characterize each garden genre become more succinct, and as a result appear more peremptory and dictatorial: obelisks and triumphal arches and you have the majestic type; moss and grottoes the mysterious; and a lake suffices for the dreamy type. To take such specifications at face value implies a certain literalism of mind, and a spirit of deference to authorities.

The example from Wurtemberg brings a crescendo in good-faith reading and understanding pushed to their limits. Notice the "*car*"—"for"—that makes of the details that follow the exemplification and proof of the statement that this garden is the most beautiful example of the fantastic genre. Those details tell us that we meet, in succession, a wild boar, a hermit, several sepulchres (a heteroclite series) followed by that wondrous boat that sails off by itself to take you into a boudoir, where you get sprayed with fountains when you sit on the sofa, which has suddenly appeared. The Wurtemberger garden is grotesque in its effect, though no doubt composed in earnest good faith. It reminds me of other useless objects lovingly described, detailed at length, in Flaubert's work: Charles Bovary's cap, which we encounter in the opening pages of *Madame Bovary*, or Emma Bovary's wedding cake, complete with its lakes of jam and nutshell sailboats, or the indescribable and useless object that Binet spends hours making on his lathe. It's as if to suggest that the world described in detail begins to cease to convey meaning. The greater the detailing of the world, it appears, the less it means. You can see it, but not make sense of it. Flaubertian description works a kind of process of designification on the world.

We are somewhere near the core of what in Flaubert distressed, and threatened, James. In the wake of Balzac, James from the outset practiced a description one might call "hypersignificant." It doesn't simply record the appearances of the real, it asks about their meaning, what they suggest and perhaps conceal, the context they provide for human thought and action. As his writing evolves, James's descriptive technique becomes more oblique, impressionistic, perspectival, but never abandons its initial premises, indeed it may become more hypersignificant than before, reading into what is seen, even merely glimpsed, an elaborate structure of meanings. Flaubert's willingness to see the world as nonsignificant or, worse, his seeming joy in robbing what the world presents to the eye of any particular significance, surely troubled James greatly. James's own premises and principles of "representation"—his touchstone word—appear to be undermined by Flaubert's practice.

Flaubert the realist seems, in passages such as this, to be undermining the whole realist project. Any novel by his disciple Zola, for instance, will have a moment of "naming of the parts," where one character leads another through the machine or institution at the center of the novel, be it the coal mine, the locomotive, the department store, the stock market. These are quasi-didactic moments where we learn how the machine functions. Description has the aspect of a user's manual: what you need to understand how your car's engine works or how to assemble your new lawnmower. The *Architecte des jardins* is also a user's manual, a how-to book. Flaubert's deadpan presentation of its instructions—sometimes citing its very words—doesn't really constitute a parody of the didactic instruction so much as a parrotry. After breaking off the composition of *Bouvard et Pécuchet* in 1875, Flaubert returned to writing with his story of a peasant woman who loves a parrot, who itself addresses the world in a limited set of fixed phrases. Here, Flaubert's parrotry of *L'Architecte des jardins* provides a user's manual that leaves us in some doubt as to its intent and significance. The reader doesn't quite know how to respond to the text.

For Bouvard and Pécuchet, however, the uses of the manual are clear: you should build the product, and then test-drive it. After reading *L'Architecte des jardins*: "Faced with this horizon of marvels, Bouvard and Pécuchet were nearly bedazzled." They are the opposite of suspicious readers. They take the manual at its word. Yet there are some limits to the realization of its instructions: "The fantastic type, it seemed to them, was reserved for princes. The temple to philosophy would take up too much room. The shrine to the Madonna wouldn't have any meaning, given the lack of assassins, and so much the worse for colonists and voyagers, American plants cost too much" (92) [39]. Their practical good sense completes the recommendations of the manual, keeping them within the bounds of the possible. Nonetheless, they are able to build a garden "which had no analogue in the whole region."

"They had sacrificed the asparagus in order to build in their bed an Etruscan tomb, that is to say a quadrilateral of black plaster, six feet high, looking like a dog kennel. Four evergreen bushes stood at the corners of this monument, which would be topped by a funeral urn and enriched with an inscription." Here the "that is to say" (*"c'est à dire"*) is a bit treacherous: who is judging that their Etruscan tomb looks like a dog kennel? There is also a great rock, which they cement together from pieces of granite dragged from a riverbank, which looks like a "gigantic potato," and a rustic cabin, and a Rialto bridge over the water. "Above the arbour six squared-off tree trunks held up a tin hat with its corners bent up, and the whole thing signified a Chinese pagoda." This is yet more treacherous, particularly in the use of the word *"signifier"*: if this grotesque construction "means" Chinese pagoda, what supports this meaning? If you start from its meaning— "this is a Chinese pagoda"—then the grotesque object does mean that. But that doesn't guarantee its meaning for those so unfortunate as to be uninformed that it *is* a Chinese pagoda. In Bouvard and Pécuchet's re-alization of the manual's instructions there is a kind of slippage from writing to reading. That is, if you read with sufficient literalness, if you take in good faith your construction as a realization of what the text says, then you are home free, in your own eyes at least. If you conceive the text, or the pagoda, from the point of view of its composition—its need to *make* the meaning it claims for itself—then things are rather more complicated.

"Like all artists, they needed to be applauded—and Bouvard had the idea of hosting a grand dinner" (94) [41]. The dinner, for all the local *notables*, is not a great culinary success, but Bouvard and Pécuchet count on the unveiling of the garden, amidst the popping of champagne corks, to provide a grand climax. They open the curtains, and the garden appears:

> In the twilight it was something terrifying. The rock like a mountain filled the lawn, the tomb made a cube in the middle of the spinach, the Venetian bridge a circumflex accent over the beans—and the hut, beyond, was a large black spot, since they had burned its roof, to make it more poetic. The yews shaped as stags or as armchairs unfolded in a line, up to the tree struck by lightning, which extended transversally from the bower to the arbour, where the tomatoes hung like stalactites. A sunflower, here and there, displayed its yellow disk. The Chinese pagoda, painted red, seemed a lighthouse over the mound. The beaks of the peacocks [sculpted from yew] reflected the glare of the sun, and behind the lattice fence, which had had its planks removed, the landscape lay flat to the horizon. (97) [44]
>
> *C'était dans le crépuscule, quelque chose d'effrayant. Le rocher comme une montagne occupait le gazon, le tombeau faisait un cube au milieu des épinards, le pont vénétien un accent circonflexe par-dessus les haricots—et la cabane, au-delà, une grande tache noire; car ils avaient incendié son toit, pour la rendre plus poétique. Les ifs en forme de cerfs ou de fauteuils se suivaient, jusqu'à l'arbre foudroyé, qui s'étendait transversalement de la charmille à la tonnelle, où des pommes d'amour pendaient comme des stalactites. Un tournesol, çà et là, étalait son disque jaune. La pagode chinoise peinte en rouge semblait un phare sur le vigneau. Les becs des paons frappés par le soleil se renvoyaient des feux, et derrière la claire-voie, débarassée de ses planches, la campagne toute plate terminait l'horizon.*

Bouvard and Pécuchet seem to have achieved Flaubert's own goal of an aesthetic object that is frightening—that approaches the dread and awe provoked by the sublime. But in the detail it somehow falls a bit short. The reaction produced in their dinner guests is one of "astonishment." While Madame Bordin admires the peacocks sculpted from yew trees, on the whole the garden is met with incomprehension, and then a series of severe judgments. "The tomb was not understood, nor the burnt-out cabin, nor the ruined wall."

Somehow the composition of a representation has gone awry here. Its reproductive function has misfired. The elements of the garden have been carefully chosen and created according to a nomenclature, a kind of repertory of elements supposed to be read according to a certain script. But what the garden is named as and what it appears as—is read as—don't coincide. There has been an inexplicable slippage between instruction and implementation, and the result is a lovingly composed and recorded absurdity. There has been a disconnect between instruction and implementation. *"Où est la règle alors?"*—what general rule can one evoke? What determines meaning? It is worth noting that when Bouvard and Pécuchet complete their work on the garden, they get an echo—apparently because they cut down the large lime tree to create their *"arbre foudroyé,"* the lightning-struck tree. They find it pleasing. But when they try it out before their guests, nothing happens—no echo.

Echo, like parrotry, doesn't appear to us a sublime form of art: it is too literally reproductive, too uncreative. And yet, if you are attempting to realize the instructions of a how-to manual, some echoing may be what you need: a kind of literalistic rendering of what you have read. This would be the equal opposite of a perfectly realist writing, which attempts a reproduction of the real in language. We know that realist writing can never be more than an aspiration, can never be literally so, since language is not the same as phenomena. Bouvard and Pécuchet seem to discover that a reproduction of linguistic reality—what is constructed in the sentences of *L'Architecte des jardins*—in the phenomenal world is also only an aspiration. It is an approximation, not a reproduction. You can get it right only if you are given the key for deciphering meanings—of the Etruscan tomb, the Chinese pagoda—beforehand. If you don't have that precious key, you are reduced to a reading that doesn't line up with the intention of the creators. You name what you see, but you also see what you name—what has been already named. At the extreme, what you see is prenamed, already-seen-and-named, or cliché.

I have perhaps belabored the experience of Bouvard and Pécuchet's garden, but it is a wholly characteristic episode that tellingly shows the pattern that will be followed in the rest of the book. By the end of the gardening chapter, for instance, they take up canning and preserving— with predictably dire results—and then the making of a liqueur named in advance "*la Bouvarine*." This dead-ends in the explosion of their still, with nearly mortal results. As a consequence, they realize that they need to study chemistry. They read many volumes. They move on to medicine, archaeology, history, biography, literature, philosophy, religion. There is a moment in their study of physiology where we are told: "They were very pleased to know that tartar of the gums contains three kinds of micro-organisms, that the seat of taste is on the tongue, and the sensation of hunger in the stomach" (112) [56]. They were very pleased to know—"*Ils furent bien aises de savoir*": their novel can be read as one of pure knowledge, knowledge acquired simply for its own sake, for the pleasure it gives, since the practical results from it seem to be nil, or worse. One is reminded of Flaubert's claim that he read over 1,500 volumes in order to compose the novel. Such an act of madness may also appear as an homage to knowledge for its own sake—even when the contents of so many of the 1,500 volumes seems to be erroneous, useless, and without general application.

When they are in their history phase, Bouvard and Pécuchet start worrying about historical accuracy and judgment. They study the French Revolution, but fall into deeper and deeper uncertainty: "To judge it impartially, one would have to have read all the histories, all the memoirs, all the newspapers and all the manuscript documents, since from the slightest omission an error might result, which would then produce other errors, on to infinity. They gave up" (174) [105]. The book of the two nerds is in this manner the novel of weariness with books and knowledge, which may be no more than error piled on error, stupidity engendering stupidity. And yet their unhappy experience with history leads only to a greater thirst for the truth: "But a taste for history had developed in them, a need to discover truth for its own sake." History itself breaks into the novel, in chapter 6, with the coming of the Revolution of 1848, in a strange reprise of material Flaubert had already used in *L'Education sentimentale*. As in the earlier novel, history itself here seems to be mainly a *sottisier*, a collection of cliché words and gestures, though given the evident bad faith of the reactionaries, those favorable to revolution—including Bouvard and Pécuchet—may appear more sympathetic here than in *L'Education*.

When Bouvard and Pécuchet launch themselves into the study of religion, becoming ever more sceptical, they are increasingly shunned by the community of Chavignolles as impious and immoral. "Then a piteous faculty developed in their minds, that of seeing stupidity and no longer tolerating it" (298) [205] [*"Alors une faculté pitoyable se développa dans leur esprit, celle de voir la bêtise et de ne plus la tolérer"*]. Are they coming more and more to resemble their creator? Perhaps, and yet the label "piteous" applied to the ability to see stupidity and not tolerate it seems to be meant in a strong sense. Perceptiveness and dissent from the commonplace do not conduce to happiness. And by the end of the chapter recounting their scepticism, which leads them to the temptation to suicide, they enter the church for midnight mass on Christmas Eve, "involuntarily" join the hymn, and feel a new dawn in their souls. The moment reminds one of the peasant Félicité in *Un Coeur simple*, which Flaubert wrote shortly before these pages of *Bouvard et Pécuchet*.

But neither scepticism nor belief provides a resting point for Bouvard and Pécuchet. They simply move on, like locusts across the pastures of knowledge. They move on, in the last chapter Flaubert completed before his death, to education. There is this much progress in the novel: that its strange protagonists do evolve from raising plants to raising children. They adopt Victor and Victorine, children of a convict who are themselves on their way to reformatories. They read all the treatises on education. They teach the children to read and write, then face the problem of what else to teach them—which in essence means a recapitulation of their own recapitulation of human knowledge. It is merely logical that their encyclopaedic thirst for knowledge should lead to the retransmission of knowledge. But with Victor and Victorine, too, the transmission of knowledge appears to be without benefit. As the children reach puberty, Bouvard and Pécuchet are distressed to discover that Victor has become a masturbator, and a thief, while Victorine is deflowered by a hunchback. They give up, once again, deciding that it is nature not nurture that has determined these results.

Nonetheless, they go on dreaming of educating their contemporaries, this time through adult education classes.

The novel breaks off here; what follows are notes left by Flaubert, which seem to indicate that Bouvard and Pécuchet give a lecture to announce their educative plans, that they cause a scandal and eventually are subject to arrest by the mayor, though through the intervention of other local *notables* who consider them mad but harmless, are let off— but not before Victor and Victorine have been taken from their custody (and have displayed no emotion at the severance). They are left with nothing to do, no more interest in life, no more projects. Both then secretly nourish a notion that eventually comes to light: the idea of returning to copying. So they take up copying again, not as a remunerated profession but simply as an occupation, a way to pass the time. "They copied . . . everything that fell into their hands . . . long enumeration . . . notes on authors read before—old papers bought by the pound from the nearby paper factory" (389) [280]. Flaubert himself had acquired old papers by the pound, as well, of course, as reams of notes on the various "authorities" read for the novel. Does he really mean to give us a "long enumeration" of all this? How would it relate to the enumerations we have had already in the course of the nerds' self-education? One thinks of the vertiginous possibility of a novel, something imagined by Jorge Luis Borges, that would at this point simply recopy itself, regurgitate (in one of Flaubert's favorite terms) the already written.

This is merely speculation. Following Flaubert's death in May, 1880, Caroline Commanville undertook to publish the first volume of *Bouvard et Pécuchet*, containing chapters 1–10: the manuscript that Flaubert had more or less finished. The Commanvilles, after all, desperately needed income. Serial publication began in *La Nouvelle Revue* on December 15, 1880. Book publication followed in 1881. Caroline asked the designated disciple, Guy de Maupassant, to edit volume 2. But on July 30, 1881, Maupassant wrote to her to say it just couldn't be done. He claimed to have spent three months going over Flaubert's notes, trying to find a way to put them in order. He concludes that this is impossible because the fragments were to have been linked and given form by the continuing narrative of the two copyists, their dialogue, their commentary on the material. Maupassant refused to write this narrative himself, and concluded that without it volume 2 would be nothing but "a mass of citations without order," and essentially unreadable. It was left for twentieth-century editors to sort through the thousands of pages of manuscript notes deposited in the Bibliothèque de Rouen, and to publish (the first version dates from 1966) "volume 2" of the novel. Any version of volume 2 is fragmentary, a choice from amongst available materials, and somewhat arbitrary in its organization.

Still, you find yourself wondering whether Maupassant quite got it right. Particularly where the *sottisier* is concerned—the material usually presented as the *Dictionnaire des idées reçues*—it may be that volume 2 was not to have been a narrative at all, but merely a carefully architected structure of citations. Flaubert in 1879 speaks of chapter 11 of the novel as being "composed almost solely of citations" and of the *Dictionnaire* as "completely done" and ready to go into the second volume. Recall his letter to Louis Bouilhet back in 1850, where he talks of the *Dictionnaire* as "arranged in such a manner that the reader would not know whether or not he was being made a fool of." The idea may have been precisely to keep the *Dictionnaire* free of any narrative or narratorial commentary, whether by Flaubert or his two copyists. It was to stand alone as the copying out of exempla of human stupidity, to be read in a spirit of irony, or perhaps simply a spirit of stupidity, vomiting (another word Flaubert uses often) the commonplaces to which we are all condemned. Two epigraphs were apparently to stand at the head of the *Dictionnaire*:

> *Vox populi, vox Dei.*

And the aphorism by the eighteenth-century *moraliste* Chamfort:

> One can wager that every public idea, every received convention,
> is stupidity, since it has suited the largest number of people.

In this clash between the voice of the people as the voice of God, and the claim that the ideas believed in by the largest number of people are stupidities, lies the enterprise of the *Dictionnaire*.

The *Dictionnaire* contains different types of definition. Often we have a particularly clichéd phrase used as definition of a word, for instance:

Blondes: "Hotter than brunettes (see Brunettes)."

If we then go to *Brunettes*, we of course get the definition: "Hotter than blondes (see Blondes)." If we pursue our research with *Negresses*, we get: "Hotter than whites (see Brunettes and Blondes)." If we move on to *Redheads*, the definition becomes a laconic: "(See Blondes, Brunettes, Whites, and Negresses)." For *Bachelors*, we get: "Madmen, egotists, and dissolutes. / They should be taxed. / They are preparing a sad old age for themselves." For *Courtesan*: "A necessary evil.—Safeguard of our daughters and our sisters. / Should be driven out pitilessly.—Are always proletarian girls seduced by rich bourgeois." The sentences capture the perfectly contradictory social construction of the prostitute in the ideologies of the time. Another kind of definition comes with *Dissection*: "Outrage to the majesty of death." Here it is a perfectly pompous and hollow phrase of the kind elicited by the mention of dissection that becomes its definition. A similar example is *Oysters*: "No one eats them any more! They're too expensive!" For *Equitation*, horseback riding, we are given: "Good exercise for losing weight. Example: all cavalry soldiers are thin. /—for gaining weight. Example: all cavalry officers have a big belly." (One hears echoes of Bouvard and Pécuchet's plaintive: "*où est la règle, alors?*") Things are a bit more treacherous with *Laconism*: "Language no longer spoken." And more political with *Worker*: "Always honest, when he is not rioting." For a final example, there is a sequence of three words with definitions that respond to one another: *Philosophy*: "Should always make one snicker." *Pity*: "Should always stay away from it." *Place* (in the sense of a position): "Should always ask for one."

Flaubert is a hero of our postmodernism partly because such a technique of citation so much characterizes the postmodernist sense of style, and its sensibility. Quotations and their setting, their montage one might say, unsettles one's faith in the stability of styles and meanings. Or perhaps it is more the opposite: meanings become all too stable, stuck in the sludge of the commonplace. They are not ours to shape, they rather shape us, make our utterances banal despite our

intentions. Flaubert hoped to make the readers of the *Dictionnaire* unable to open their mouths, for fear of uttering nothing but clichés. In
this sense, the *Dictionnaire* demonstrates our imprisonment in what
Nietzsche called the "prisonhouse of language." It stands at the opposite end of a spectrum from the romantic notion of the ineffable: according to Flaubert, it's not a matter of sentiments and ideas that are
unspeakable, beyond expression. On the contrary, everything is all too
speakable. It's already coded. Everyone has been there already, and
said that.

It seems entirely appropriate that *Bouvard et Pécuchet* should end
with a dictionary: a final, arbitrary (because alphabetical) classification
of things through words, which are used to define one another. The
dictionary, like the encyclopaedia the reading of the two nerds (and of
their creator) so often evokes, is a summa of sorts in the organization of
human knowledge, the outcome of lines of investigation and study.
The most characteristic form of the nineteenth-century novel may be
the *Bildungsroman*, the novel of education, development, achieving
maturity. Turgenev's title, *Fathers and Sons*, speaks of the matter of
many novels of the time, from Stendhal to Joyce, that consider the difficulty and the necessity of transmission of knowledge, wisdom, and
power from one generation to the next. Biological fathers very often
seem to be lost or rejected in favor of an elective father, someone who
imparts not merely personal knowledge but the ways of the world. Bouvard and Pécuchet apprentice themselves to all the surrogate fathers
and teachers they can find in their reading—only to find them contradictory, uninstructive, inapplicable to the case at hand. And then they
try to retransmit what they have (not really) learned to their adoptive
children, who seem to demonstrate that nature is far stronger than cultural nurture.

Bouvard et Pécuchet offers a general housewrecking: of the systems
of thought of which Western culture is most proud, especially of the
application of thought to action—in the "mastery of nature" often
taken to characterize advanced civilizations—and the organization of
knowledge into learnable systems, and then the transmission of systematic knowledge to other learners. Nothing works. It is an antinovel of
non-education, based on the acquisition of knowledge that is useless,

of experience that turns to nought. In the lecture sketched out in Flaubert's notes for volume 2, Pécuchet predicts a future in which "America will have conquered the earth." This apparently entails: "Universal loutishness. There will be nothing but a great drunken blowout of the workers. End of the world from a lack of heat" [*"Pignouflisme universel. Tout ne sera plus qu'une vaste ribote d'ouvriers. Fin du monde par la cessation du calorique"*] (386) [277]. The novel reaches to this vision of a future in which stupidity has triumphed, and then the world comes to a cold end.

On its publication (without the second volume) in 1881, the novel received a largely hostile reaction. It is not surprising that James was among those who found the novel simply aberrant. To begin with, it *is* aberrant, by any definition of a novel. Then, James's definition of the novel does not reach to the kind of satire of ideas that Flaubert presents. One recalls T. S. Eliot's famous remark that James had "a mind so fine no idea could violate it," which in a positive interpretation means that James so turned ideas into human emotions and dramatized interactions that they were fully integrated into life. He does not, for instance, indulge in the famous narratorial reflections of George Eliot. His characters tend to be more intelligent than not—even the "fools," as he called them, who perceive what is going on only partially, and even children such as Maisie Farrange and Morgan Moreen. Whereas Flaubert's copyists are imbecilic in many ways, but serve toward a kind of fiction of ideas. While Flaubert expressed a wish, in that letter to Turgenev, to make a narrative of their tragicomic exploration of knowledge, that narrative was surely for James too inhuman, too abstract, virtually didactic. It curiously smacked, though with an entirely different savor, of the didactic demonstrativeness he so deplored in Thackeray.

There is even more at stake, I think, in James's negative reaction to *Bouvard et Pécuchet*, when it is set in the context of his reservations about all Flaubert's work, with the single, and qualified, exception of *Madame Bovary*. As James repeatedly makes clear, his deepest allegiance lies with Balzac, with a novel devoted to character and dramatic action, to plots that arrive at theatrical enactments where moral and intellectual confrontations are played out in the verbal clash of persons.

His repeated praise for Balzac's respect for the "liberty of the subject" · suggests why, despite all the lapses from taste and plausibility he finds in Balzac, he chose this novelist as icon of the novel's project: the novelist to study, he tells us, if the novel is ever to recover its "wasted heritage." Respect for the liberty of the subject, the love of character playing out its destiny, even when grasping and evil—as with Madame Marneffe— becomes James's touchstone for an attitude at once aesthetic and moral. It is the right aesthetic position because it gives fictions that are free of that "damning interference" of the author in his work, his all-too-visible manipulation of his created world. It is the right moral position because it argues against the exploitative manipulation of the weak by the powerful, or the lover by the beloved, or simply one person by another. James appears to have a morbid fear of interference, of meddling in another's existence.

Flaubert's fictions all suffer, in James's view, from an insufficient grant of freedom. It is not that Flaubert interferes in blatant ways, in Thackeray's manner: he is after all the theoretician of the invisible author who, in the famous phrase, should be everywhere present in his creation but nowhere visible. ("An author in his book should be like God in the universe, present everywhere and visible nowhere," he wrote to Louise Colet.) But he does control his created life, and his created world, very tightly, in prose that defines, delimits, and tends to sever any possibility of realizing one's dreams. One may feel James's objections to Flaubert most strongly in his strictures on *L'Education sentimentale*, which he surely misestimates and even misunderstands, but for very plausible reasons. That novel strips away any possibility of a world, a career, a love brought to us by the "beautiful circuit and subterfuge of our thought and our desire," to recall James's celebrated definition of romance. At least *Madame Bovary* contains Emma's own romance sensibility, her aspiration to something else. Frédéric Moreau seems incapable of a wish or a desire that has any consistency, or any staying power. He is an ineffective "register and reflector" of life as James saw it—and no doubt disquieting in his implication that finally there is less to register and reflect than James believes. The diminishment of the novel's high project that James finds in *L'Education sentimentale* is also a diminishment of life as James wants and needs it to be.

Bouvard and Pécuchet are not given a chance to be anything more than what is needed for Flaubert's demonstrative project. They are, like Tweedledee and Tweedledum, or Hamm and Clov, or Rosencrantz and Guildenstern, two intellectual ciphers in a comedy of knowledge. They don't matter in themselves, and they don't persuade us that how we lead our lives matters—and I think that is a vital issue for James. His American moral strenuousness—what he satirizes in the Reverend Babcock, in *The American*, but to a degree shares with him, as with his brother William—can encompass Balzacian moral melodrama, even when lurid and impurpled and "immoral" by Cambridge standards, but not Flaubert's cosmic nihilism, if that is the right term for it. I sense that James finds *Bouvard et Pécuchet* not merely boring and baffling but also profoundly subversive of his own enterprise for the novel.

Flaubert, I mentioned, had set *Bouvard et Pécuchet* aside shortly before James arrived in Paris, during the Commanville crisis, and would not pick it up again until 1877. But in the fall of 1875 he began to write himself out of his depression with the novella *La Légende de Saint-Julien l'Hospitalier*, which would be followed in the spring and summer of 1876 by *Un Coeur simple*, and then by *Hérodias*, the three constituting the *Trois Contes* published in 1877. One would think that the most admired, famous, anthologized of the three tales, *Un Coeur simple* [A Simple Heart] would have appealed to James. Flaubert's story of a simple heart was dedicated to George Sand—who died on June 8, 1876, shortly after Flaubert began its composition. And more than that: it was conceived to answer her complaints that Flaubert was hardhearted, unfeeling, even cynical in his writing. One needs, she wrote to him on January 12, 1876, "to go straight to the highest morality one has in oneself and not make a mystery of the moral and useful meaning of one's work." If *Un Coeur simple* was not to be precisely Sandesque in this manner, Flaubert claimed to a correspondent that "it is not at all ironic, as you seem to think, but on the contrary wholly serious and sad."

James in his 1902 essay on Flaubert calls the *Trois Contes* "preponderantly of the deepest imaginative hue," but almost pointedly leaves out *Un Coeur simple* while noting the "'classic' fortune" of its two companion tales, *La Légende de Saint-Julien l'Hospitalier* and *Héro-dias*. It is earlier, in 1884, in the essay "The Art of Fiction," that he al-ludes to the novella, contrasting it to Turgenev's "tale about a deaf and dumb serf and a lap-dog," which he finds "touching, loving, a little masterpiece." James's description of *Un Coeur simple* perhaps tellingly foregrounds the parrot: "Gustave Flaubert has written a story about the devotion of a servant-girl to a parrot, and the production, highly fin-ished as it is, cannot on the whole be called a success. We are perfectly free to find it flat, but I think it might have been interesting" (56–57). Then comes the contrast to Turgenev, and the conclusion that Tur-genev "struck the note of life where Gustave Flaubert missed it." This may strike us as unnecessarily obtuse. *Un Coeur simple* would seem, at least superficially, to answer some of James's doubts, as well as Sand's, about Flaubert's moral vision. To be sure, the Norman peasant Félic-ité, servant to Madame Aubain in Pont l'Evêque for over half a century, is not one of the complicated and civilized characters who most inter-est James. But perhaps there is something more in his denigration of the tale: a sense that although it is not engaged in the housewreckings of *Bouvard et Pécuchet*, and indeed is not at all ironic, *Un Coeur simple* nonetheless takes us close to an aesthetics and ethics of stupidity that James found troublesome. It is of course speculative to propose a Jame-sian reading of a text he scarcely commented on. Yet the perspective of the Jamesian novel—and novella, since this was a form James grate-fully adapted from the French tradition and used often—allows one to see something about the kind of "morality" Flaubert proposes or prac-tices in *Un Coeur simple*.

I agree with Flaubert that *Un Coeur simple* is not ironic. There would be no point in exercising irony on the limited and unambitious mental and emotional world of Félicité. Irony is to be exercised on the pretentious, on the bourgeois who claim to understand things and to tell us how to live, such as Homais the pharmacist in *Madame Bovary*; or on any aspiration that makes a claim to human agency in a world subject to chance, if not ruled by chaos. The vehicle of Flaubert's irony is very often indirect discourse, where he folds the words of his charac-ters into the narrator's discourse in such a way that context, juxtaposi-tion, sentence rhythm, and the occasional narratorial comment smuggled in create an ironic distance on the represented world and word. (One could make a case for the whole of the *Dictionnaire des idées reçues* as a kind of indirect discourse, the words of others reset in a new context, though in this case without any clear signals of ironic perspective.) There is very little indirect discourse in *Un Coeur simple*, and when present it seems oriented, like the descriptive and narrative prose, toward an attempt to imitate Félicité's world of sensations and ideas. For instance, when Félicité accompanies the beloved Virginie, her employer's daughter, to catechism, she learns the rudiments of the Testaments from the priest, and works out her own understandings of them, rooted in her lived experience of the farm: the stable, sowing and harvesting, cider presses, lambs, doves. The Holy Ghost is more taxing to her imagination:

> She had difficulty imagining his person, since he was not only a bird but also a fire, and at other times a breath. It's perhaps his light that flits along the edges of the marsh at night, his breath that pushes the clouds in the sky, his voice that makes the churchbells melodious; and she dwelt in adoration, taking pleasure in the cool walls and the tranquillity of the church.

Such simplicity, and good faith in simplicity, appears beyond irony.

This is not the view of M. Bourais, the retired attorney, who undertakes to explain to her the whereabouts of her adored nephew Victor, who has sailed off to Havana:

> He reached for his atlas, then began explaining longitude; and he had a condescending smile at Félicité's amazement. Finally, with his pencil holder, he indicated in the indentations of an oval spot an imperceptible black point, adding: "There it is." She bent over the map; the network of colored lines tired her sight, without teaching her anything; and when Bourais asked her to say what was bothering her, she begged him to show her the house where Victor was staying. Bourais threw up his hands, sneezed, laughed enormously; such naiveté provoked his hilarity, and Félicité couldn't understand why—she who maybe expected to see the very picture of her nephew, even, so limited was her intelligence! (37) [36]

It's not clear that Bourais' superiority triumphs in this confrontation. After all, maps (and longitudes) are arbitrary systems of representation, and if you don't possess the key to them, or can't make the system clear to another, the kind of result Félicité looks for—the appearance of Victor's house on the map—is just as logical as any other. The naïve, the simple view here shows up the arbitrariness, the lack of necessity, of a form of the language of representation used by humans to signify things that are not present—and used also to exercise power over those who are not initiated in the conventions of the form. There may be an oblique commentary on the atlas offered by the illustrated geography book that Bourais gives the Aubain children: "The illustrations represented different scenes from around the world, cannibals with feathered headdresses, a monkey kidnapping a young maiden, Bedouins in the desert, a whale being harpooned, etc." The "etc." constitutes the treacherous narratorial comment here: a comment on the heteroclite and stereotyped and finally unreliable nature of such "knowledge."

Flaubert borrowed a stuffed Amazon parrot from the Rouen Museum of Natural History on July 15, 1876, in a curious gesture toward reproductive realism, imitation. The parrot, Loulou, in *Un Coeur simple* indeed is described in precise detail, but his imitative function aligns him with the deconstructive enterprise of *Bouvard et Pécuchet*. Loulou, who learns three phrases, offers a strange, repetitive relation to speech, and a kind of mirror inversion of reality. He finds Bourais an object of laughter, for instance—he laughs so hard that Bourais takes to slipping along the outside wall, hat down over his face, and entering the house only through the garden gate. Bourais will later die an apparent suicide, and be exposed as a thoroughly fraudulent accountant. It's as if Loulou saw through Bourais' social manners to another reality by way of his capacity for imitation. His function becomes yet more significant when Félicité has gone deaf, and the parrot's imitations of sounds are the only thing that reach her:

> The narrow circle of her ideas contracted still further, and the chiming of the bells, the lowing of the cattle were no more. All living things functioned silently as ghosts. Only one sound now reached her ear, the voice of the parrot.

As if to distract her, he would reproduce the tic-tac of the spit in the fireplace, the high-pitched call of the fishmonger, the saw of the cabinetmaker who lived across the way; and when the door-bell rang, he imitated Mme Aubain: "Félicité! the door! the door!

They had dialogues, Loulou serving up endlessly the three phrases in his repertory, and she responding with words that had no more sense, but in which her heart overflowed. (56–57) [47]

Language in this passage reverts to a kind of primordial, almost prelin-guistic state, as an imitation of the noises of the world. The world speaks to Félicité only through the parrot's imitation of it—which makes Loulou the artist of reality, the one true practitioner of mimesis. But his speech doesn't quite constitute language, even though it can function as a simulacrum of language, as in the order to open the door. And the dialogues with Félicité are carried out in a language that is both meaningless and full of affection. Or rather: we know Félicité's side of the dialogue is a lover's discourse, but Loulou of course remains opaque, hidden behind a language that he speaks but does not use.

Parrotry, as I have called it, is disturbing in that it imitates the mean-ingful utterance in a way that is purposeful but (we assume) devoid of intention. Or at least: without the intention that presided at the com-position of the utterance, but perhaps with another intention, which could be a demand for attention, an expression of affection, or simply a penchant for imitation. A mirror of reality that reflects only effects without their causes, effects that may have no real motivation behind them, disquiets because it suggests that our causes, motives, intentions may themselves be without merit, and our speech mere babble—as much speech between human interlocutors surely is. In this sense, Loulou's three phrases are a kind of distillation of the *Dictionnaire des idées reçues*, the world as repetitive babble.

James may have read *Un Coeur simple* with a certain awareness of the disturbing force of parrotry—that is, as something other than the sentimental tale it is often taken to be. And beyond the troubling re-flections on language and art introduced by Loulou there is the ques-tion of stupidity—not in this case the stupidity of cliché, of the already-said-and-repeated, but rather of the lack of ideas. Félicité's mind remains close to the sensations of the physical world. Her mental horizon is restricted, and as she grows older, deafer, and eventually blind as well, there is no possible passage for new ideas. She doesn't understand the processes by which mind works on the world, the work of representation or symbolization. She gets things backwards. A colored engraving of the Holy Ghost becomes a portrait of Loulou—now dead and stuffed by the taxidermist. When she buys a copy of the engraving and hangs it in her room, she prays as much to the stuffed parrot the engraving resembles as to the Holy Ghost that is the supposed subject of representation. Loulou eventually, with the parish priest's permission, becomes part of the Corpus Christi altar, as if in authentication of her concrete view of the spiritual.

The famous final paragraph of the tale takes us to the very threshold of death. Félicité smells the incense from the altar outside:

> A blue vapor rose up to Félicité's bedroom. She opened wide her nostrils, inhaling the scent with mystic sensuality; then her eyelids closed. Her lips were smiling. Her heartbeats slowed one by one, softer each time, less marked, like a fountain running dry, like an echo fading away; and when she exhaled her last breath, she thought she saw, in the opening heavens, a gigantic parrot, winging above her head. (73) [56]

Ultimately the tale confers a kind of absolute dignity on simplicity of heart and mind. Félicité is not an object of irony; her story is, as Flaubert claimed, "wholly serious and sad." But it is precisely its seriousness, its lack of irony and buffoonery, that makes its representation of life disturbing as well as moving. Is this all there is to life, we may want to ask? Flaubert convincingly suggests that such is the case, not only for Félicité, who is merely a more severe form of a generalized human limitation. James, who found Emma Bovary and Frédéric Moreau too limited as "registers and reflectors" of existence, might find in Félicité confirmation that Flaubert never could take on the civilized and complicated human character. He might recognize that Félicité's limitation as reflector and register is wholly appropriate to her case, to the extremely narrow range of experience allotted to her, while finding that the case itself, Flaubert's choice of subject, reveals a

lack of interest in the kind of psychological and moral drama that
James wanted.

Recall James's reservation about Flaubert's "gift" as a writer: that
"there are whole sides of life to which it was never addressed and
which it apparently quite failed to suspect as a field of exercise." And
he concludes the paragraph in which this sentence figures with the
somewhat arch remark: "*L'âme française* at all events shows in him but
ill." That "French soul" so copiously chronicled by Balzac becomes
constricted, simplified, and limited in Flaubert. Yet one might from a
Flaubertian perspective ask: yes, but what if one doesn't believe in the
soul? What if the very point of Flaubert's fiction—all the more radically so in his latest work—is to suggest that any notion of the soul is a
romantic fiction that needs to be dismantled? Near the outset of *L'Education sentimentale*, there is a sentence concerning the "soul" of its
protagonist, Frédéric: "He found that the happiness that he deserved
for the excellence of his soul was slow in coming" ["*Il trouvait que le
bonheur mérité par l'excellence de son âme tardait à venir*"]. His story
will tend to demonstrate that excellence of soul gets you nowhere, that
the very concept is indeed an illusion that prevents one from a more
lucid engagement with the real. Flaubert belongs to a long line of disil-
lusioners and dissenters, and he becomes the inspiration of those dis-
abused ironists of the next century, Joyce, Beckett, Kafka, Svevo.

James's plea for attention to the "soul" is surely not overtly a declaration of religious commitment, or even of spirituality. James tends to
ironize overt practices of spirituality, as in *The Bostonians*. He is of
course deeply preoccupied with the ethical, and perhaps particularly
alert to the presence of evil in the world—evil allied to dread, to death
of the soul, to forces mysterious and exploitative. Flaubert could not
help him here, since Flaubert had eliminated that aspect of the problem of the human. Balzac, for all the romantic claptrap still cluttering
his imagination, had much more to offer. Still, James turns away from
the lesson of Flaubert only with regret because the craft of fiction and
the métier of the novelist have never been given a higher illustration.
Flaubert, almost single-handedly in James's view, made fiction a serious art form, and all his successors are in his debt. "May it not in truth
be said that we practise our industry, so many of us, at relatively little

cost just *because* poor Flaubert, producing the most expensive fictions ever written, so handsomely paid for it?"

Poor Flaubert, indeed. When James's admiration for Flaubert reaches its limits—when he encounters what he sees as Flaubert's limitations—he tends toward condescension. As in his letters to Cambridge from Paris in 1876, he assumes a somewhat patronizing attitude toward this towering figure of French letters ("I easily—more than easily—see all round him intellectually," for instance). I suppose it is his form of exorcism, or avoidance of the weight of Flaubert's influence. There is no evidence that Flaubert paid much attention to the views of the whippersnapper from Cambridge. But he might have replied that James's own practice was too timid, too much of a compromise with Victorian conventions of storytelling. And yet, some ten to twenty years after Flaubert's death—in the mid to late 1890s—James's practice of the novel becomes more radical, more filled with anguish about the very existence of the subjects that interest him and the moral forces at play in world, more doubtful about our capacity to know reality with any certainty, and more fully committed to a limited viewpoint or perspective on human action and motive. James does not want to travel Flaubert's path to its end (one might figure it as ending in Bouvard and Pécuchet's garden) but he does absorb, without full acknowledgment, no doubt without full awareness, Flaubert's lessons on perspective. If James will continue to write novels where the spiritual is at issue, the issue of how it is at issue will be brought to the foreground.

5. The Quickened Notation
of Our Modernity

A Certain Faint Convergence

On June 23, 1897, James left Bournemouth, where he was vacationing, and took the train up to London. It was not a very good day to travel: on June 22, London had lavishly and loudly celebrated Queen Victoria's Diamond Jubilee. These celebrations James had studiously avoided, but the 23rd still displayed their aftermath, with London "a huge dusty cabless confusion of timber already tottering, of decorations already stale, of *badauds* already bored. . . . Millions of eyes, opening to dust and glare from the scenery of dreams, seemed slowly to stare and to try to recollect." The cab ride across the city from Waterloo Station to Paddington was slow and difficult. Then he was on the train to Oxford, to hear the French novelist Paul Bourget deliver a lecture at the Taylorian Institution—Oxford's center for modern languages—on Gustave Flaubert. "That the day should have come for M. Bourget to lecture at Oxford, and should have come by the same stroke for Gustave Flaubert to be lectured about, filled the mind to a degree, and left it in an agitation of violence, which almost excluded the question of what in especial one of these spirits was to give and the other to gain."

James made the long trip to Oxford because he wanted to find symbolism in what he called "a certain faint convergence." On the one hand of this convergence was the novelist who in the seventeen years since his death had come to seem, despite his limitations, more and

129

more a classic. James's major essay on Flaubert would come in 1902, as a preface to a new English translation of *Madame Bovary*, henceforth ensconced among the indispensable works of European literature. James had known him, and that acquaintanceship had by now begun to bathe in a glow of reminiscence. On the other hand stood the representative of a younger generation of French novelists—Bourget was nine years James's junior—who had publicly declared himself James's disciple. A somewhat awkward and unwieldy disciple, in that Bourget was fast evolving toward the right wing and Catholic ideology that would make him a rabid anti-Dreyfusard and antisemite when *l'Affaire Dreyfus* broke out, the following year.

Bourget had recently published a novel entitled *Le Disciple*, which could be read to cast a strange light on his discipleship to James. In that novel, the master is an unworldly and egotistical philosopher, the disciple a would-be cold-hearted seducer and manipulator, and the relation of master to disciple one of responsibility for a mind and a life gone astray. But Bourget's admiration and affection for James seem to have been real and durable. They exchanged visits on both sides of the Channel. There was even a week at Costebelle, Bourget's country house near Hyères, in 1899, at the height of *l'Affaire*, though James found this visit somewhat painful. James mentioned Bourget in print as a leading novelist of the younger French generation, while more and more admitting in his correspondence—including some letters to Bourget himself—not to like his fiction. One senses that James was highly flattered by having a French writer declare allegiance to him: it was a pleasing reversal of his own earlier unrequited discipleship to French masters.

"Un héros intellectuel" Bourget called Flaubert toward the end of his lecture. The intellectual heroism was that scrupulous, disinterested devotion to the art of the novel that James, too, felt to be Flaubert's greatest claim to the novelist's undying gratitude. James underlines the "degree of poetic justice, or at least of poetic generosity," in Flaubert's entry into the academic pantheon: "it was impossible not to feel that no setting or stage for the crowning of his bust could less have appeared familiar to him, and that he wouldn't have failed to wonder into what strangely alien air his glory had strayed." Thus the occasion becomes "a little miracle of our breathless pace." A novelist present on the occasion could not fail to feel himself "becoming rather more of a novelist than before." Here was the modern novel, the contemporary novel—as written by someone James had known in person—entering into the hallowed academic precinct: a precinct not at all known for its welcome of the contemporary. On the contrary, what James feels to be so distinctive about the occasion is its exceptional quality, since there is generally "a certain usual positive *want* of convergence, want of communication between what the seat and habit of the classics, the famous frequentation and discipline, do for their victims in one direction and what they do not do for them in another. Was the invitation to M. Bourget not a dim symptom of a bridging of this queerest of all chasms?" (1410).

James probably expresses something of a fond hope here: Oxford as an institution was not about to embrace contemporary literature (and Flaubert's disciple Zola, for instance, could still be banned in England for indecency). The hope is one with his dream of a convergence of fiction and criticism, and his effort to establish the novel as a serious art form. His choice to write novels never seemed morally quite up to snuff for the values of Quincy Street, especially the values of the philosopher older brother. The answer was to prove that the novel was a serious criticism of life if only it were practiced with higher conviction, and read with finer discrimination. James did more than any other novelist to establish the writing and reading of novels as a discipline. And his difficult creative years in the 1890s were absolutely crucial in his own discovery of the vast and challenging possibilities of the novelistic form.

The Flaubert-Bourget encounter stands for James as part of "the quickened notation of our 'modernity.'" Looking at Bourget's lecture in the context of the volume of Taylorian Lectures in which it was published, in 1900, one realizes that it stands in an emerging tradition of the new that avant-garde Oxford, at least, was prepared to recognize. We find that the Taylorian over the years 1889–99 invited, in addition to Bourget, W. M. Rossetti, Walter Pater, Ernest Dowson, and Stéphane Mallarmé—the last of these offering as his lecture *La Musique et les lettres*, a major statement of the most advanced thinking about poetic practice of the time. I doubt that James ever read Mallarmé: he wasn't up to date on experimental French poetry of the 1890s. Nonetheless, I think one could say that James at this time was making a self-conscious encounter with "modernity" of a sort postponed from his Paris stay of 1875 and 1876. It is significant of course that James had very much maintained contacts with members of the Flaubert circle following the death of the Master in 1880.

Alphonse Daudet, Guy de Maupassant, and Emile Zola had all been visitors to London, as well as objects of visits in Paris. James's standing among French novelists had clearly improved since the Paris stay—even though it seems likely that, with the exception of Bourget, they did not read him. His ease with spoken French and his complete familiarity with French culture made him a friendly point of entry into Victorian London for visiting French writers. And while much that James publishes in these years about French writers seems to want to maintain a clear sense of distinction between their vision of the novel and his, it is evident that he is keeping up with the novelistic avant-garde. But he had other preoccupations as well.

Following his novelistic exploration of the world of the theater in *The Tragic Muse*, published in volume form in 1890, he had moved, cautiously but with strong fascination, into literal theater: into becoming a playwright. He undertook a dramatization of his novel *The American* for the Compton Comedy Company, which in 1891 had a decent success in the provinces, and moderate success in London. In the process of self-adaptation, James made the latent melodrama of the novel all too overt: the staginess of the novel literalized on the stage tended to efface much of the wit and nuance furnished by the narrative voice of the novel. James, who of course had spent innumerable evenings of his life at the theater—especially in Paris—was always attracted to the worldly, public, sociable fame brought by successful playwriting, and he continued for the next three years or so to write plays, mainly social comedies, that found no takers. Then the actor-manager George Alexander undertook to produce and act in the strange late-romantic drama James had begun in 1893, *Guy Domville*. The play opened on January 5, 1895, in a famous débâcle, with the author booed, as well as applauded by some, at the end. The play held on for five weeks, but it was never a success.

The wounding James suffered at the première of *Guy Domville* was severe. But he determined to profit from his unsuccessful theatrical venture by putting its lessons of technique to work in his novels. The highly scenic *The Spoils of Poynton*, begun in 1895, finished and serialized as *The Old Things* in 1896, then published as a book in 1897, was a striking example of theater transmuted into the novelistic form. Between the passages of exposition and narration James tended to call "summary," the novel developed as a series of major "scenes," played out in the living spaces of Poynton or Ricks (or at a crucial moment in Fleda Vetch's father's London flat), amidst stage properties—the famous "things"—that also held resonant symbolic value. Then in 1896 he converted his play *The Other House*—written under the impact of his discovery of Henrik Ibsen—into a novel, in a process he later said gave him "a divine little light to walk by." Again in 1899, *The Awkward Age*, written almost entirely in dialogue, would be a novel resolutely modeled on the scenic form. And throughout James's later novels, what he called his "scenic method" would be crucial.

But the mid-1890s brought something else as well as the attention to theatrical form (which after all had been something of a Jamesian preoccupation from very early on). It brought a concern with how we see and know a story, with the bases of our knowledge of what is going on around us. From approximately the time of *The Figure in the Carpet*, in 1896, through *What Maisie Knew* (1897), *The Turn of the Screw* (1898), *In the Cage* (1898), to *The Sacred Fount* (1901)—and then, belatedly, *The Beast in the Jungle* (1903)—James's fiction appears to evidence a radical dis-orientation, a displacement of the observer from a central or frontal position to a marginal one, a position that might be described in the parlance of the theater as "partial view": behind a pillar, in the side balcony. Knowledge had of course always been important in James's fictions, which were indeed often centrally dramas of knowledge—perhaps most notably *The Portrait of a Lady*, where Isabel Archer's discovery of the latent meanings of her disastrous marriage constitutes the core of the drama. Bafflement leading to recognition was perhaps always the principal Jamesian scenario. What seems new in the fiction of the mid- to late 1890s is the emphasis on the bafflement itself, and the difficulty or even impossibility of assuring that the recognition is real, rather than the product of a partial, misinformed, or even unhinged imagination. It is in this work that James appears to discover some of the radical issues in perspective that we associate with modernity in French painting, and with the later work of Flaubert. As Leon Edel has noted, post-1895 James seems already to have left the nineteenth century behind, and to be launched toward the fictional experimentation of Joyce, of Woolf, of Proust. For all his earlier rejection of impressionism, he now experiments with techniques not unlike those of the emerging post-impressionists and cubists, recording the same figure or scene from more than one perspective at once, seeking unfamiliar angles of vision to make us see anew. It's as if the lessons explicitly not learned in Paris in 1876—where he rejected modernist experimentation—had dropped into that "deep well of unconscious cerebration" to re-emerge as lessons now important and salutary.

Maisie's "Innocence Saturated with Knowledge"

It is no accident that the final scenes of *What Maisie Knew* are played out in France, in Boulogne-sur-Mer, where James had spent several months as a child. Boulogne was, and still is, one of the ports of cross-Channel traffic, and that's precisely why the climax of *Maisie* takes place there. Sir Claude, Maisie's stepfather, has more or less abducted her, in order to "save" her from the adults who conspire to declare their undying attachment to her at the same moment they are rejecting her. Sir Claude is partner to Mrs Beale, formerly Miss Overmore, Maisie's governess who married Beale Farrange, Maisie's father, who divorced Ida, Maisie's mother, who then married Sir Claude. These two stepparents to Maisie have ended up as her informal guardians, since the two biological parents have made it clear that they want nothing to do with her—though done so in such a way as to claim that it is Maisie who is rejecting them. Ida indeed has followed Sir Claude and Maisie as far as Folkestone—on the English side of the Channel—to make it clear that Maisie must choose Sir Claude and thus renounce herself. As Sir Claude formulates it to Mrs Wix the governess in Boulogne, "She has chucked our friend here overboard not a bit less than if she had shoved her, shrieking and pleading, out of the window and down two floors to the paving-stones." The violence of the image is justified, and an indication of how Jamesian psychological and moral melodrama keeps breaking through into this novel of (bad) manners.

Boulogne is important precisely as an escape from England: a respite from Beale Farrange and Ida and their various past and current lovers and other hangers-on, and a potential liberation from the law, both formal and informal. Sir Claude and Mrs. Beale are not married—both are still legally wed, to Ida and to Beale respectively—though they regard themselves as morally free to live together because each has been effectively repudiated by his and her spouse. There is a good deal of talk about their freedom. But if that's an acceptable French notion of freedom to pursue a life together, an English interpretation would not have it that way. And England comes marching into the hotel at Boulogne in the formidable person of Mrs Wix, the governess to Maisie who has made herself an even more powerful claimant to parenthood.

Mrs Wix denounces Maisie's want of moral sense, since Maisie appears willing to go off to live with Sir Claude and Mrs Beale in their "sin." Mrs Wix confronts them with the impossible immorality of their intentions, and suggests that Sir Claude renounce Mrs Beale in order to keep Maisie—and Mrs Wix herself (who, like Maisie, adores Sir Claude, who indeed seems destined to please all women, which is a problem). Sir Claude in turn puts it to Maisie that if she is to stay with him and Mrs Beale she will have to give up Mrs Wix. The ultimate, searing choices are forced on Maisie herself. She proposes the truly impossible solution: she'll give up Mrs Wix if Sir Claude will give up Mrs Beale—leaving stepfather and stepdaughter to carry on alone, in some unimaginable prefiguration of *Lolita* told from the point of view of the pubescent girl (which is what Maisie, though her age is unspecified, appears to just about be by this point in the novel). Sir Claude ruefully recognizes that he can't give up Mrs Beale—and Maisie leaves with Mrs Wix, to catch the Channel ferry back to Folkestone.

There are two moments where Sir Claude lapses into French in these final chapters of the novel: first, with the *patronne* of the hotel, whom he asks to send up breakfast to Mrs Wix, and who then queries:

> "*Et pour Madame?*"
> "*Madame?*" he echoed—it just pulled him up a little.
> "*Rien encore?*"
> "*Rien encore.* Come, Maisie." She hurried along with him, but on the way to the café he said nothing. (240).

The issue—what makes Sir Claude hesitate a moment—is that Mrs Beale is not "Madame" in the sense of being his wife, though in French she *is* Madame, as any married woman—married to whom is not the point—must be. After their time in the café, Maisie and Sir Claude return toward the hotel by way of the railroad station, to buy newspapers and books, "one yellow and two pink": the yellow French novel is in James often an emblem for French fiction of an audacity (particularly in matters of sex) denied to the English (French novels have important moments onstage in both *The Awkward Age* and *The Ambassadors*), and the pink represents the "Bibliothèque Rose," the series of educative novels for proper young girls written, most famously, by the Comtesse de Ségur, novels that represent a particularly French sense of traditional young womanhood.

They notice a train about to start for Paris. Maisie expresses the wish that Sir Claude would take her off to Paris. As she makes the proposal, Maisie is "conscious of being more frightened than she had ever been in her life," and perceives that Sir Claude has gone white from his own fright (254). They appear to be at a moment of dramatic choice: Sir Claude appears to take her wish seriously, though he will use it to turn the tables on her, to ask her for a renunciation of Mrs Wix, so that the scene becomes one more manipulation of Maisie. The porter tells him the train is due to start in two minutes, and asks if he should go get them tickets. He says they just barely have time:

> "*Et vos billets?—vous n'avez que le temps.*" Then after a look at Maisie, "*Monsieur veut-il que je les prenne?*" the man said.
> Sir Claude turned back to her. "*Veux-tu bien qu'il en prenne?*"

It was the most extraordinary thing in the world: in the intensity of her excitement she not only by illumination understood all their French, but fell into it with an active perfection. She addressed herself straight to the porter. "*Prenny, prenny. Oh prenny!*"

"*Ah si mademoiselle le veut—!*" He waited there for the money.

But Sir Claude only stared—stared at her with his white face. "You *have* chosen then? You'll let her go?"

Maisie carried her eyes wistfully to the train, where, amid cries of "*En voiture, en voiture!*" heads were at windows and doors banging loud. The porter was pressing. "*Ah vous n'avez plus le temps!*"

"It's going—it's going!" cried Maisie.

They watched it move, they watched it start; then the man went his way with a shrug. "It's gone!" Sir Claude said. (254)

Here is the climax and the end of Maisie's "dream," her fantasy of sole possession of Sir Claude. That it should play out in French—and that in the excitement of the moment Maisie should have a transient but effective access to that language—makes what James is doing here even more extraordinary. Sir Claude at the climatic moment of choice speaks to her in the optative subjunctive: "*Veux-tu bien qu'il en prenne?*" making it her decision whether or not the porter goes to buy the tickets. Her Anglicized French answer, "*Prenny, prenny. Oh prenny!*" is taken as good currency by the porter, but Sir Claude merely uses it to turn the screw of choice one more turn, to demand her explicit renunciation of Mrs Wix—and with this new demand of his the time expires in a banging of carriage doors. One could say that the French language both glosses and glosses over the moral drama of the novel.

By this I mean that "Frenchness," so actively represented here toward the end of *What Maisie Knew*, in both setting and language use, evokes a kind of literature—playfully emblematized in the yellow-covered novel—that we might call Flaubertian, not only for its realist exploration of all sorts of subjects very much including nonmarital sex but also for its perspectivalism, its address to all issues of life and the world through someone's perspective, with all the limitations of vision and understanding that this implies. The main drama of *What Maisie Knew* turns precisely on the kinds of knowledge that we, as adult observers, can detect in or impute to the child Maisie. The last sentence of the novel—which follows hard on Maisie's choice of Mrs Wix over Mrs Beale and Sir Claude—comes on the ferry as they steam back across the Channel. Maisie admits that she looked back at the balcony of the hotel as they left Boulogne harbor, and that Sir Claude wasn't there.

> Mrs Wix was also silent a while. "He went to *her*," she finally observed.
> "Oh I know!" the child replied.
> Mrs Wix gave a sidelong look. She still had room for wonder at what Maisie knew. (266)

Taking the measure of the growth of Maisie's knowledge over the course of events recounted in the novel is of course the reader's problem as well. The fact that it should at the last be Mrs Wix who wonders about the question may be evocative of the way in which everything French glosses over what the staid governess sees as the problem: not only the question of what Maisie knows, but as well the moral content of this knowing.

Mrs Wix's problem lies in her belief that she must cultivate Maisie's moral sense without further contaminating her with forbidden knowledge. This constitutes very much of a double bind, for both of them. Following her arrival in Boulogne, Mrs Wix considers what it would mean to stay on as Maisie's governess in the employ of the unmarried Sir Claude and Mrs Beale. To the claim of each of these to be "free," Mrs Wix comments that nobody is free to commit a crime.

> "A crime!" The word had come out in a way that made the child sound it again.
> "You'd commit as great a one as their own—and so should I—if we were to condone their immorality by our presence."
> Maisie waited a little; this seemed so fiercely conclusive. "Why is it immorality?" she nevertheless presently inquired.
> Her companion now turned upon her with a reproach softer because it was somehow deeper. "You're too unspeakable! Do you know what we're talking about?" (207)

The extent to which Maisie knows what they are talking about is uncertain and variable. She learns enough, one might say, to survive her necessary relations with the adult world but not enough to participate fully in that world's games of knowledge offered, withheld, forbidden, made alluring.

Throughout her adventures as the simultaneously fought-over and rejected bone of contention in *Farrange v. Farrange and Others*—the divorce case that leads to a "solution" of joint custody—Maisie has learned to practice "the pacific art of stupidity" (77). And again: "she had never been safe unless she had also been stupid" (176). In fact, her discovery of the uses of stupidity to protect herself from adult prying at her knowledge is closely allied to her discovery of her selfhood, in a passage where, daringly, James seems to take us into the dawning of consciousness in a young child:

> She had a new feeling, the feeling of danger; on which a new remedy rose to meet it, the idea of an inner self or, in other words, of concealment. She puzzled out with imperfect signs, but with a prodigious spirit, that she had been a centre of hatred and a messenger of insult, and that everything was bad because she had been employed to make it so. Her parted lips locked themselves with the determination to be employed no longer. She would forget everything, she would repeat nothing, and when, as a tribute to the successful application of her system, she began to be called a little idiot, she tasted a pleasure new and keen. (43)

The sense of the inner self is born together with the idea of concealment, of mendacity, and an assumed stupidity. Maisie anticipates Michel Foucault in the understanding that knowledge that would be power must conceal its face. All the more so when this knowledge is imperfect, even faked, as is the case with what underlies the behavior of the adult world: sex. "Everything had something behind it: life was like a long, long corridor of closed doors. She had learned that at these doors it was wise not to knock—this seemed to produce from within such sounds of derision." (54–55) The Balzacian premise of the "beneath and behind" here is explicitly sexual, and the passage goes on to describe how Maisie imitates the adult world in playing with her

French doll, Lisette. The naïve questions she attributes to Lisette produce convulsions of laughter in Maisie. Faced with such innocence, she imitates "the shrieking ladies. There were at any rate things she really couldn't tell even a French doll. She could only pass on her lessons and study to produce on Lisette the impression of having mysteries in her life, wondering the while whether she succeeded in the air of shading off, like her mother, into the unknowable" (55). So that the cultivation of mystery—the implication of possession of hidden or forbidden knowledge—is the counterpart of the practice of stupidity.

Mrs Wix faces the traditional problem of teaching ignorance: that is, of inculcating that "moral sense" she wants Maisie to have without providing the essential knowledge of good and evil on which it must be based, knowledge about sex. Following her accusation that Maisie is "unspeakable" in proposing they live with the unmarried couple of Sir Claude and Mrs Beale, Mrs Wix laments that Maisie's adventures have led the respectable governess to know more than she wants to know. "Now I know too much, too much!" the poor woman lamented and groaned" (214). She laments also that she may have brought to Maisie knowledge that she ought rather to have concealed: "I've gone from one thing to another, and all for the real love of you; and now what would anyone say—I mean anyone but *them*—if they were to hear the way I go on? I've had to keep up with you, haven't I?—and therefore what could I do less than look to you to keep up with *me*?" One may think here of the words spoken by the governess of *The Turn of the Screw* when for one instant of lucid self-judgment she asks if she not be the bearer of the evil knowledge that she attributes to the child Miles: "For if he *were* innocent what then on earth was I?" Mrs Wix suggests that while Maisie's various guardians were in the process of "ruining" her, they might have completed the job, and so spared Mrs Wix. "Then I shouldn't have had to do whatever it is that's the worst: throw up at you the badness you haven't taken in, or find my advantage in the vileness you *have*! What I did lose patience at this morning was at how it was that without your seeming to condemn—for you didn't, you remember!—you yet did seem to *know*. Thank God, in his mercy, at last, *if* you do!" (214).

This is not much more specific than Maisie's conversation with her

French doll. If Maisie does know the immoral from the moral without the vileness of that knowledge having been imparted by Mrs Wix then she is reprehensible, in Wixian terms, for not condemning it. But does Mrs Wix's "thank God *if* you do" refer to condemnation, or to knowledge? What would be the content of any knowledge Maisie might now possess, since we have seen that her knowledge of sexuality takes the form of a pragmatics—how to handle adults so motivated—rather than anything more specific? And how could there be any basis for condemnation, since morality has to mean, for her in the first instance, self-preservation? The very first paragraph of chapter 1 tells us: "It was to be the fate of this patient little girl to see much more than she at first understood, but also even at first to understand much more than any little girl, however patient, had perhaps ever understood before" (39). (The lines echo the first paragraph of *In the Cage,* another, nearly contemporaneous Jamesian tale of ways of knowing and the problems of innocence as ignorance.) "Point of view" in *What Maisie Knew* is correspondingly complex: what we see her seeing, and what we learn that she is learning, don't perfectly coincide—the latter is not only delayed in relation to the former, it also is imperfectly understood by us, perhaps also by Maisie herself. And when we add to this situation her discovery of the uses of stupidity in her relations with the adult world, the result is a complex and treacherous drama of seeing and knowing.

I don't think there is any work of James's prior to *Maisie* in which he is quite so willing to permit a kaleidoscopic play of meaning, perspective, interpretation without trying to order it, hierarchize it, control at least the principles of interpretation. Here there is an astonishing fluidity to everything, of a sort we encounter later, for instance in certain passages between Millie Theale and Kate Croy in *The Wings of the Dove*, between Maggie and the Prince in *The Golden Bowl*. To be sure, the story isn't told in Maisie's voice—in the first person, for instance—or in a third-person narration focalized exclusively on her. Nor is it seen wholly through her eyes, though mostly the sense data reaching us are filtered through her interpretive consciousness. Jamesian point of view allows for a narratorial voice that speaks over and beyond all the characters, so to speak. The text is radically perspectival nonetheless, since this narratorial voice (except possibly in the introductory chapter that briskly announces the divorce and custody arrangement) renounces the perspective of any adult (and the adults are all callow and self-interested in any case) in favor of Maisie's progressive rendering of their perspectives, a confusion and muddle out of which emerges as a principle of knowing and acting simply one's self-interest—to the extent that that "self," in its formative years, can know its interests. If *What Maisie Knew* inevitably reminds us of the tradition of the *Bildungsroman*, here "education" is another moving target that enlists the reader's active quest to find out and to understand.

"What there was no effective record of indeed was the small strange pathos on the child's part of an innocence so saturated with knowledge and so directed to diplomacy" (150). James's extraordinary stereoscopic technique in this novel—both recording what Maisie sees, and probing the limits of what she does and doesn't understand—reaches this kind of oxymoron of consciousness. Maisie is at once innocent and saturated with knowledge, though a knowledge that is particularly developed for its usefulness in relations with the adult world. The phrase comes during her brief interlude with her father, Beale—whom she has not seen for some time, and who in this scene will precisely maneuver her into excusing him from any care for her in the future, "with all the appearance of virtue and sacrifice on his side" (153). It is a frightening scene of seduction and rejection.

> There was a passage during which, on a yellow silk sofa under one of the palms, he had her on his knee stroking her hair, playfully holding her off while he showed his shining fangs and let her, with a vague affectionate helpless pointless "Dear old girl, dear little daughter," inhale the fragrance of his cherished beard. (148)

For all the indirection of narrative presentation in the novel, here—as in other key moments—we cut through to the primal story of child abuse that is at the heart of *What Maisie Knew*. See those wolfish, folk-tale-like "shining fangs" in Beale's mouth. James never is far from the terror underlying human relations—think, for instance, of Prince Amerigo's line to Maggie in *The Golden Bowl*: "Everything's terrible, *cara*—in the heart of man." But terror and pity become most explicit in James where children are concerned, as they are with remarkable frequency and poignancy in his work, in *The Turn of the Screw* and *Owen Wingrave* and *The Pupil* and a number of other tales. Here, the apparent paradox of James's complex indirection of presentation—his hesitant and discreet attempts to enter the mental processes of a young girl whose very being is intricated with the falsehoods she needs to state and perhaps to believe in order to survive—is that it ushers out onto terrifying moral melodrama.

So caressed by her father, Maisie's emotional bent is toward self-sacrifice. "To give something, to give here on the spot, was all her own desire. Among the old things that came back was her little instinct of keeping the peace" (149). She is ready for "an immense surrender"—of everyone except Sir Claude and Mrs Beale:

> The immensity didn't include *them*; but if he had an idea at the back of his head she had also one in a recess as deep, and for a time, while they sat together, there was an extraordinary mute passage between her vision of this vision of his, his vision of her vision, and her vision of his vision of her vision. What there was no effective record of indeed was the small strange pathos on the child's part of an innocence so saturated with knowledge and so directed to diplomacy. (150)

Maisie's complex vision here mimics the "ratiocination" made famous by Edgar Allan Poe's Inspector Dupin ("the robber's knowledge of the loser's knowledge of the robber," as the narrator formulates it in *The Purloined Letter*). But Maisie's knowledge and diplomacy only serve to her recognition that her father's offer to take her with him (and "the Countess," alias Mrs Cuddon and various uncomplimentary epithets) to America is wholly insincere, and that indeed she is being given a final farewell by Beale.

> Wasn't he trying to turn the tables on her, embarrass her somehow into admitting that what would really suit her little book would be, after doing so much for good manners, to leave her wholly at liberty to arrange for herself? She began to be nervous again: it rolled over her that this was their parting, their parting for ever, and that he had brought her there for so many caresses only because it was

important such an occasion should look better for him than any other. For her to spoil it by the note of discord would certainly give him ground for complaint; and the child was momentarily bewildered between her alternatives of agreeing with him about her wanting to get rid of him and displeasing him by pretending to stick to him. So she found for the moment no solution but to murmur very helplessly: "Oh papa—oh papa!" (152)

There is here a kind of moral and psychological pathos that Flaubert never approached, even what you might call an ethical terror that children can be so abused by their parents.

So it is that in *What Maisie Knew* James seems able to combine the perspectival lessons of Flaubert with a moral vision that evokes a wholly different tradition in the novel: that of George Eliot, perhaps— eminently a novelist of moral terrors—or even Balzac, who also was sensitive to tortured children, or the puritan Hawthorne. Note that James's title refers us not to what Maisie saw—which we might consider to be more the realm of Flaubert and other French realists and impressionists concerned with the look of things—but to what she knew. James emphasizes this point in his preface to the New York Edition of the novel, where he refers to his subject as "the small expanding consciousness" of the child, and then poses indirectly the question of how such an approach can repay "the favour of our attention." In answer to this question, he pauses over the scene between Maisie and her father that I discussed above:

The facts involved are that Beale Farrange is ignoble, that the friend to whom he introduces his daughter ["the Countess"] is deplorable, and that from the commerce of the two, *as* the two merely, we would fain avert our heads. Yet the thing has but to become a part of the child's bewilderment for these small sterilities to drop from it and for the *scene* to emerge and prevail—vivid, special, wrought hard, to the hardness of the unforgettable; the scene that is exactly what Beale and Ida and Mrs Cuddon, and even Sir Claude and Mrs Beale, could never for a moment have succeeded in making their scant unredeemed importances—namely *appreciable*.

What I take this somewhat obscure passage to mean is that the play of Maisie's evolving consciousness gives the sordid scene, and others throughout the novel, a kind of significance that presentation of the scene in other ways—through an adult observer, for instance—would not. The scene between Beale and "the Countess" is in itself the stuff of the more deplorable varieties of French fiction. As part of Maisie's struggle to understand, however, it is transformed into the drama of consciousness.

As James continues in discussion of the problem of mixing up a child with an adult world of such immorality, he allows that a reaction of aversion to such a treatment is also part of his subject. This modulates into one of his defenses of his own art:

> The effort really to see and really to represent is no idle business in face of the *constant* force that makes for muddlement. The great thing is indeed that the muddled state too is one of the very sharpest of the realities, that it also has colour and form and character, has often in fact a broad and rich comicality, many of the signs and values of the appreciable. Thus it was to be, for example, I might gather, that the very principle of Maisie's appeal, her undestroyed freshness, in other words that vivacity of intelligence by which she indeed does vibrate in the infected air, indeed does flourish in her immoral world, may pass for a barren and senseless thing, or at best a negligible one. (1164)

He answers the self-generated charge with the claim that Maisie's case is made remarkable "exactly by the weight of the tax on it"—the tax "would have done little for us hadn't it been monstrous" (1164).

To some extent, this is James attempting to ward off an Anglo-American reaction to the gross immorality of the adult world into which he has thrust his innocent child. But it also, I think, declares a certain allegiance to the Anglo-American moral reaction. If life offers muddlement, the "effort really to see and to represent" needs to render both the muddlement and the "monstrous" moral realities. It is Flaubert's limitation that the ethical consciousness never emerges from his efforts to see and represent the world by way of our experience of it—an experience that in the case of *A Simple Heart* has some of the innocence and simplicity of the child's. But Félicité in *A Simple Heart* remains largely an uneducated consciousness throughout her story—whereas Maisie gains a knowledge all the more embracing and portentous in that we can't at the end exactly say how far it extends. And like our surrogate Mrs Wix, we can't ask in order to find out, since asking might precisely rob Maisie of whatever innocence remains to her. Never has the Jamesian uncertainty principle been so fully in evidence as here: an attempt to penetrate the opacities of Maisie's moral consciousness would risk destroying what is seen as most valuable, possibly redeeming, in it.

The novel also makes the claim that Maisie's developing consciousness changes those adults from whom she must learn, stimulates their own production of knowledge. The claim is advanced in a startling passage where the narrator, speaking as "I," intervenes in the novel for the first time. It comes during the Boulogne episode, following Mrs Wix's accusation of Maisie's lack of moral sense. In the relations of knowledge between Mrs Wix and her charge, the narrator comes on to speak of Maisie and his own inability to track fully her consciousness: "I so despair of courting her noiseless mental footsteps here that I must crudely give you my word for its being from this time forward a picture literally present to her" (212). What is present to her is the manner in which she has elevated Mrs Wix to a level that might "pass almost for sublime." The sublimity in fact seems to be of Maisie's doing, and of this she may in part be aware. "I am not sure that Maisie had not even a dim discernment of the queer law of her own life that made her educate to that sort of proficiency those elders with whom she was concerned. She promoted, as it were, their development." This makes quite an extraordinary claim to the reciprocity of the learning process between Maisie and her instructors. The claim leads in turn to Maisie's reflection on her own future completion of knowledge:

As she was condemned to know more and more, how could it logically stop before she should know Most? It came to her in fact as they sat there on the sands that she was distinctly on the road to know Everything. She had not had governesses for nothing: what in the world had she ever done but learn and learn and learn? She

looked at the pink sky with a placid foreboding that she soon
should have learnt All. (213)

The passage is nearly Miltonic, or otherwise Calvinist, in her own apprehension of her predestination to knowledge—knowledge that lies
before her in a "placid foreboding," knowledge of the coming, inevitable lapse from innocence into knowing good and evil. To suggest
how such a proleptic understanding of the nature of knowledge and
the process of its impending arrival comes to consciousness in the
young girl, and in turn affects all relations with the adult world, James
produces an exceptionally complex play of perspectives and a complexity of novelistic knowing perhaps never before attempted.

What Maisie Knew was published in volume 11 of the New York
Edition along with *The Pupil* and *In the Cage*, the former another tale
of a child dispossessed of childhood, the latter another tale of partial
knowledge, knowledge acquired through an inadequate perspectival
position ("in the cage"), its gaps filled in through the work of the imagination (trained on romance from the lending library), and ultimately a
knowledge that the young woman at the center of the novella can't
have access to since it belongs to another social class, to people who
use her and discard her. When James in his preface comes to *In the
Cage*, he pauses for a curious piece of self-criticism: he accuses himself
of reading "rank subtleties into simple souls and reckless expenditure
into thrifty ones," endowing the telegraph girl of his story with a more
active consciousness than such a person in reality would probably
have. "The matter comes back again, I fear, but to the author's irrepressible and insatiable, his extravagant and immoral, interest in personal character and in the 'nature' of a mind, of almost any mind the
heaving little sea of his subject may cast up." If this irrepressible, extravagant, and immoral author—immoral, note, in his desire to get
into others' minds and impute a drama of consciousness to them—
resembles a precursor, it would have to be Balzac.

It was during the composition of *Maisie* that James recorded in his
notebook an admonition on method that has often been cited since: "I
realize—none too soon—that the *scenic* method is my absolute, my imperative, my *only* salvation." He draws the lesson of his failed attempts to

be a playwright: that he must create drama in his novels by moving their action toward, and by way of, climactic scenes. In this notebook entry, he refers to having just read Henrik Ibsen's "splendid" *John Gabriel Borkman* in proof, and goes on: "I must now, I fully recognize, have a splendid recourse to it to see me out of the wood, at all, of this interminable little *Maisie: 10,000 more words* of which I have still to do. They can be magnificent in movement if I resolutely and triumphantly take this course with them, and *only if I do so.*" The last 10,000 words of *Maisie* do include the highly dramatic scenes played out in Folkestone and then in Boulogne. And yet compared to *The Awkward Age*, for instance—which is almost exclusively dramatic dialogue—*Maisie* is a curiously skewed drama because so much of it is witnessed by a person not of adult height, someone who can't always see over the seatback in front of her. If it is scenically represented, the scenes at times remind us of that "other stage"—that *anderes Schauplatz*—that Freud defined as the representational space of the dream. Maisie's experience is nightmarish, hallucinatory, a kind of unresolved bind between innocence and the saturation of knowledge.

James tells us that *Maisie* and *In the Cage* were the first novels that he dictated to his first amanuensis, William MacAlpine, and while I think much of *Maisie* may have been written out by James before MacAlpine arrived on the scene, the challenging, radical fluidity of the novel may be connected to the practice of dictation—which would soon become standard for James, and surely inflected his late style. One is tempted to use the word "impressionist"—except that James's objection to the impressionists in painting was founded on a real difference of artistic belief. James continues to believe in a representative function of art, one that may appear to be in love with a luminous, complex, shifting surface but is also intent to ask about what lies behind it, not just what Maisie sees but what she knows. Even though the content of that knowledge may ultimately be indeterminate because we never can find a way to observe it without altering or destroying it, we have to believe it is there, and that trying to get at it is what our work is all about. That knowledge, however inaccessible, represents the realm of meaning and value.

We might recall Virginia Woolf's report of Roger Fry's attempt to explain to a James baffled by the postimpressionists that "Cézanne and Flaubert were, in a manner of speaking, after the same thing." James's reaction is remarkably close to that of Zola, Cézanne's boyhood class-mate and friend who praised his early painting but then was unable to understand his more experimental work—the work that to us defines Cézanne—because Zola, too, was committed to a kind of representa-tion that he no longer finds in later Cézanne. (The notational style of such a late Cézanne landscape as *Houses on the Hill, 1900–06* seems nearly analogous to James's stylistic reticences in his late work.)

Recall that James, shortly after his year in Paris and his negative comments on the impressionists, comments on Whistler (in a remark I quoted in chapter 3): "It may be a narrow point of view, but to be inter-esting it seems to me that a picture should have some relation to life as well as to painting. Mr. Whistler's experiments have no relation what-ever to life; they have only a relation to painting." This, one might say, is dumb-smart-dumb: James indicates that he understands the origins of "modernism" as a preoccupation with the medium itself, yet rejects his insight out of fidelity to an older tradition of representation. Does he blind himself to the process by which Whistler, like the impres-sionists, is teaching us to see in ways that can change our understand-ing of representation? A year later—in 1878—James encountered Whistler in his path again: "His manner is very much that of the French 'Impressionists', and, like them, he suggests the rejoinder that a picture is not an impression but an expression—just as a poem or a piece of music is."

Here is where Fry and Woolf may encounter an impasse in their ef-fort to convert James to the experimental modernism that by 1912 so clearly commanded their allegiance. James announces his fidelity to expressionism over impressionism—and despite the radical perspecti-valism of the work of the 1890s and beyond, I don't think he ever en-tirely renounces his expressionist premises. By "expressionism," I mean something that characterizes the writing of Balzac as well as the paint-ing of Edvard Munch, for instance: the effort to make surface yield something that is not purely of surface, that drama of ethical substance that requires "going behind" (to use James's phrase from the preface to *The Tragic Muse*). James is himself too morally tortured to find any serenity in impressionism or in an experimentalism that is only "about" the relation of the artwork to its medium. While he writes allegories of the artist that at moments appear to be largely about the aesthetic— *The Figure in the Carpet* is the most famous, but others, such as *The Birthplace*, are relevant too—the aesthetic often plays a deceptive role in them. As with *The Lesson of the Master, The Middle Years, The Death of the Lion, The Bench of Desolation*, the aesthetic without the expressionist impulse or ambition is sterile and mannered. It is not the lesson one should take from Flaubert but precisely where Flaubert, for all he has to teach the writer, falls short.

The other experimental fiction of the 1890s, I think, fits the description I have tried to give of *What Maisie Knew. Maisie* is from 1897. It is followed by: *The Turn of the Screw* (dictated in 1897, published in 1898), *In the Cage* (1898), *The Awkward Age* (1898–99), *The Sacred Fount* (1900–1901), and *The Beast in the Jungle* (1903). In most of these novels and novellas, the limitations of the narrative point of view are radical, challenging, even taxing for the reader; disorienting, even debilitating for characters within the fiction. *The Turn of the Screw* is notoriously a study in interpretive undecidability: it can be read as a story of the governess' obsessions that bring the postulated presence of the ghosts and kill Miles, or as a true ghost story that can't properly be registered by a skeptical intelligence. It is both of these—but it can't be both at once, so to speak. *In the Cage* is yet more radical from an epistemological point of view. The telegraph girl—never named in the course of the novella, which is significant—sits in the cage, a wired-off telegraph office in the corner of Cocker's grocery store, and counts words as numberless as the sands of the seashore all day long. In her caged position, she also participates imaginatively in the life of the society folk (Cocker's is in Mayfair) who come in to send off telegrams, most of them expensively arranging social (and amorous) rendezvous. She becomes particularly caught up in the correspondence of Captain Everard and Lady Bradeen, and nurtures a growing fantasy romance with Everard—which at one moment seems to offer a possibility of realization, though on terms that couldn't be acceptable to her, since she is not "a bad girl." She ends, I think, thoroughly exploited by a social system to which even her imaginative access is eventually thwarted. Fictions, romance, even language itself appear by the end to have a class definition: they are expensive, you can't have them simply by wanting them. She has to settle for Mr Mudge, the grocer.

James—in a detail that passes so quickly that many readers miss it—tells us that the telegraph office at Cocker's is a small one that only sends messages and doesn't receive them. Thus the girl sees only one half of the correspondence she is privy to—she has to reconstruct the replies through the play of her imagination on the outgoing messages. The situation could stand for the problem of knowledge and interpretation that we find throughout James's work at the end of the century. At first, the telegraph girl finds benefits in the incompleteness of her knowledge: "she pressed the romance closer by reason of the very quantity of imagination it demanded and consumed." Yet at the crisis of the story, she will realize that what she hasn't known has been of crucial importance: "Then it was that, above all, she felt how much she had missed in the gaps and blanks and absent answers." If the telegraph girl is like a reader according to the literary theorist Wolfgang Iser—someone who creatively fills in the "gaps" of a text—she finally discovers the limits to this kind of construction of meaning. By the end, she has lost any relation to Everard, and must learn of the dénouement of his affairs through the tattling of the butler Mr Drake. The whole principle of her epistemology is superseded by something far less glamorous, and far less susceptible to reformation by the imagination.

Each of these experimental works of the end of the century treats in its own manner questions of how we know, and how we construct meanings with knowledge that necessarily is limited, confined to a single perspective, and never sufficient to gain certainty. With *The Awkward Age*, readers have often had trouble figuring out just what happens in the novel, particularly in its climactic scene of exposure, where an untitled "French novel" makes the rounds of Mrs Brookenham's social circle, and it is revealed that the virginal Nanda has actually read it—which apparently destroys her chances on the marriage market. With *The Sacred Fount*, the majority of readers over the years have simply given up, writing the novel off as incomprehensible, or a kind of Jamesian self-parody. It is the most extreme of his fictional experiments, and

fare only for readers who enjoy a complex game of ratios and relationships that has no certain outcome. The narrator (it is one of James's
rare novels in the first person) spends a weekend enclosed in the
sphere of the country house, Newmarch, attempting to figure out the
pairings of the other guests, according to a rule by which one is drink-
ing at the sacred fount of the other—becoming younger and more vigorous while the other declines into exhaustion. It is a vampirish view of
erotic relations, as well as a somewhat sadistic principle of seeing and
knowing. By the end, the person who has seemed to be the narrator's
collaborator in his mental constructions, Grace Brissenden, tells him
that he's got everything wrong, that he's built a house of cards—which
she proceeds to make tumble down. Yet it's not clear whether she is
right, or rather seeking to protect her own illicit romance from the narrator's prying attentions. We are left with a kind of narrative construction kit without any clear instructions for assembly.

It is tempting to designate *The Beast in the Jungle* as the last in this
series of fictions, not only because it overlaps with the start of "the major phase" of James's work—the three great final novels, *The Ambassadors*, *The Wings of the Dove*, *The Golden Bowl*—but also because it
takes the principle of uncertainty in knowing, sets it as the central preoccupation of the protagonist of the novella, then proceeds to chart the
ethical drama that unfolds from dedicating your life to such a principle. John Marcher confides to May Bartram that he has long felt himself marked out for some special destiny, something exceptional that is
to happen to him, something lurking like a beast in the jungle. May
agrees to wait and "watch" with him. The years pass, he waits—and she
eventually recognizes that it is this waiting itself, Marcher's incapacity
to do anything because of his uncertainty about what awaits him, that
is the beast. In particular, she realizes that Marcher's egotism and self-
absorption are such as to blind him to the possibility of the love relation with her. She dies—and in the Jamesian presentation, it's as if she
dies from want of loving (the case of Milly Theale in *The Wings of the
Dove*, one could argue), from the perception of Marcher's egotism.
She expresses the hope that he will never find out what he was watching and waiting for. But after a time of pursuing what he thinks of as
"the lost stuff of consciousness," revelation does come.

It comes in the cemetery, in the perception of the stricken face of a mourner at another grave—a face that shows him what loss can mean, hence what passion could mean, and how what he has missed has been love, May Bartram herself, the chance of relationship with another, the knowledge provided by eros. He now stands gazing at "the sounded void of his life." He discovers that "he had been the man of his time, *the* man, to whom nothing on earth was to have happened. . . . all the while he had waited the wait was itself his portion." Knowledge at the last comes as pain. The very ending of the novella offers an extraordinary moment of overt melodramatic enactment of Marcher's smiting by this knowledge:

> This horror of waking—*this* was knowledge, knowledge under the breath of which the very tears in his eyes seemed to freeze. Through them, none the less, he tried to fix it and hold it; he kept it there before him so that he might feel the pain. That at least, belated and bitter, had something of the taste of life. But the bitterness suddenly sickened him, and it was as if, horribly, he saw, in truth, in the cruelty of his image, what had been appointed and done. He saw the Jungle of his life and saw the lurking Beast; then, while he looked, perceived it, as by a stir of the air, rise, huge and hideous, for the leap that was to settle him. His eyes darkened—it was close; and, instinctively turning, in his hallucination, to avoid it, he flung himself, face down, on the tomb.

The Beast in the Jungle both thematizes the void of knowledge—the problem of not having enough knowledge perfectly to know and to interpret—and moralizes it, gives an ethical dimension to the void, so that Marcher's failure is not merely epistemological but ethical as well, a failure in relation to other human beings. It's an extraordinary demonstration of how the preoccupation with ways of knowing and perspectives of interpretation in James's hands leads us back from the apparently modernist premises of the tale to what almost appears as old-fashioned Victorian melodrama. This is, I think, as James wants it: a kind of unimaginable combination of Flaubert and George Eliot.

There have been many readers inclined to identify James with John Marcher, as a self-portrait of the man who all his life avoided romantic entanglement in favor of dispassionate if voyeuristic observation. There has also been a temptation to read the novella as a coded reference to James's life in the homosexual closet, and surely it lends itself fully to this kind of reading. Yet the analytic self-awareness of the tale strikes me as the work of someone who has seen such possible selves and repudiated them. There is a very late story, *The Jolly Corner*—from 1907—that seems a rewrite of *the Beast in the Jungle* in a gentler mode, and with an uncharacteristically happy ending, as Alice Staverton and Spencer Brydon embrace. I'm not so convinced as some critics that James was "unhappy" (whatever that means) with his life, including his version of sexuality. The erotic passion he invests into knowing, into finding out (and here *The Sacred Fount* is highly characteristic) could well be called "epistemophilia" (James Strachey's translation of the term Freud used in discussing the highly intelligent obsessional neurotic known as the "Rat Man," *Wisstrieb*). The eros usually associated with the object of knowledge becomes invested in the search for knowledge, in knowing. What this might translate to in James's personal life is hard to fathom, since he was so good at covering his tracks. It becomes clearer and clearer as he grows older that he entertains passionate attachments to a number of good-looking young men, Hendrik Andersen, Jocelyn Persse, Howard Sturgis, Hugh Walpole, among others. As was the case with Paul Zhukovsky, there is no evidence of his having had sex with any of them. Was James exclusively masturbatory? That might fit with the voyeuristic preoccupations. Or there may have been liaisons with men that were hidden from sight so thoroughly that we cannot now uncover them. What does seem certain is that James's imagination is far from sexless—that he is more often than not preoccupied and indeed fascinated by what he called "the great relation." This I think becomes clearer when we come to the final three novels, which all turn on the demands of sexual relations.

To conclude on what I see as the experimental fiction of the turn of the century: James appears to reach back to lessons learned in Paris in the mid-1870s—to the lesson of Flaubert, of course, but also more generally to what he picked up in the city that was beginning to invent modernism. It's as if what James rejected in 1875–76 had lain dormant in him ever since, to come to flower at the *fin de siècle*—a moment that of course favored experimentation as well as decadence, a moment that promoted a good deal of self-consciousness about transitions and transformations. What prompts James to reach back toward kinds of perspectivism he learned from Flaubert and others cannot be denoted with any certainty: to us in retrospect, this seems a natural evolution of his art. Leon Edel designated this period in James's life as "the treacherous years," and certainly—beyond the treachery of time that anyone may feel in moving from his 50s to his 60s—there is the very painful comeuppance of *Guy Domville*; the arrival to stay in London and then the death of his invalid sister, Alice; the death by suicide of Constance Fenimore Woolson (who may have wanted something more than friendship from James). All this may have contributed to the treacherous epistemological situation dramatized over and over again in the fiction. Yet that kind of treachery was also part of the time, of a moment on the threshold of Wittgenstein and Einstein and Heisenberg as well as Proust, Joyce, and Woolf. New forms of uncertainty loomed. And while James's turn of the century is full of anguish, it is notable how serenely he adapts uncertainty to his uses. After the try-outs of *Maisie* and *In the Cage* and *The Sacred Fount*, he seems to take a great breath and launch himself into his most memorable works—works that all dramatize uncertainty in knowing while moving, in the hands of a master, toward a kind of moral clarity.

6. The Death of Zola, Sex in the French Novel, and the Improper

Emile Zola died on September 28, 1902, asphyxiated by carbon monoxide fumes, apparently because of a blocked chimney in his apartment. Many of Zola's friends, and many French in general, believed he was murdered, the chimney intentionally blocked by one of the multitude of enemies he had made for himself during his defense of Captain Dreyfus. (Decades later, a deathbed confession—of somewhat uncertain reliability—confirmed this hypothesis.) Zola had by this point returned from his exile in England, where he fled after a court convicted him of libeling the French Army. He had been pardoned by the president of the republic. Alfred Dreyfus himself had not yet been rehabilitated at the time of Zola's death, but the process was underway. Zola's funeral became one of those national "events" the French manage to stage from time to time, not only an expression of grief and remembrance but a symbolic moment in dramatization of ideas of justice and dignity. Some 50,000 compatriots followed the funeral cortège. The casket was buried under a mound of wreaths and flowers. Even the miners from the north of France—those whose grim lives were chronicled in Zola's *Germinal*—sent their delegation. Zola, Anatole France declared in his funeral oration, "was a moment in the history of human conscience."

James was from the outbreak of the *Affaire Dreyfus* resolutely pro-Dreyfus and distressed and disgusted by the antisemitism of the anti-Dreyfusards, including his friend Paul Bourget, to whom he paid a long-promised visit in the midst of the *Affaire* — in 1899 — but only with acute discomfort. (Later on, he referred to the now successful and *mondain* novelist as "the inflamed Academician," yet continued to see him in Paris, where he was a key member of Edith Wharton's circle.) With the publication of Zola's *J'accuse* and his trial, James wrote to a correspondent that he felt as if he were "every a.m. in Paris by the side of the big brave Zola, whom I find really a hero." He declared *J'accuse* "one of the most courageous things ever done." He apparently dashed off a letter of support to Zola, though the letter has not been found, and may never have reached the French novelist, en route to his refuge in Surrey, at just about the time James was moving into his new home, Lamb House, in Sussex.

Yet James in the retrospective essay on Zola that he published in the *Atlantic Monthly* in August 1903 somewhat perversely offers a view of Zola as a writer sheltered and indeed cut off from life. He recalls his impression of Zola during his visit to London in September 1893, one that confirmed James's earlier sense — when he saw Zola at Flaubert's in 1876 — of what he promised to become. That impression "consisted, simply stated, in his fairly bristling with the betrayal that nothing whatever had happened to him in life but to write Les Rougon-Macquart. It was even for that matter almost more as if Les Rougon-Macquart had written *him*, written him as he stood and sat, as he looked and spoke, as the long, concentrated, merciless effort that made and stamped and left him." Zola in James's impression begins to sound like John Marcher of *The Beast in the Jungle*, the man to whom nothing happened, whose fate was to be precisely to have nothing happen in his life. The inference that James has turned Zola into the sad protagonist of his novella, written at nearly the same moment, may largely be reinforced when he continues to speak of what did happen in Zola's life, as a result of his courageous intervention in the Dreyfus Affair. "Something very fundamental was to happen to him in due course, it is true, shaking him to his base; fate was not wholly to cheat him of an independent evolution. Recalling him from this London hour one strongly felt during the famous 'Affair' that his outbreak in connection with it was the act of a man with arrears of personal history to make up, the act of a spirit for which life, or for which at any rate freedom, had been too much postponed, treating itself at last to a luxury of experience."

One could fairly treat this as astounding, coming from James—whom numbers of readers have wanted to see as nearly as poor in life experience as the self-deluded Marcher. Zola, after all, had the experience of commerce—he had begun as a publicist for the publishing house of Hachette—and his famous investigations among the miners, and the department store workers, and the stockbrokers, and the jobbers of Les Halles, in any number of the productive sectors of society—and then the experience of a double life between his wife and his mistress (at one time his wife's maid), the second life developing into the richer experience, complete with children and an elaborate ménage. And when the Dreyfus Affair arrived, Zola was in a position unimaginable for James: to print his famous open letter to the president of the republic—*J'accuse*—on the front page of the daily newspaper *l'Aurore*. To see Zola's act here as a spirit "treating itself at last to a luxury of experience" may strike us as a bit mean-spirited.

What James means becomes reasonably clear over the course of the essay. It is perhaps best captured in his recollection of a conversation with Zola during that London visit, about travel to Italy. Zola allowed that he'd only been to Genoa, and that for only a few days. Since he had at this moment just published the final volume of *Les Rougon-Macquart*, *Le Docteur Pascal*, James inquired into his future writing plans. Oh, said Zola, I shall start at once on the series of *Les Trois Villes*. And which are those three cities to be? asked James. "Lourdes, Paris, Rome," came Zola's reply. James is left "gaping" but also now in possession of "the key, critically speaking, to many a mystery." James continues some lines later:

> It flooded his career, to my sense, with light; it showed how he had marched from subject to subject and had 'got up' each in turn—showing also how consummately he had reduced such getting-up to an artifice. . . . One would leave him, and welcome, Lourdes and Paris—he had already dealt, on a scale, with his own country and people. But was the adored Rome to be his on such terms, the Rome he was already giving away before possessing an inch of it?

One thought of one's own frequentations, saturations—a history of
long years, and of how the effect of them had somehow been but
to make the subject too august. Was *he* to find it easy through a
visit of a month or two with 'introductions' and a Baedeker?

Rome to James is evidently a love object long courted and jealously
possessed. How dare Zola stake his claim on the equivalent of a one-
night stand.

Possession, frequentation, saturation: these are of course recogniza-
ble as terms of the Jamesian novel, ways of knowing not only cities but
also people, and the matter of novels. The three nouns represent both
themes of Jamesian novels and characterizations of the ways of being
of a number of his fictional persons. They suggest also something
about the mode of his novels, their ways of representation. While
James recognizes that Zola's strengths lie in his representations of "the
Common," of the crowd and the people—rather than in any nuance
of individual psychology—he nonetheless can't help but see Zola's
methods as constituting something of a shortcut. The result is that
"his whole process and its results" constitute "the most extraordinary
imitation of observation that we possess." He contrasts Zola's elaboration of a novel cycle to Balzac's: for all his own categories and appeals
to science, "Balzac affects us in spite of everything as personally overtaken by life, as fairly hunted and run to earth by it." Zola in contrast
never had to leave his "magnificent treadmill of the pigeonholed and
documented—the region we may qualify as that of experience by imitation." James will give a further twist of the critical screw in "The Lesson of Balzac" (1905), where he contrasts Balzac's effort at representation to what he calls Zola's "extraordinary show of representation
imitated."

To the reader who appreciates Zola's novels, these strictures appear
mean, and unfair. Despite them, however, the 1903 essay is largely
generous and appreciative of Zola's strengths. It singles out for especial praise three of Zola's novels, *L'Assommoir*—that epic of the
proletarian—*Germinal*, and *La Débâcle*, this last Zola's account of
the Second Empire's defeat and collapse in the Franco-Prussian war.
The essay ends on an evocation of James's first reading of *La Débâcle*,

in the summer heat in an old Italian town, and his rereading, in order to write his essay, with the fear that he might have overestimated it. But no, this is Zola at his greatest, comparable in his own way to Tolstoy in the portrayal of war.

Zola's inadequacy to a Rome demanding frequentation and saturation for possession may be matched by his perfect fit to a city he never saw: New York. In his record of his return to the United States in 1904–5, *The American Scene*, James writes almost obsessively of New York—his native city, but one that has come to represent all the reasons he fled to Europe. Amidst the embryonic skyscrapers of downtown Manhattan, James keeps telling us how he cannot deal with New York. He offers a kind of promissory note:

> I must dip into these depths, if it prove possible, later on; let me content myself for the moment with remembering how from the first, on all such ground, my thought went straight to poor great wonder-working Emile Zola and *his* love of the human aggregation, the artificial microcosm, which had to spend itself on great shops, great businesses, great "apartment houses," of inferior, of mere Parisian scale. His image, it seemed to me, really asked for compassion—in the presence of this material that his energy of evocation, his alone, would have been of a stature to meddle with. What if *Le Ventre de Paris*, what if *Au Bonheur des Dames*, what if *Pot-Bouille* and *L'Argent*, could but have come into being under the New York inspiration?

To wish New York and Zola on one another is characteristically ambivalent praise. James is surely sincere, and perhaps even accurate, in his view that Zola could render the human urban agglomeration better than any other novelist—for all his failings, he surely has more artistic discrimination and range than Theodore Dreiser (a young writer whose *Sister Carrie* James doesn't appear to have read), for instance. But "poor great wonder-working Zola" shares something of the wasted effort James sees in New York itself. And yet in the paragraphs that follow, even "Zola" subsides into a gentler mode, a sensibility formed before the extent of the New York scene became what it is. That this chapter of *The American Scene* concludes with James's visit to Ellis Island—

where the "visible act of ingurgitation" of aliens brings "a new chill in his heart" and a "sense of dispossession"—makes the point in a way that even the dedicated Jamesian may find discomforting.

The 1903 essay on Zola on the whole strikes a note of reconciliation and even reparation. James had reviewed *Nana* upon its publication in 1880, and mainly lamented its "filth" and "foulness." While protesting that the English novel labors under too much of a burden of self-censorship—"a good thing for virgins and boys, and a bad thing for the novel itself"—he sees *Nana* as somehow casting discredit on realism. The 1903 essay doesn't really revise his opinion of *Nana*, but it does dismiss the critical preoccupation with the "improper" as blinding critics to anything else. Here, *Nana* evokes Hogarth for James. It's a work that because of its ungrateful and "formidably special" subject matter "represents a kind of technical intrepidity." This is not much of an appreciation of one of Zola's greatest novels, but it at least moves us beyond prissiness. And no one would ever claim that James would be comfortable with the topic of sexuality and women that *Nana* more or less exists to talk about.

"It is in the great lusty game he plays with the shallow and the simple that Zola's mastery resides." That's neither the manner nor the matter of the Jamesian novel, but one senses James's desire to get things right, to state fully the reasons for an appreciation of Zola, despite all his reservations. This can of course be attributed in part to the memorializing aspect of an essay written shortly following Zola's death. But the impulse toward summing-up, toward the balanced assessment, and toward reparation when he felt that was due, characterizes James's essays from this moment on all the French novelists he cared about, as indeed it characterizes his self-inspection in the prefaces to the New York Edition, which would follow shortly after these essays. James's major essays on Balzac, Flaubert, and George Sand—all of them later collected in *Notes on Novelists*—date from 1902, and the lecture "The Lesson of Balzac" follows in 1905, and there are then later (and lesser) essays on Balzac and Sand. It's almost as if James, here entering the productive novel-writing moment of his "major phase," turned back to his French masters to redo the essays collected in 1878 as *French Poets and Novelists*. And what is most notable is that in every case, he is more relaxed in his critical judgments, less stuffy, more appreciative than he was in his thirties. One senses that he is by this point far more assured of who he is, as novelist and as reader, than in the earlier essays. He feels less need to play to Anglo-Saxon prejudices and puritanisms, and in fact often goes out of his way to say so. He is more open to appreciation of other kinds of novelistic writing than his own, though also intent to define the specific nature of the Jamesian novel against the tradition. Above all, I think it is remarkable that James, now the successful and celebrated novelist, feels the need to return to those we might see as the Masters of 1875, to reassess them, to get them right this time.

I have already talked at some length about the 1902 essay on Flaubert—written as a preface to a new translation of *Madame Bovary* published by William Heinemann. It represents a very long distance traveled from his narrow strictures on the novel in the 1876 "Charles de Bernard and Gustave Flaubert." The 1902 essay on Balzac—this an introduction to a translation of *Two Young Brides*—not only reiterates the continuing allegiance to Balzac, it makes specific amends for a moment of rather arch criticism in the 1875 essay. I have mentioned this reparation before, but it bears revisiting since it can take us to the core of what James sees as the reach of his late fiction. What's at stake is an important episode in the keystone novel of Balzac's *Comédie humaine*, *Lost Illusions*. The hero Lucien Chardon—poet and later journalist—has arrived from the provinces in Paris as the protégé and still (but barely) platonic lover of Louise de Bargeton, herself provincial nobility but allied to the greatest of Parisian grandes dames, the Marquise d'Espard. Lucien, who styles himself "de Rubempré"—annexing to the name of his father, a pharmacist, his mother's more aristocratic moniker—has been invited, along with his beloved Louise, to the Opéra in Madame d'Espard's box. But this queen of Parisian sociabilities finds his costume and coiffure and manner ridiculous. When during the interval she discovers from Louise that he is the son of a petit-bourgeois and has usurped his mother's noble name without authorization, she commands that the two of them leave, abandoning Lucien alone in the box, and that Louise declare her rupture with so compromising a creature.

Recall that in the 1875 essay, James declares that Balzac's aristocratic women "really seem at times to be the creatures of the dreams of an ambitious hairdresser." As illustration, he cites the episode of Lucien's night at the opera. "The ladies, accordingly, beat a precipitate retreat, leaving Lucien the master of the field. The caste of Vere de Vere in this case certainly quite forgot its repose." Balzac's efforts here to do the Parisian upper class merely reveal, for James, his irredeemably plebeian origins. But in 1902, James declares that the whole episode is "either a magnificent lurid document or the baseless fabric of a vision," to decide: "The great wonder is that, as I rejoice to put it, we can never really discover which, and that we feel as we read that we can't, and that we suffer at the hands of no other author this particular helplessness of immersion." James goes on to use a term that is always, for him, among the highest terms of praise for a novelist: "It is *done*—we are always thrown back on that; we can't get out of it; all we can do is to say that the true itself can't be more than done and that if the false in this way equals it we must give up looking for the difference."

James has had to move beyond his earlier apparent commitment to a kind of reasonable realism of presentation to reach the serenity of this judgment, which allows a less restrictive mode of representation. We may of course sense that James's earlier understanding of what the Jamesian novel was up to was somewhat blinded—that his brand of fiction was always closer to the conflation of the "magnificent lurid document" and the "fabric of vision" than he realized—as indeed he would discover in his act of self-analysis in the preface to *The American*, composed around 1907. In response to remarks such as these, I think he would have argued that he had by his maturity got beyond the particular dichotomy of realism and romance that characterized *The American*. But perhaps he did so only by accepting the permanently romantic strain in his fiction, and his need for a play of different perspectives within it in order to preserve both the romantic and its realist critique. He argued back in 1877 that the French actors appealed by being at once "realistic to the eye and romantic to the imagination." This ideal now seems to argue for a greater fusion of the two terms: document and vision inseparably joined.

What ultimately makes Balzac the novelist who most inspires others of the same trade is "that he truly cares for nothing in the world, thank goodness, so much as for the free play of character and the sharp revelation of type, all the real stuff of drama and the natural food of novelists." This is, once again, what the novel as genre is all about. That "free play" of character points to the further development of Balzac's "lesson" to novelists in the lecture prepared for the American visit, "The Lesson of Balzac" (1905). We may recall that the key passage comes when James picks up from the French critic Hippolyte Taine a contrast between Thackeray and Balzac. Thackeray, says Taine in James's paraphrase, displays a "marked jealousy" of Becky Sharp's freedom; he's overly concerned with judging her. Whereas, in Taine's phrase, "Balzac aime sa Valérie"—referring to "the awful little Madame Marneffe" of Balzac's *La Cousine Bette*, to whom Balzac allows "the long rope, for acting herself out." Noting that an English reviewer of Taine had claimed Balzac's love of Madame Marneffe "only showed Balzac's extraordinary taste," James ripostes:

> the truth being really, throughout, that it was just through this love of each seized identity, and of the sharpest and liveliest identities most, that Madame Marneffe's creator was able to marshal his array at all. The love, as we call it, the joy in their communicated and exhibited movement, in their standing on their feet and going of themselves and acting out their characters, was what rendered possible the saturation I speak of; what supplied him, through the inevitable gaps of his preparation and the crevices of his prison, his long prison of labor, a short cut to the knowledge he required. It was by loving them—as the terms of his subject and the nuggets of his mine—that he knew them; it was not by knowing them that he loved.

James could be said to advance here a principle of love as epistemology that characterizes not only his literary criticism but also much of his late fiction—and more than any other *The Golden Bowl*.

From the 1876 Sundays at Flaubert's apartment, James also formed a lasting friendship with Alphonse Daudet, the writer from Provence, creator of the comic latter-day Don Quixote known as Tartarin of Tarascon—James was even drafted into translating one of the later volumes of the Tartarin series. But Daudet was never a novelistic master in the sense of Balzac, Flaubert, or Zola—he had nothing to teach James. On the other hand, another, younger writer met at Flaubert's— he was then in his twenties—very much did. Guy de Maupassant returns frequently in James's thinking about novelistic representation. There is no summary essay from the time of those on Balzac, Flaubert, and Zola, perhaps mainly because Maupassant died in 1893, aged only 43, from the sequels of syphilis. But James probably saw more of Maupassant, personally, than most of his other French connections. In particular, Maupassant visited London in August of 1885, and called upon their earlier acquaintance at Flaubert's to make James his principal English sponsor—a task James assumed with his usual seriousness and tact, organizing a dinner at Greenwich (the London clubs being closed for summer vacation) that included George Du Maurier and Edmund Gosse, to which Maupassant added Count Joseph Primoli, a Bonaparte descendant. The more savorous incident of this visit is recounted by Oscar Wilde, who claims that Maupassant, dining in a London restaurant with James, repeatedly requested that his host pick up attractive women at neighboring tables for him. James's demurrals provoked Maupassant's irritation; he was there in large part to sample English womanhood.

It is one of those Oscar Wilde anecdotes that at least ought to be true, since it conveys something essential in the James-Maupassant relation: the problem of sex. James's summings-up on Maupassant—the longer essay published in 1888, then a shorter one in 1889, essays earlier and of lesser maturity than those on Balzac, Flaubert, Zola—seem a bit embarrassed. James indeed will say so. "M. de Maupassant would doubtless affirm that where the empire of the sexual sense is concerned, no exaggeration is possible." Yet "as we Anglo-Saxons see it," the human spectacle "has less analogy with that of the monkeys' cage than this admirable writer's account of it." He goes on to say that "his point of view is almost solely that of the senses," and if this makes him an interesting case, it also makes him an embarrassing one—"embarrassing and mystifying for the moralist." Maupassant is a "lion in the path," one that should not "be made light of by those who have really taken the measure of the animal." For James finds in Maupassant a perfection in the art of narrative never surpassed by anyone. Maupassant presents the disturbing paradox of a high, scrupulous artistic conscience combined with an absence of moral scruples.

James goes on to argue that (like Flaubert) Maupassant achieves his high artistry only by sacrificing a major term of the problem: he has no interest in inwardness and moral complexity. "The very compact mansion in which he dwells presents on that side a perfectly dead wall." We are once again in a kind of prison house—longing for the freedom of the smashed window-pane practiced by Balzac. This omission of one of the items of what James sees as any novelist's task "has made the problem so much easier that it may almost be described as the short cut to a solution. . . . M. de Maupassant has simply skipped the whole reflective part of his men and women—that reflective part which governs conduct and produces character." This leads James back to sex in the concluding paragraph of the essay: "The erotic element in M. de Maupassant, about which much more might have been said, seems to me to be explained by the same limitation, and explicable in a similar way wherever else its literature occurs in excess. The carnal side of man appears the most characteristic if you look at it a great deal; and you look at it a great deal if you do not look at the other, at the side by which he reacts against his weaknesses, his defeats." The standard Anglo-Saxon prudishness—James is after all dealing with a writer considered "shocking"—seems to be doubled by a more complex Jamesian equation of "the carnal side" with "weaknesses, defeats." I suppose this takes a Victorian view of sexual virtue in terms of which any concession to the carnal is a "defeat," but one wonders if there is some more private Jamesian scenario at work.

It will, I think, be part of James's evolution over the next decade and a half—from around 1888, when the principal Maupassant essay was published, to 1903–4, when he wrote *The Golden Bowl*—to make peace with, or at least to make allowance for, the carnal side. It may be significant that in concluding this final paragraph of the Maupassant essay, James uses his very stricture about what you take to be typical to suggest that the novel must not be confined and censored:

> Hard and fast rules, *a priori* restrictions, mere interdictions (you shall not speak of this, you shall not look at that) have surely served their time, and will in the nature of the case never strike an energetic talent as anything but arbitrary. A healthy, living and growing art, full of curiosity and fond of exercise, has an indefeasible mistrust of rigid prohibitions. Let us then leave this magnificent art of the novelist to itself and to its perfect freedom, in the faith the one example is as good as another, and that our fiction will always be decent enough if it be sufficiently general.

This sounds like Madame Carré's defense of art in *The Tragic Muse*: morality is equated with high artistic seriousness. In that case, the problem with sex may be that it is too "special"—or perhaps only put in the category of the special by a certain capacity to deny and repress, as in the case of John Marcher in *the Beast in the Jungle*, a story that can be read as a critique of too much ignoring the carnal side. The Maupassant essay hasn't yet reached that critique; it is too much concerned with the other, the claim that Maupassant represents his own kind of denial.

Citing Maupassant's belief that psychology should be hidden in the novel (a corollary of Flaubert's invisibility of the author), James queries the status of this hidden: hidden from whom? "For me an act, an incident, an attitude, may be a sharp, detached, isolated thing, of which I give a full account in saying that in such and such a way it came off. For you it may be hung about with implications, with relations, and conditions as necessary to help you to recognise it as the clothes of your friends are to help you know them in the street. You feel they would seem strange to you without petticoats and trousers." These three sentences offer a full contrast between the Flaubertian novel (Maupassant's kind) and the Balzacian (James's also, on balance). It is interesting that those "implications," "relations," and "conditions" that we recognize as the world of Jamesian fiction—where what matters is less the "sharp, detached, isolated thing" than ways of looking at the thing—should end up resembling clothes. And that it is suggested we couldn't recognize our friends stripped of their petticoats and trousers. We are left with a slightly uncomfortable sense that Jamesian refinement of motive and perspective are possibly being used as covers for a nakedness that makes him deeply uncomfortable. We may want to protest that people are subject to our recognition even when naked.

James reiterates his strictures on the carnal in the French novel in an essay he published in *North American Review* in October 1899 following a return to France the previous spring, "The Present Literary Situation in France." He finds French fiction in this last year of the century afflicted by "that demon of staleness who hovers very dreadfully, at this time of day, everywhere." He repeats his charge that Emma Bovary is "a poor case" that would have been improved if "more relations had been shown." In general, the antidote to the repetitive insistence on sexual relations lies in "cultivating just this possibility of the vision of more relations." For, says James, "There *are* others, after all, than those of the eternal triangle of the husband, the wife and the lover, or of that variation of this to which we are too much condemned as an only alternative—the mistress, the first and the second, or the second and the third, the third and the fourth, lovers." He proposes that "passion" for Anglo-Saxons may have its wings clipped, but "it lives a great variety of life, burns with other flames and throbs with other obsessions than the sole sexual." Here, the plea seems to be less that one needs to avoid the sexual than that one needs to complicate it, perspectivally, to see it through other "relations." The demon of staleness may most of all lie in the obsession with eternal triangles.

One further set of critical remarks on the French attention to the "carnal side" seems to me full of interest. These remarks come not in a published essay but in a letter written, in French, to Paul Bourget following the publication of Bourget's novel *Mensonges* in 1887. This appears to be a second letter of critique, replying to Bourget's response to James's first. While acknowledging Bourget's gracious response to the "rudesse" of his first, James in the present letter is brutally honest in his opinion that *Mensonges* sacrifices to "false idols." James was famously incapable of flattering work he didn't like—he nearly drove his friend Howard Sturgis to despair by his critique of a novel in manuscript. Edith Wharton in particular has left a witty and convincing account of

how he would begin a critical response with slight praise, then bring
the full weight of his damning analysis to bear. In this letter to Bourget
of February 23, 1888, he first dismisses all the characters in *Mensonges*—
who pretty much conform to one version of the eternal triangle—as
trivial. When Bourget offers us the point of view of a character such as
Mme Moraines (older mistress to the young protagonist), her subjectiv-
ity becomes something of a bad joke: "vous lui consacrez, à elle et à
son *underclothing*, une attention toute spéciale et toute malsaine"
("you devote to her, and to her underclothing, a very special and thoroughly unhealthy attention"). What moral inwardness can such a creature have? James asks. To an extent, his critique resembles that of
Flaubert's choice of limited "registers and reflectors": "Life reflects so
poorly in such a nature that the reader feels outraged and deceived by
the promenade that you invite him to make here, under pretext of a
psychology of suffering!" As for René Vincy, the young hero "making
his début in adultery," he only makes Anglo-Saxon readers want to give
him "a kick in the rear."

That "underclothing" isn't there by chance. James in the next paragraph takes up the "dirtiness" of the novel, its "saleté": "Vous me direz
encore que cette épithète de 'saleté' est un *begging of the question* et
que cette saleté-là caractérise essentiellement la vie" ("You will tell me
further that the epithet of 'dirtiness' is a begging of the question, and
that the dirtiness in question characterizes life essentially.") Here is a
crux of sorts: sex equals dirtiness equals the essence of life. James takes
up the defense of love as not dirty—but by that he appears to mean
love that leaves the description of sex under a heavy veil. One needs to
leave out the petty details, such as "the number of embraces, their
quality, the place where they occur, the manner in which it's done [la
manière dont ça se fait], and a thousand other particularities more intensely personal and less *producible* in the daylight than anything else
in the world." If this is squeamish, at least James now is being particular
in regard to what he is squeamish about—at least he is acknowledging
the existence of physical lovemaking. He goes on:

> What do we know about it moreover and how can one speak, in
> this whole business, for anyone other than oneself? That is why one

should speak of it as little as possible because there is a fatuousness, a lack of taste and a lack of modesty, to speak about it for oneself. The gestures of lovemaking [les procédés de l'amour] seem to me to constitute a completely special part of our being whose special character is to lend itself to *action*, and not to reflection. This element of action is everyone's business but from the moment reflection gets involved—from the moment one begins to muck about in it intellectually, as novelist, as painter, the thing becomes unhealthy and disagreeable [malsaine et déplaisante]. . . . How can it matter to us, the details of the foreplay that Desforges, or René and his mistress, did to one another when they slept together and the greater or lesser number of shifts and corsets they were wearing? It never would cross my mind to want to know what is going on in their bedroom, in their bed, between a man and a woman; and I really don't see what difference is made (especially in the matter of publicity) by the fact that these persons aren't married.

In the next and final paragraph, James brings his letter to a conclusion in expressing the hope that Bourget will be indifferent to his "almost feminine harshness." It is almost as if he is claiming at the end a privileged private world of lovemaking—note his repeated use of the word "special" in reference to sexual activity—which Bourget has violated in his descriptions of sex in *Mensonges*.

Bourget in reply gracefully evades James's critique: he says that in his future work he will try not to "exaggerate this sexuality that seems to exasperate you in what I write." But then he cites a line from La Fontaine: *"Quiconque est loup agisse en loup"* ("Le loup devenu berger") (freely translated, Let wolves be wolves). Bourget may be claiming such wolfish nature as part of the French inheritance that Anglo-Saxons don't understand. One more cross-Channel misunderstanding, then—a position that James sometimes appears to subscribe to, especially in a later letter to Edith Wharton where reading George Sand's correspondence leads him to reflect that French erotic behavior is predetermined by cultural and linguistic forms:

To have such a flow of remark on that subject, and everything connected with it, at her command helps somehow to make one feel that Providence laid up for the French such a store of remark, in advance and, as it were, should the worst befall, that their conduct and *moeurs*, coming *after*, had positively to justify and do honour to the whole collection of formulae, phrases, and as I say, glibnesses— so that as there were at any rate such things there for them to inevitably *say*, why not simply *do* all the things that would give them a *rapport* and a sense?

The perception is Flaubertian: we not only are spoken by our language and its clichés, our very "conduct and *moeurs*" are kinds of behavioral clichés, cultural "glibnesses" in action. French sex is simply a cultural commonplace.

To return to the letter to Bourget: I don't claim to know what to make of James's reactions to Bourget's novel here—a novel that, read today, strikes us as a bit like second-rate Balzac with extra psychological padding. If *Le Disciple* still carries something of an impact by its subject and its somewhat over-the-top attributions of intellectual responsibility for one's students' acts, *Mensonges* seems a rather faded novel of ambition and society. James's very "Anglo-Saxon" reaction of wanting to give the young René a kick in the rear suggests the arousal of more emotion than the novel deserves. In his reaction to the sex of the novel, James speaks more directly and intimately than usual, in that he doesn't simply efface or cover over the sex but rather argues, as I construe him, that physical acts of sex belong to the realm of bodily actions that don't bear talking about, that they are personal in a way that should resist exposure and does not lend itself to sharing in language. The French tendencies to talk about sex as a kind of shared social experience (Catherine Millet's *La vie sexuelle de Catherine M.* is a recent example) and to create a metaphysics of sex seem to strike James as the wrong path to follow. Yet he is not simply refusing to look at sex here. He indeed sounds as if he is claiming a personal knowledge of it.

His strictures on what he sees as Bourget's excessive attention to underclothing might bear comparison to his later repeated critique of his young friend Hendrik Andersen's excessive and grandiose statues of naked bodies. "You ought absolutely to get at Busts, at any cost of ingenuity—for it is fatal for you to go on indefinitely neglecting the

Face, never doing one, only adding Belly to Belly—however beautiful—and Bottom to Bottom, however sublime." James ostensibly is concerned for Andersen's prospects of commercial success: in busts, as in Nick Dormer's portraits, there is money to be made, whereas Andersen's colossal nudities find no buyers. Yet for all his censoriousness, one senses James's pleasure in evoking those beautiful bellies and sublime bottoms. And not only in this letter. Earlier, responding to photos of his work that Andersen has mailed him, he writes that he is dissatisfied with the faces in the statues. And he continues: "Also I sometimes find your sexes (putting *the* indispensable sign apart!) not quite intensely enough differentiated—I mean through the ladies resembling a shade too much the gentlemen (perhaps as in the case of this last *ballerina*, through your not allowing her a quite sufficient luxury—to my taste—of hip, or, to speak plainly, Bottom. She hasn't *much* more of that than her husband, & I should like her to have a good deal more.)" This call for a greater marking of sexual difference could long engage us. It is of course important to note that James is writing to a young man to whom he feels an intense and quite openly stated physical attraction: the letters to Anderson are full of epistolary touching and embracing. And the denigration of Andersen's female figures may be a coded homoerotic sign of greater interest in the male.

The point that needs making, I think, is that James by his late maturity—he is into his sixties at the time of these letters to Andersen—shows a certain pleasure in talking about the sexual body. The letters to Andersen, like those to James's other young male admirations—Jocelyn Persse, Hugh Walpole, and the openly gay Howard Sturgis—are full of a kind of erotic warmth that may be easier for James to express because one senses that by this point in his life—whatever may have been the case earlier—he doesn't intend to pass from word to deed. The Andersen letters are particularly interesting because the sculptor's nudes give him a chance to take pleasure in talking about the sexual body. The name of Fanny Assingham verbally realizes what he finds missing in Andersen's women, which may in both cases be a coded way of acknowledging what is present in the men: both Andersen's sculpted ones—marked by "indispensable sign"—and James's phallic Prince Amerigo. One more instance from the Andersen correspondence, a letter of October 18, 1906, suggests under its scolding a kind of wistful nostalgia for the denuded body:

> When you speak of your Poverty, however, I could howl—howl with anguish—over your continued *parti-pris* never apparently to do any blessed helpful pot-boilers—but only your vast stripped stark sublime Family—on whose myriad of penises & bottoms & other private ornaments how can you *ever* financially "realize" in America? Forgive this anxious cry from your tenderest

> HJ

Despite the harsh realism of judgment here, one senses that the tenderness is not indifferent to those private ornaments.

Naming is always important in James—the Notebooks are full of trial names—and critic Hugh Stevens accurately suggests that "James's wordplay seems to recover a joyish sense of childish defilement." Stevens's *Henry James and Sexuality* is perhaps the most interesting of recent studies to take up the vexed question of its title in the light of a new attention to gay studies and queer theory. Stevens subtly and convincingly demonstrates that whatever the sexual acts committed or not by James, he constitutes himself as gay in his writing, ever more openly as time passes, most openly in his correspondence with close friends. The final decades of the nineteenth century may have created the modern concept of "the homosexual" as a distinct (recognized and repressed) social (and medical) category. The 1890s not only witness James's most daring experimentations with narrative point of view and ways of knowing, they also bring acutely to his attention what it could mean to be gay in the trial and imprisonment of Oscar Wilde. James did not like Wilde or his work: the person seemed to him indiscreet, attention-mongering, outrageous, and his work trivial (and, on the stage, far more successful than James's own). But his exposure and downfall elicit in James, if not much pity, certainly a kind of terror at the fact of such exposure. If there may be a certain homosexual self-loathing in James, as Stevens suggests—registered in such works as *The Beast in the Jungle*—the principal Jamesian fear seems to be outing, the overt exposure of a homosexual identity. That takes us back to Paul

Zhukovsky and his outed life with Peppino in Posilippo, and James's outraged reaction to it. This is of course consonant with James's whole style of being, which tends to avoid the overt, and to substitute for it the playfulness of the stylish and even the camp. If you can't talk about sex—as even Zola can't wholly, directly—it is fun to talk around it.

The letter to Bourget, for all its censure of *Mensonges*, points toward the greater acknowledgment of sex not only in James's later correspondence but also in his later novels. It's a somewhat strange progress in acknowledgment, to be sure. *What Maisie Knew* and *The Awkward Age* are in some large measure about the great sexual secret at the center of society, and the impossible bind a girl and a young woman are placed in with relation to the secret. *The Beast in the Jungle* is all about the failure to make the move toward sexual "action": James's term in the Bourget letter seems wholly appropriate to Marcher's failure in his long, unconsummated relationship with May Bartram. In all these works, it is of the essence of what is centrally at issue to be unspeakable. Then, *The Ambassadors* seems to turn centrally on Strether's failure, both naïve and willful, to see sex where it obviously is. *The Wings of the Dove* and *The Golden Bowl* finally stage scenes of sex that are crucial to their dramas. Kate Croy comes to Merton Densher's bed in Venice under duress, as part of the bargain by which he will continue to court Millie Theale only if Kate becomes his lover. Prince Amerigo and Charlotte Stant go to a hotel in Gloucester specifically and explicitly for sex. Neither scene is described, of course. Each indeed is recorded as a kind of blank between chapters. But the content of each never is in doubt, and each makes an enormous difference. *The Golden Bowl* in particular is all about sexuality—suppressed, rediscovered, denied, finally acknowledged. It's thus in many ways a breakthrough for James, something of an acknowledgment of the unspoken in his own prior work.

So perhaps the strangely vehement critique of Bourget's *Mensonges*— does the fact it is written in French liberate James to be more explicit than he otherwise would?—may be a step toward a certain liberation, a move toward coming to terms with James's considerable obsession with sex. I see this relative self-liberation in regard to sex as moving in parallel to his increasingly relaxed attitude toward his French novelistic

masters and confrères. If he over and over again criticizes the narrow-
ness of Flaubert's vision, the shortcuts practiced by Zola and Maupassant, he nonetheless is on the whole willing to grant that they produce
works that require and reward discussion in a way that is rarely the case
for the English novel. At the time he is writing *The Tragic Muse*, for instance, his notebook entries are full of references to Maupassant. The
reference to Balzac as the true master continues, but his admiration of
Balzac, too, is less hedged with strictures and reservations. James seems
to be coming to terms with his artistic points of reference as well as
with himself. His praise of Balzac's respect for the "liberty of the subject" in the 1905 "Lesson of Balzac" needs to be read as covering a
range of meanings from artistic technique to moral attitude.

James more and more claims the right to be himself and to engage
the full range of life. Strether in *The Ambassadors*, though sometimes
interpreted as James himself in his regret at not having "lived," may
strike us as an almost crudely monitory figure. To the extent that he is
based on William Dean Howells—supposed to have delivered a version of the "Live all you can: it's a mistake not to" speech enunciated in
the novel by Strether to Little Bilham—the failure to have claimed sexual activity and sexual pleasure when one could may represent an
American destiny that James feels that he has happily escaped. In that
sense, James may be not Strether only but also Chad Newsome, sati-
ated with the sexual attentions of a beautiful, aristocratic woman. As he
wrote to his "Belovedest Hugh" Walpole on August 21, 1913:

> We must know, as much as possible, in our beautiful art, yours &
> mine, what we are talking about—& the only way to know it is to
> have lived & loved & cursed & floundered & enjoyed & suffered—
> I don't think I regret a single "excess" of my responsive youth—I
> only regret, in my chilled age, certain occasions & possibilities I
> didn't *embrace*.

Strether or not Strether? One cannot of course tell, but certainly the
note of regret is matched by the embrace of life. This is not to suggest
that James was in fact leading an active sexual life during his youth or
later, but rather that he at least now admits its possibility. That possibility, he almost regretfully concludes in his Notebook entry for what

would become *The Ambassadors*, must for Americans always be connected to Paris, the too banal but inevitable setting for dramas of sexual relations. The return to the French novelists of 1875–76 just after the turn of the century prepares his work not only on *The Ambassadors* but also his final completed novel, which he originally thought of as set in Paris, *The Golden Bowl*.

7. For the Sake of This End

What was James thinking of in choosing to build his American lecture tour on "The Lesson of Balzac"—an extended plea that practitioners of the craft of fiction should return to the French novelist if the novel were to "recover its wasted heritage"? It's not clear to me that that the audiences to whom James lectured in Philadelphia and Chicago, not to mention Saint Louis, South Bend, Indianapolis, and San Francisco, had any idea that there *was* a heritage of the novel, or that it had been wasted, and particularly that one had to look toward a Frenchman dead for over half a century to mend things. The choice to entertain American audiences with talk of a French novelist seems odd, if somewhat characteristic of James's sense that his native land was in need of European cultural imports. The literary clubs and circles that invited him to speak consisted of course mainly of the somewhat self-consciously "cultured" elite. And it is probably true that for that American cultural elite in 1905, Balzac was more of a living presence than he is today. Not only did a higher percentage of the elite feel the need for French culture—French painting, both academic and avant-garde was, for instance, in demand among American collectors with new or old money—this was the time when complete editions of Balzac's works in English translation were available in bookstores. The translations were largely the work of James's acquaintance Katherine Prescott Wormeley, who lived in the shadow of Mount Chocorua in New Hampshire—near William James's summer place—and worked her way patiently

177

through the ninety-odd novels and tales of the *Human Comedy*. James visited Wormeley during his American tour. In some curious sense, one could say that James's long-delayed and extended visit to native ground was emblazoned with the name, and the tradition, of the most famous of French novelists. The seeming incongruity may have been conscious.

The American trip would eventuate in the publication of *The American Scene*, a travelogue that records a somewhat painful homecoming and sense of estranged recognition of what American culture had developed into. If in James's book on Hawthorne (dating from 1879) America is famously a landscape of absences—"No sovereign, no court, no personal loyalty, no aristocracy, no church, no clergy . . . no castles, nor manors, nor old country-houses, nor parsonages, nor thatched cottages nor ivied ruins . . . no great Universities nor public schools—no Oxford, nor Eton, nor Harrow . . ."—in *The American Scene* it is filling in, but scruffily, vulgarly, in a way that makes the choice of expatriation seem entirely justified. The orderliness of the enclosed and finished Sussex landscape seems more and more necessary, Lamb House a true refuge from disorder.

And the French novel had by this point in James's evolution become more necessary than ever. We have seen that his major essays on Balzac, Flaubert, and Zola date from the early years of the new century, and they are more generous in their praise, and less narrow-mindedly Anglo-American in their "moral" stance, than the earlier ones. What most emerges from these is perhaps above all James's concern with the meanings of representation, almost, you might say, his concern with what it means to be a novelist. In his dialogue with the masters of French fiction—whom he more and more sees as the writers he most needs to measure himself against—he seems to be taking stock of his own choice in life. The monument of the New York Edition of the novels and tales, published from 1907 to 1909, was of course explicitly modeled on Balzac's *La comédie humaine*, to the very number of volumes originally projected. There was in James a residue of Cambridge Puritanism in his evident worry that novel writing might not appear to be a wholly serious way to spend one's life and talents—as opposed, say, to William's illustrious academic career—to which he opposed the insistent plea that novels were serious business, that the representation of life as undertaken by committed artists was worthwhile.

James's last completed novel, *The Golden Bowl*, was published in England and the United States while he was on his American tour. Even though it includes three Americans among its four major characters, in all sorts of ways it is the least American novel imaginable. One can take some measure of this from brother William's reaction. Not that William read it upon first publication. Henry's American tour—which, as the lecture invitations and the newspaper articles multiplied, became something of a triumph—became also the occasion of William's uncharacteristic declaration that he was going to take a vacation in the Greek isles. That was in the spring of 1905, when Henry, in the Midwest, was preparing to take the train to California. Nonetheless, one senses that the vast expanse of the country was too big to accommodate both of them—just as William refused membership in the newly formed Academy of Arts and Letters because, as he put it, his "younger and shallower and vainer brother is already in the Academy"—elected two ballots earlier than William.

And when William did read that novel, in the fall, he sent Henry the most overtly critical letter yet, one that indeed bordered on hostility. The novel, like most of his brother's recent work, had put him "in a very puzzled state of mind"; its manner went "agin the grain of all my own impulses in writing." He went on:

> Why won't you, just to please Brother, sit down and write a new book, with no twilight or mustiness in the plot, with great vigor and decisiveness in the action, no fencing in the dialogue, or psychological commentaries, and absolute straightness in style. Publish it in my name, I will acknowledge it, and give you half the proceeds. Seriously, I wish you *would*, for you *can*; and I should think it would tempt you to embark on a "fourth manner."

The aggressiveness of this comment is evident, perhaps most of all in the suggestion that Henry publish something straightforward in William's name, with the admonition that he could write well (like his brother) if he chose. We note also that William, the champion of vigorous manhood, implicitly accuses Henry of femininity, deviousness, perhaps of an allegiance to gay stylishness that he ought to repudiate ("for you *can*").

Henry in response did not back down. To write what William wants would be possible—"but let me say, dear William, that I shall greatly be humiliated if you *do* like it, and thereby lump it, in your affection, with things, of the current age, that I have heard you express admiration for and that I would sooner descend to a dishonored grave than have written." He goes on: "I'm always sorry when I hear of your reading anything of mine, and always hope you won't—you seem to me so constitutionally unable to 'enjoy' it, and so condemned to look at it from a point of view remotely alien to mine in writing it . . ." And here comes the stinger: "you appear even to assume that the life, the elements forming its subject-matter, deviate from felicity in not having an impossible analogy with the life of Cambridge." To think that the life of Cambridge defines civilization, defines what's interesting in existence, is ever, for Henry, a measure of utter provincialism. *The Golden Bowl* is a European novel. In Henry James's first sketch of it, it was in fact in its setting a French novel.

It is perhaps strange, though certainly characteristic, that the father of pragmatism was so wholly unable to appreciate his brother's late novels, which all are perspectival, indeed are both in method and in theme about ways of looking at things, and in that sense the restriction of usable knowledge to what you can make your own—which is not unlike pragmatism. The division of *The Golden Bowl* into two books, the first labeled "The Prince," the second "The Princess," implies a divergence in ways of seeing things, but the radical perspectivalism of the novel goes much further. It's not only that people see things in different ways, but that seeing at all is problematic. It has to take place in the interstices of evidence, it has to shape clues that look like nothing into hypotheses. And then it has to conceal what it is up to. If James's late heroes and heroines sometimes give the impression of stalking around like Sherlock Holmes, looking at minute clues under the magnifying glass, they differ from Holmes in that they have to conceal their investigative enterprises. As a "case," *The Golden Bowl* may resemble the Freudian even more than the Holmesian: there is from the outset a postulate that everything that needs to be known is present somewhere in the present or the past of its four principal characters. But much of it lies under a bar of repression.

James's initial Notebook sketch for *The Golden Bowl*—it dates back to 1892—saw it as taking place in Paris, and conceived the Prince as a Frenchman, "charming always, to 'the other woman.' The other woman and the father and daughter all intensely American." The identity of the Prince as Frenchman seems supposed to make readily available to the reader his lack of moral rigidity. In shifting his scene to London, James in fact made his Prince Italian, with a kind of baroque and super-subtle moral sense that can understand almost anything except the Americans, daughter and father, with who he has united himself. James did, however, set a key moment of the novel in Paris, where Adam Verver and Charlotte Stant await word from the newly married Prince Amerigo and Maggie Verver, who have traveled to Rome. Adam, Maggie's father, has decided to ease his solitude by asking Charlotte to marry him. Charlotte, American friend of Maggie's since childhood, has conditioned her final acceptance on Maggie's approval. Maggie has responded with a telegram to her father: "We start tonight to bring you all our love and joy and sympathy," which fully satisfies Adam but apparently not Charlotte, who wonders why they are cutting short their Italian sojourn and rushing back. Adam infers that Charlotte wants to have words of approval from the Prince as well. As their conversation unfolds in the atrium of the Paris hotel, a telegraph boy enters, and delivers an envelope to the portress—who brings it to Charlotte: "Cette fois-ci pour Madame!" When Charlotte has silently studied its message "without a sign," she looks up: " 'I'll give you,' she simply said. 'what you ask.' " The text continues: "The look on her face was strange—but since when had a woman's at moments of supreme surrender not a right to be?" (177)

James's text dissembles with us here. First of all, it's not for another forty pages that we are given the contents of the Prince's telegram, and then his words have more than normal telegraphic opacity:

"A *la guerre comme à la guerre then*"—it had been couched in the French tongue. "*We must lead our lives as we see them; but I am charmed with your courage and almost surprised at my own.*" (212)

The telegram makes us ask in retrospect to whom Charlotte has offered her "supreme surrender." We have by this point in the novel been made privy, mainly through Fanny Assingham's late-night dialogues with her husband the Colonel, to the fact that the Prince and Charlotte had a romance before the Prince ever met Maggie—a romance abandoned because they were both too poor to marry one another. Fanny, to the Colonel's skepticism, insists that they never became lovers. "There wasn't time." But by Fanny's own further accounts, this is far from certain. By one elaboration of her scenario, Charlotte left Rome and the Prince in order that he be free to marry money—and now that he has, she has come back to him. It is hence Fanny's idea that Charlotte in turn must be married off to keep her out of mischief. The Prince's telegram seems to applaud Charlotte's courage in choosing a spouse who is bound to bring them into close proximity, and he announces his matching courage—as a kind of promissory note that he will not fail her? The phrase in French, "A *la guerre comme à la guerre*," means approximately that one has to make the best of it, whatever the conditions, which doesn't bring any specificity to the Prince's meaning but does imply that he is ready for anything.

The scene in the Paris hotel courtyard thus plays out a double drama, the one apparent to Adam, the suitor crowned with success, the other to Charlotte, though this one is seen by the reader, initially at least, only through a glass darkly. When Charlotte has read the telegram from the Prince, she holds it out to Adam, offering to let him read it.

> "Don't you want to read it?"
> He thought. "Not if it satisfies you. I don't require it."
> But she gave him, as for her conscience, another chance. "You
>   can if you like." (178)

When Adam again declines, she crumples it in her pocket—but we will discover later that she has smoothed it out, preserved it, and often reread it. What are we to make of her "as for her conscience" offering it to Adam's eyes? She reflects later that if he had read it, it probably would "have dished her marriage; that all the future had in fact hung by the single thread of Mr Verver's delicacy . . . and that her position, in the matter of responsibility, was therefore inattackably straight" (213). Charlotte is as ever somewhat morally opaque: her sense of the "straight" is most of all to preserve a certain illusion of good behavior — though that is a moral standard to which all of the characters, even Maggie, eventually repair.

Part of the opacity of the scene in the Paris hotel comes from how it is registered: the chapter begins by following Adam's perspective: "He had talked to her of their waiting in Paris, a week later, but on the spot there this period of patience suffered no great strain" (168). And to the extent that the scene is reflected in his consciousness, Charlotte's un-readability is wholly understandable. Yet at moments — as when the telegraph boy enters the courtyard — the tracking consciousness seems momentarily to be Charlotte's. There is in fact a certain cinematic flu-idity of vision here. What then are we to make of James's claim, in the preface, that his story is told only through two observers: "the whole thing remains subject to the register, ever so closely kept, of the con-sciousness of but two of the characters" — the Prince and Maggie. He goes on to stake the whole "compositional value" of his novel on the idea that Book 1 approaches Maggie only through the Prince's vision of her, whereas Book 2 symmetrically gives us the Prince in Maggie's view. Not only does this leave in limbo such as this chapter describing Adam and Charlotte in Paris — the Prince and Maggie are in Rome, re-member, and cannot be witnesses — it also makes short shrift of what to any reader is a memorable and key aspect of the novel: the role of Fanny Assingham, choral commentator and protonovelist. James does note this "disparity," the moments when Mrs Assingham "functionally" supersedes the Prince, but he dismisses it as "superficial."

I'm not so sure. Fanny's role seems far from superficial. Fanny's role in the novel seems to me to have much to do with its particular texture as an exploration of kinds and ways of knowing. In some sense, she represents the intrusion of the reader into the text, and in this manner a far more radical use of points of view than James sees, or acknowl-edges, in his rereading of the novel. When we first meet Fanny, she expresses the fear "that anything of the past . . . should come back *now*" (52). As the person with the greatest synthetic knowledge of the past—Charlotte's romance with the Prince, Maggie's meeting with the Prince—she appears the psychoanalyst wary lest a return of the repressed work ravages on the decorous though flawed present. The image of the golden bowl, gilded glass with a hidden crack, is readily available as a symbol of the relation of past to present, and when the object resurfaces to establish the adultery of Charlotte and the Prince, Fanny reacts by destroying the symbol itself, smashing the bowl, as if in sign of her failure as therapist. But Fanny's role early on begins to extend beyond a kind of damage control of the past, to become a shaping commentary on the status of that past in the present and on the future unfolding of the plot.

The first ratcheting up of Fanny's consciousness occurs during her carriage ride home from the grand London evening during which the Prince and Charlotte have appeared without their respective spouses. She slips into an anxious reverie about her role in bringing the two couples together, and the possible "ends that were now bearing fruit and that might yet bear a larger crop" (202). Thinking on possible outcomes, "the misery of her fear produced the next minute a reaction; and when the carriage happened, while it grazed a turn, to catch the straight shaft from the lamp of a policeman in the act of playing his inquisitive flash over an opposite house-front, she let herself wince at being thus incriminated only that she might protest, not less quickly, against mere blind terror." The terror is such that she can give it "no name," which is "a help, in turn, to not making out that her hands were embrued, since if she had stood in the position of a producing cause she should surely be less vague about what she had produced." Notice that the vocabulary of Jamesian psychic melodrama breaks through here: the illumination of conscience—and consciousness— breaks through like the flash of the policeman's lamp, producing terror. Has her analysis discovered her to be a kind of Lady Macbeth with bloody hands?

Fanny continues in her conversations with the Colonel to plot out the possible adultery and its possible consequences. Meanwhile, Charlotte and the Prince move closer and closer to erotic fulfillment. Their "pledge" to protect the "sacred" status quo of their marriages is sealed by what is no doubt the sexiest kiss that James permitted himself:

"It's sacred," he said at last.

"It's sacred," she breathed back to him. They vowed it, gave it out and took it in, drawn, by their intensity, more closely together. Then of a sudden, through this tightened circle, as at the issue of a narrow strait into the sea beyond, everything broke up, broke down, gave way, melted and mingled. Their lips sought their lips, their pressure their response and their response their pressure; with a violence that had sighed itself the next moment to the longest and deepest of stillnesses they passionately sealed their pledge. (229)

It is tempting to read the passage as a figural rendition of intercourse of some sort: "through this tightened circle, as at the issue of a narrow strait into the sea beyond." But it remains figural. Soon after this the Prince and Charlotte manage so that they can use a weekend at the country house, Matcham, as cover for a return to London by way of a hotel in Gloucester, scene of what promises to be a passionate encounter. "These days, yesterday, last night, this morning, I've wanted everything," says Charlotte as they move to leave Matcham for the train to Gloucester; to which the Prince replies: "You shall *have* everything" (266).

Fanny witnesses neither the kiss nor the rendezvous in the Gloucester hotel; nor, of course, does the reader witness the latter. But it is she nonetheless who figures out what is happening, and, in particular, what it will mean for the future. In a dialogue with her husband that stretches over the two final chapters of Book 1, she finally confesses her own authorship of the plot up to now—"I did it all" (279)—and then hands future authorship off to Maggie. "She'll see me somehow through," Fanny says of Maggie, and then: "The way it comes to me is that she *will* live. The way it comes to me is that she'll triumph" (281). To "live" in this sense—see *The Ambassadors*, see *The Wings of the Dove*—always for James has a sexual connotation: Maggie's triumph will be erotic. And that, Fanny intuits, is why it must be Maggie's alone. The kind of matchmaking Fanny has performed up till now takes one only into the formal bonds of marriage. Beyond that, it is up to the couples to become lovers. As she postulates how Maggie will take over the situation, Fanny suggests that it won't be a matter of her struggling to get the Prince back: " 'To "get him back" she must have lost him, and to have lost him she must have had him.' With which Fanny shook her head. 'What I take her to be waking up to is the truth that, all the while, she really *hasn't* had him. Never.' 'Ah, my dear—!' the poor Colonel panted" (281).

We may, like the Colonel, feel we are panting to keep up with Fanny. But we would be nowhere without her. Our participation in the novel would be wholly different if we didn't have her to explore ways of reading the action so far, and to plot out its possible future courses. She represents us in the unfolding narrative. Not only does *The Golden Bowl* present different perspectives on its central action, it offers in the dialogues of the Assinghams a kind of representation of and commentary on perspectivalism itself. They constantly put before us questions of reading, interpretation, and indeed the very process of novelistic creation. Fanny may at times come perilously close to a kind of postmodernist sense of the arbitrariness of narrative: the way it would take only a shift of authorial whim to make everything come out differently. But this step toward exposing the fictionality of fiction is one that James refuses to take: he wants his reader to believe in the world he has created and to take seriously its moral compass points. He in fact uses Fanny in this same conversation to pose the moral stakes of the drama to come. Fanny says of Maggie: "Her sense will have to open. . . . To what's called Evil—with a very big E: for the first time in her life" (282). Fanny's invitation extends to the reader, whose sense—if he or she is to be a reader of the type James wants—must also open.

For all the possibilities of commentary provided by the Assinghams, a person looking very much like an overall narrator also intervenes from time to time. For instance, at the start of chapter 9: "So much mute communication was doubtless, all this time, marvellous, and we may confess to having perhaps read into the scene, prematurely, a critical character that took longer to develop" (114). This "we" appears to be both witness and creator, writer and reader. Or at the start of chapter 20: "The main interest of these hours for us, however, will have been in the way the Prince continued to know . . . a certain persistent aftertaste" (239). This "us" posits a community of reader and writer. In one more, somewhat complex, example concerning Charlotte in guarded conversation with a Fanny intent to know how things stand: "Her opportunity had accordingly, after a few minutes of Mrs Assingham's almost imprudently interested expression of face, positively acquired such a price for her that she may, for ourselves, while the intensity lasted, rather resemble a person holding out a small mirror at arm's length and consulting it with a special turn of the head" (186). Here Charlotte in her moment of self-regard—figuring out how best to preserve her own freedom of maneuver—has a different figuration for the reader than for Fanny.

My examples here—and they could continue to multiply—are meant to suggest that James's rereading of *The Golden Bowl* in his preface for the New York Edition is partially blind to what he has in fact done. The novel has a fluidity and suppleness in the play of perspective that reminds one of the future, not the past, of the novel: of Proust and Virginia Woolf in particular. If James doesn't quite match Woolf's (or Joyce's) stream of consciousness, it may be that the "for us" remains normatively more important for him: he feels the need to maintain a play of moral consciousness *on* the recordings of consciousness. It is not the meanders of consciousness that interest him so much as the detective work on the way humans behave that consciousness performs.

But is also true that Book 2 of *The Golden Bowl* more consistently follows Maggie's perspective than Book 1 does the Prince's. The reason, I think, is that as Book 2 develops, Maggie becomes the novelist, the person pulling the strings of the action, more than Amerigo ever claimed to do in Book 1. She gains the knowledge she needs—the knowledge she did not have before, that heretofore was mainly Fanny's—in order to assert her role as privileged observer. In fact, she progressively takes over the novelistic function from Fanny Assingham, so that by the very end she assigns all the characters their role and their place—dispatching Charlotte to American City with Adam, bringing the Prince back into his marriage and into her explicitly sexual embrace.

It's especially hard to describe this second half of the novel, where the victim turns the table on her victimizers, who all the while see what is being done to them without being in any position to protest. To describe it as a matter of victims and victimizers of course sounds melodramatic—but it is a melodrama that James very much wants to keep hovering over his refined actors. As the Prince reflects late in Book 1, the family he has married into doesn't support his traditional Italian sense of intrigue and drama: "He might vulgarly have put it that one had never to plot or to lie for them; he might humorously have put it that one had never, as by the higher conformity, to lie in wait with the dagger or to prepare, insidiously, the cup" (230). The dagger and the cup have this latent presence in the text, but precisely as what will never have to be brought to realization, never brought into the open. Book 2 follows a rhythm of revelation and recognition, yet neither the exposure of "evil" (Fanny's "Evil—with a very big E") nor the recognition of its meaning is ever allowed to achieve overt status—is not allowed to occupy the front of the stage.

From the onset of her inner itinerary of discovery, Maggie feels, along "with the throb of her deeper need to know where she 'really' was" (340), simultaneously the imperative that "the specific, in almost any direction, was utterly forbidden her" (360). The specific is forbidden because it would bring the melodrama into the open, and would thus precipitate a crisis: the crisis named specifically as adultery, as treachery, with the probable result of two marriages broken, or at least explicitly compromised. Maggie early on in her discoveries realizes that the preservation and renewal of her marriage, not its dissolution, is what she will strive for. This means that she must in the same process: gain her new knowledge of good and evil; use it to exert pressure on the Prince; yet repress it from any public articulation; and, perhaps especially, keep it from her father (the deceived husband), at least in any "specific" and articulate form. Book 2 of the novel is all about knowledge gained and used but also set aside and repressed. It's an extraordinary representation of a performance on Maggie's part, and on James's part an extraordinary performing of all the premises of his kind of fiction—a kind of demonstration that he can be George Eliot and Gustave Flaubert at the same time, which might be to say an updated and altogether more subtle and sophisticated Balzac.

When the Prince and Charlotte are late in returning from Matcham—because they have gone to Gloucester to consummate their adultery, it seems—Maggie does not wait for them at her father's in Eaton Square, which would have been her traditional refuge from the shortcomings of her marriage, but returns instead to Portland Place, where she dresses for dinner and awaits Amerigo's return alone. This, as she later reflects, makes the initial difference in the situation she wishes to change: it creates a moment of uncertainty on his part, the beginning of his wondering about what she may have learned. Her choice to await the Prince at Portland Place constitutes for her "proof" that "she was no longer playing with blunt and idle tools, with weapons that didn't cut. There passed across her vision ten times a day the gleam of a bare blade" (304). This and all the ensuing imagery—of Maggie as a crouching tigress, for instance—signal the advent of moral melodrama. Maggie feels like the actress "who suddenly, on the stage, before the footlights, had begun to improvise, to speak lines not in the text" (322). The improvisation then begins to alert the Prince that the scenario has somehow changed. He reacts to it mainly with the attempt to seduce—a seduction that Maggie holds at arm's length, wishing to give in to him, but fully conscious that to do so would be to defeat her purpose. She wants him back, but disencumbered of Charlotte.

The process of Maggie's discovering the sexual liaison of her husband and Charlotte is hence both a simple whodunit, a more momentous venture into knowledge of good and evil, and a further discovery that her new knowledge can only be used without apprising others that it exists as knowledge. Because her new knowledge is not publicly serviceable—only to be used occultly—the initial crisis of the novel is in some measure unneeded, superfluous. That crisis takes the form of the return of the golden bowl that Charlotte and Amerigo discover in an antiques shop when seeking a wedding gift that Charlotte would give Maggie. The bowl of gilded crystal is rejected by the Prince since he suspects it to have a hidden flaw. Maggie's own loitering in the antiques shops leads her to it—and to her purchasing it. But the antiques dealer then has a compunction, and comes to tell her of the flaw in the bowl, and in doing so sees photographs of the Prince and of Charlotte in Maggie's drawing room. This leads to the revelation that they had together considered purchasing the bowl back before the wedding. This is the relevant fact: that they were on a basis of intimacy before the twin marriages necessarily brought them together. They were, as Maggie puts it in displaying the bowl to Fanny, "too intimate . . . to let me know anything about it" (417). The bowl thus represents "the outbreak of the definite" (423), the coming of that "specific" knowledge Maggie wished to keep under the erasure of denial. When Fanny responds to learning of the crack in the bowl by hurling it to the ground, where it breaks into three pieces, the Prince enters to view the fragments, which "reminded him, unmistakably though confusedly, of something known, some other unforgotten image" (432).

This "unforgotten image" rising confusedly from the past gives an effective image of the return of the repressed that Freud was contemporaneously theorizing. The past returns in the form of the cracked bowl that names the novel. The gilded bowl with the hidden flaw within is almost too blatant a symbol of Maggie's marriage to the Prince. And in fact that symbolism may be less important than the process by which the bowl brings backs the past, breaks through the different kinds of bars of repression that Maggie, and the Prince, and Fanny have all placed upon it. The way in which the past resurges into the present is very like the double structure of Freudian trauma, where a later occurrence retrospectively, by retroaction, sexualizes and gives traumatic content to an earlier incident. Here, the moment of the Prince's return from the Matcham excursion, always troubling but never quite understood, takes on its true meaning: how his face "had flashed a light into her troubled soul the night of his late return from Matcham" (432). As she insists in the ensuring dialogue with the Prince, she has ceased "to be as I was. *Not* to know" (447).

A bit earlier in this scene, there occurs one of those extraordinary Jamesian moments of mute communication, where what the characters' words don't say becomes more important than their articulations:

She had done for him, that is, what her instinct enjoined; had laid a basis not merely momentary on which he could meet her. When, by the turn of his head, he did finally meet her, this was the last thing that glimmered out of his look; but it came into sight, none the less, as a perception of his distress and almost as a question of his eyes; so that, for still another minute, before he committed himself, there occurred between them a kind of unprecedented moral exchange over which her superior lucidity presided. (438)

I imagine this is the kind of thing that most drove brother William to distraction. This exchange of glances that becomes an "unprecedented moral exchange" takes a convention of stage and novel writing—how characters' facial physiognomies are supposed to betray their emotions and even, as in melodrama, their moral identity—and gives it a kind of witty, metareal existence. We don't have simply the exchange of glances between Maggie and the Prince. We have a reading of that exchange, a claim of meaningfulness attributed by the reader. Just as Freud was to claim (in 1905, contemporaneously with James's novel) that no mortal could keep a secret because he "chatters with his fingertips; betrayal oozes out of him at every pore," James posits a victory of knowing over the apparently insignificant.

By the end of this chapter, 34, Maggie knows all there is to know, and so does the Prince and so does Fanny. What Charlotte knows and what Adam knows is not clear, and indeed never can be made clear since once Maggie has gained her unwanted new knowledge she will put all her efforts to once more keeping it from becoming public knowledge. If the climactic scene of the breaking of the bowl was in some sense an almost unnecessary overt representation of what she has learned, the true climax of the novel will come, I think, soon after, when the six principal characters have gathered at the country house Fawns, and Maggie reaches her true moral crisis: how to use the knowledge she has gained. She feels herself to be a young actress "suddenly promoted to leading lady and expected to appear in every act of the five" (449–50). But at the moment of climax, she is not only actress but potentially theater director.

That climax comes as Adam, the Prince, Charlotte, and Fanny Assingham play bridge following dinner. The Colonel is writing letters, and Maggie, never a card player, sits with a copy of "the last salmon-coloured French periodical" (467)—we may guess it by the color to be the *Revue des Deux Mondes*—and watches the foursome, and thinks of the knowledge she is concealing. "There reigned for her, absolutely, during these vertiginous moments, that fascination of the monstrous, that temptation of the horribly possible, which we so often trace by its breaking out suddenly, lest it should go further, in unexplained retreats and reactions" (468). This almost sounds like a temptation to Balzac's smash of the windowpane: a breaking though of the surface of manners to get to the thing "hideously *behind*" (471). She realizes that she has the capacity to say the repressed truth, in the manner of the melodramatic heroine-victim: "springing up under her wrong and making them all start, stare and turn pale, she might sound out their doom in a single sentence, a sentence easy to choose among several of the lurid" (468). The "lurid" is always James's word of choice for moments of melodramatic showdown. What is going to be so striking about this showdown is what Maggie does with its potential.

She wanders out on the terrace, and looks in through the windows: "they might have been figures rehearsing some play of which she herself was the author," she thinks (470). In that key Jamesian word for novelistic writing, they *represent*: "They might in short have represented any mystery they would; the point being predominantly that the key to the mystery, the key that would wind and unwind it without a snap of the spring, was there in her pocket—or rather, no doubt, clasped at this crisis in her hand and pressed, as she walked back and forth, to her breast." That is, what is to be represented on this stage is her choice: "Spacious and splendid, like a stage again awaiting a drama, it was a scene she might people, by the press of her spring, either with serenities and dignities and decencies, or with terrors and shames and ruins, things as ugly as those formless fragments of her golden bowl she was trying so hard to pick up."

But here comes the Jamesian turn, highly characteristic ever since *The American*, yet here in *The Golden Bowl* a turn that comments almost explicitly on James's progressive understanding of the melodrama of consciousness. Maggie understands that she cannot give herself to "the vulgar heat of her wrong." To do so would be to reveal to Adam his status as cuckold, but Maggie's refusal goes beyond this, to a larger refusal of the melodramatic mode itself. That is figured as an outlandish experience: "a wild eastern caravan, looming into view with crude colours in the sun, fierce pipes in the air, high spears against the sky, all a thrill, a natural joy to mingle with, but turning off short before it reached her and plunging into other defiles" (471). The operatic is not for her, and she moves on beyond its temptation to a full discovery, yet almost simultaneous repression, of the bared truth of her situation:

> She saw at all events why horror itself had almost failed her; the horror that, foreshadowed in advance, would, by her thought, have made everything that was unaccustomed in her cry out with pain; the horror of finding evil seated, all at its ease, where she had only dreamed of good; the horror of the thing hideously *behind*, behind so much trusted, so much pretended, nobleness, cleverness, tenderness. It was the first sharp falsity she had known in her life, to touch at all, or be touched by; it had met her like some bad-faced stranger surprised in one of the thick-carpeted corridors of a house of a quiet on a Sunday afternoon; and yet, yes, amazingly, she had been able to look at terror and disgust only to know that she must put away from her the bitter-sweet of their freshness. (471)

Maggie discovers evil—Fanny's Evil—seated "all at its ease"; she discovers in particular "the thing hideously *behind*." She is thus initiated into the full panoply of Jamesian melodrama, which is more than anything else about evil hidden behind the trusted appearance. This discovery then takes the shape of the "bad-faced stranger" lurking in the house, a figuration that cannot help but recall a tale written two years after *The Golden Bowl*, *The Jolly Corner*, which tells of Spencer Brydon's encounter with his hideous but potent alter-ego on his return to his childhood home in New York after some thirty-three years of absence. Maggie's encounter with the familiar stranger, though, leads to a decision—or more precisely, to the *knowledge*—that she must put aside the bittersweet solace of terror and disgust. The sight of her companions inside the house dictates her seemingly instantaneous recognition that the unleashing of such emotions—the lifting of the bar of repression that keeps them latent—belongs to a melodramatic mode of enactment that is not available to her. "It was extraordinary: they positively brought home to her that to feel about them in any of the immediate, inevitable, assuaging ways, the ways usually open to innocence outraged and generosity betrayed, would have been to give them up, and that giving them up was, marvelously, not to be thought of."

Note that Maggie's deeply ethical decision is figured as a renunciation of a certain aesthetics: that associated with "innocence outraged and generosity betrayed," which we can unhesitatingly identify as the unrepressed acting-out of melodrama. James seems to be indicating in this manner that the Jamesian novel contains both a temptation to melodrama and an overcoming of it, internalizing it as melodrama of consciousness and then renouncing its uses. Yet for all Maggie's designated role as actress and stage-director who chooses the mode of her unfolding play, James has not done with melodrama: he wants, in fact, to have eaten his melodramatic cake while having it too. On the very next page, Maggie realizes that Charlotte has arisen from the card table and come seeking her. "The splendid shining supple creature was out of the cage, was at large" (472). When Charlotte tracks her down on the terrace, Maggie has the sense "of having been thrown over on her back with her neck, from the first, half broken and her helpless face staring up" (475). The violence refused overt expression comes to inhabit the metaphors of Maggie's inner experience.

Charlotte has come to ask whether Maggie believes that Charlotte has done her a "wrong," indicating that she has at least partially penetrated Maggie's dissimulation of her sense of betrayal. Maggie in response realizes that she can only tell a lie—a lie that eventually takes the form precisely of a denegation of melodramatic utterance: "I accuse you—I accuse you of nothing" (480). Charlotte indeed states that what she has come for is "your denial" (481). On Maggie's side: "She saw soon enough what more was to come. She saw it in Charlotte's face, and felt it make between them, in the air, a chill that completed the coldness of their conscious perjury. 'Will you kiss me on it then?'" That is Charlotte's final move, sealing the perjury in a gesture that, with the arrival of their companions at the open door to the terrace, takes on a "high publicity" (482). Which is where the chapter ends.

This climactic episode is faithful to James's theatrical premises, all the while playing out another drama within Maggie's consciousness: a drama that is imagistically melodramatic while overtly renouncing the solace of the melodramatic mode. The exterior drama ending in the public Judas kiss is doubled by a drama that often seems to be playing out on what Freud called that "other stage" (*anderes Schauplatz*) of the dream, in a world always verging on the nightmare, as in the discovery of a bad-faced stranger lurking in your house, or finding yourself metaphorically on your back with a broken neck. We have here the most fully achieved form of James's most masterful mature fiction, where the theater of manners in which Maggie figures as actress and director but finally, and perhaps most importantly, as spectator as well, requires an inner theater in which that grotesque Evil that must be repressed in reality is given free play to produce the deformations of fear, flight, evasion, entrapment.

The rest of *The Golden Bowl* tracks the consequences of Maggie's realizations and renunciations during the great scene at Fawns. Maggie's pressure on characters and their actions will both produce the dénouement and keep its latent meanings—what it really signifies about relations among the four principals—from erupting through the surface of manners. The emblematic moment comes when a baffled and unhappy Charlotte has taken the wrong volume of an old "triple-decker" out to the garden to read—or rather, not to read, since the novel is simply a makeshift cover for her flight to the garden. "I saw you come out—saw you from the window," says Maggie, "and couldn't bear to think you should find yourself here without the beginning of your book. *This* is the beginning; you've got the wrong volume, and I've brought you out the right" (526). Placing the others in the right volume is the work of Maggie's endgame. With her father, her pressure works to produce a result she would have deplored earlier in the novel, but now endorses: his return to American City, with his wife. The solution to the adultery of son-in-law and mother-in-law is to separate them by an ocean.

This makes of the adulterous pair, in Maggie's vision of them, no longer "high Wagnerian lovers . . . interlocked in their wood of enchantment" (503). (When he and Charlotte go off to their tryst in Gloucester, Amerigo exclaims: "I feel the day like a great gold cup that we must somehow drain together" [263]: Tristan and Isolde lurk in the background.) They are doomed by Maggie's decision to rearrange everyone without ever articulating their loss of arrangement. The lie between Charlotte and herself ties Charlotte's tongue. And Adam's decision ties Charlotte's future to an America without Amerigo. As Charlotte shows guests around the treasures of Fawns—the richest of them destined for Adam's museum in American City—Maggie hears her voice as like "the shriek of a soul in pain" (512). And then she has "some vision of Io goaded by the gadfly or of Ariadne roaming the lone sea-strand" (523)—the evocation of Ariadne, abandoned by Theseus, sister of the Phaedra who will fall in love with her son-in-law Hippolytus, is particularly interesting given the quasi-incestuous relations of the novel. The price of Maggie's emergence as the master plotter of the novel is indeed the sacrifice of Charlotte, forced into separation from her lover, forced into exile to an America she knows only too well. There is a measure of cruelty in the punishments meted out to Charlotte toward the end of the novel, as if the sexiest of James's women characters had to be heavily scapegoated.

Maggie is aware of Charlotte's torment, and at the heart of it she sees Charlotte's ignorance: her inability to figure out what Maggie really knows—and what Adam really knows. This latter quantity is a mystery to Maggie as well—who maybe prefers not to know: it would kill her, she tells Fanny, to know that her father knew of his deceived status. Fanny says to Bob Assingham back in Book 1, "what is morality but high intelligence?" (66). Not to know dooms one—unless one knows but chooses not to know, which may be a still higher form of intelligence. The ultimate cruelty to Charlotte may come from the Prince, who in the next-to-last chapter of the novel says of her, to his wife: "She's stupid" (552). Stupid, it seems, because she ought to have known Maggie better, ought to have been better prepared to play the role of deceiver, and detective.

With the Prince himself, Maggie's pressure is really the avoidance of what would be the usual pressure—the pressure to confess his wrongdoing. She doesn't want his confession. She wants him to know that she knows, but does not want any further articulation beyond that. On the verge of Adam and Charlotte's departure for the voyage back to America, Maggie reflects that this sundering of the tight foursome they had constituted would have been impossible, "would have torn them to pieces, if they had so much as suffered its suppressed relations to peep out of their eyes" (562). This is what we might call the repression of the repressed: the conscious decision not to face the terror of the truths they have repressed. The closest the Prince comes to a confession is his comment when Maggie expresses the terror and pity of Charlotte's situation, her status as a kind of Emma Bovary or Anna Karenina:

"It's terrible"—her memories prompted her to speak. "I see it's *always* terrible for women."

The Prince looked down in his gravity: "Everything's terrible, *cara*—in the heart of man. She's making her life," he said. "She'll make it." (553)

The reader can't tell whether the Prince's "heart of man" stands in gender distinction to Maggie's "terrible for women" as a comment on male infidelity, or if it rather refers to all mankind. Both, probably; and the Prince in this manner at least alludes to the latent content of the repressed. It is the stuff of terror and pity.

This articulation of the "terrible" calls to mind a much earlier exchange between Maggie and Fanny about why she has chosen to rearrange the disarranged marriages rather than allowing their dissolution. She tells Fanny, "I can bear anything."

"Oh, 'bear'! Mrs Assingham fluted.
"For love," said the Princess.
Fanny hesitated. "Of your father?"
"For love," Maggie repeated.
It kept her friend watching. "Of your husband?"
"For love," Maggie said again. (384)

For love: it is characteristic of the Jamesian melodrama of consciousness that it should at key moments break through indirections and repressions to speak the truths that the conflict is all about.

The love that Maggie subscribes to is by the end of the novel specifically erotic. From the moment of suspicion of the Prince's relations with Charlotte—the night of his return from Matcham by way of Gloucester—Maggie has feared and fought against surrender to his

sexual presence. And at some point the Prince himself seems to es-
pouse this sense of a durance, a test—like Tristan and Isolde with the
sword between them on the bed—that appears to keep them apart as
they work to come back together. In the next-to-last chapter, Maggie
refuses his offered embrace, telling him to wait. Then, at the very end,
with Adam and Charlotte gone, Maggie once again keeps at bay what
she sees as the possibility of the Prince's confession, and chooses instead to celebrate Charlotte's dazzling manner in her refusal to let on
that anything has happened to any of them "That's our help, you see,"
she tells Amerigo, who then comes over to her; and now the embrace
occurs.

> . . . close to her, her face kept before him, his hands holding her
> shoulders, his whole act enclosing her, he presently echoed:
> "'See'? I see nothing but *you*." And the truth of it had, with this
> force, after a moment, so strangely lighted his eyes that, as for pity
> and dread of them, she buried her own in his breast. (567)

The novel ends with these words, which seem to record the Prince's
choice of Maggie over Charlotte as the object of desire. This for Maggie elicits "pity and dread"—for the abandoned Charlotte? For her own
subjection to his desire—and then what seems like surrender? It is a
moment of fulfillment, but not without its costs.

These final lines need to be read in conjunction with Maggie's reflections, on the preceding page, on "her reason for what she had
done."

> She knew at last really why—and how she had been inspired and
> guided, how she had been persistently able, how, to her soul, all
> the while, it had been for the sake of this end. Here it was, then,
> the moment, the golden fruit that had shone from afar; only, what
> *were* these things, in the fact, for the hand and for the lips, when
> tested, when tasted—what were they as a reward? Closer than she
> had ever been to the measure of her course and the full face of her
> act, she had an instant of the terror that, when there has been sus-
> pense, always precedes, on the part of the creature to be paid, the
> certification of the amount. Amerigo knew it, the amount; he still

held it, and the delay in his return, making her heart beat too fast
to go on, was like a sudden blinding light on a wild speculation.
She had thrown the dice, but his hand was over her cast. (566)

"For the sake of this end": she has guided things to the restoration of
her marriage, and to a moment that promises—with a certain terror as
well as exhilaration—erotic fulfillment. The Prince at the last reaffirms
the kind of phallic presence he has latently maintained throughout the
novel, as the marker of sexual desire, now brought home to Maggie.

"For the sake of this end" figures also, of course, the work of Maggie
as novelist who, having taken the relay from Fanny Assingham, has
plotted the novel's action with this end in mind. So that James passes
responsibility for "authorship" from himself to the character who, originally deceived and manipulated, emerges as his most forceful surrogate. Maggie's active management of the novel reinterprets in interesting ways what one might take to be the underlying mythic material of
the novel. That is, one could take the novel to be a replay of the legend
of Sleeping Beauty. Recall that in the Grimm Brothers' version of the
tale, *Briar Rose (Dornröschen)*, there is an initial failure to invite to the
newborn princess' christening a thirteenth fairy—to whom Charlotte
likens herself when she shows up unexpected in London for Maggie's
wedding, which is slated to take place "before twelve assistants exactly"
(45). Charlotte queries the Prince: "Twelve including *me*?" To which
he replies: "You'll make the thirteenth. It won't do." In the folk tale,
the uninvited fairy then curses the baby: on her sixteenth birthday, she
will prick her finger on a spindle and fall down, dead. But one of the
other fairies manages to commute the sentence: she will rather fall into
a deep sleep, lasting for a century. Her father then reacts by hiding all
the spindles in the kingdom. Nonetheless, on her sixteenth birthday
Briar Rose manages to make her way into a hidden tower room, where
she finds an old woman—transform of the thirteenth fairy?—making
thread on a spindle. Her curiosity cannot be contained, she touches
it—with the predicted results. The whole castle falls asleep, and a thick
hawthorn hedge grows up around it. Over the hundred years of her
sleep, dozens of young men try to make their way to her—but merely
impale themselves on the hawthorns. Only when the appointed time

has come can the chosen prince make his way through the hedge, which parts of its own accord before him.

The sexual symbolism of the story is too overt to need much comment. And one could read a strong parallel in Maggie's story: originally her marriage with the Prince seems to be lacking in sexual passion, or at least mature, intelligent sexual passion. There is a kind of failed transition to maturity, as in *Briar Rose*. In Maggie's case, it is figured as an inability to break from the (incestuous) embrace of the father—a situation played out in many another folk tale, *All-Kinds-of-Fur* (*Allerleirauh*), for instance. Only when Maggie undertakes to rewrite the story of her marriage "for the sake of this end"—to bring it to another dénouement—does she appear to awaken to erotic possibility. There is a kind of woman's *Bildungsroman* here, comparable to that dramatized by George Eliot in Gwendolen Harleth's story in *Daniel Deronda*. It seems to me a fairly astonishing feat on James's part. In much of his fiction—*Portrait of a Lady* may be the most famous example—James undertakes to write of the inner experience of women (renewing a tradition reaching back to Samuel Richardson). *What Maisie Knew* and *The Awkward Age* may appear as transitions from *Portrait* to *The Golden Bowl*, in that sexual knowledge assumes greater importance. But Maggie's novel seems to include not only sexual knowledge but also sexual experience.

If this marks a "French" aspect of the novel—as it very much does in *The Ambassadors*, all about tracking down the sexual nature of Chad's liaison with Madame de Vionnet—James in his preface insists rather on the "French" indirection of narrative presentation in the novel. The preface—which in this case follows original publication by only five years—begins with the assertion: "Among many matters thrown into relief by a refreshed acquaintance with *The Golden Bowl* what perhaps stands out for me is the still marked inveteracy of a certain indirect and oblique view of my presented action." He notes his "preference," especially in his shorter pieces, for avoiding the direct presentation, so that his narratives "have ranged themselves not as my own impersonal account of the affair in hand, but as my account of somebody's impression of it." He goes on to argue the enhanced interest of experience reported as it becomes personal experience of "some other conscious and confessed agent." There is a kind of doubling of interest by this method, particularly when the agent in question is also a major actor in the story, as is the case for the Prince and Maggie. James at this point in his novelistic career has reached the proposition: "Anything, in short, I now reflect, must always have seemed to me better—better for the process and the effect of representation, my irrepressible ideal—than the mere muffled majesty of irresponsible 'authorship.'"

This cuts to the heart of James's theory of the novel and what it is for. While his "always" in the sentence quoted no doubt reflects honestly his preoccupation from the beginning of his career with states of consciousness, certainly the obliquity of representation, and the avoidance of that "mere muffled majesty of irresponsible 'authorship,'" become far more marked in the 1890s and after. And as he notes in passing, the shorter fiction, often novellas—typical of the 1890s—is often the place where such an oblique point of view is being worked out: *What Maisie Knew* is a telling example. The form and the technique can accurately be called French. Think in contrast of the practice of James's most important English master, George Eliot, for whom the majesty of authorship was a constant temptation—whose explicit narratorial interventions and reflections indeed are most characteristic of her style, and who in them may succumb rather too much to mere muffled majesty. Yet James also makes a point of describing his first agent of reflection, the Prince, as "having a consciousness highly susceptible of registration." Recall his strictures on Flaubert for using such "limited reflectors and registers" as Emma Bovary and Frédéric Moreau. The novel is more interesting, in James's claim, when that central consciousness is highly developed, sensitive, a recording apparatus that distinguishes nuance and subtlety, that is attuned to the surface of manners and aware also of those things that can lie "hideously *behind*."

Following this justification of his commitment to ways of looking at the thing in preference to any direct presentation of the thing itself—is the preface in some measure an answer to William, then in the last year of his life?—James uses most of his text for a justification of the project of revision itself. The notion of revising one's earlier work for a definitive edition has over the decades struck many, perhaps most, readers as a strange waste of time, and there are many who express a preference for the original versions of such early novels as *The American*. *The Golden Bowl*, representing his most mature work, underwent very little in the way of revision, but he uses its preface to scold those who stand up for the unrevised versions of his novels—of *The American*, for instance. James argues that in rereading that novel, he found it inadequate to its subject, like "a garment misfitted, a garment cheaply embroidered and unworthy of it." This is a curious view of his early fiction, yet doubtless one that fits well with his understanding that the novel must always be seen from the point of view of the reader. Recall those occasional summonses in *The Golden Bowl* to consider how things look "to us." James's rejection of the "mere muffled majesty of irresponsible 'authorship'" is most of all a call to include the reader in the text, or perhaps more accurately, the reading process in the text. The novel is in essence about decipherment, discovery, learning to read the signs.

It is striking that James summons as tutelary presence for the project of revision none other than Balzac. "He . . . re-assaulted by supersessive terms, re-penetrated by finer channels, never had on the one hand seen or said all or had on the other ceased to press forward. His case has equal mass and authority—and beneath its protecting shade, at any rate, I move for the brief remainder of these remarks." It is true that Balzac was never done altering his novels. They tended to appear first in periodical form, then in volumes, then in one of the various and progressively restructured editions of the *Comédie humaine* published during his lifetime. They were rewritten for the occasion, and often reworked to fit in a different context, as part of something larger. As the cast of returning characters of the *Comédie humaine* grew, many of them were retrospectively written into the earlier texts. Balzac is indeed a good example of "supersessive" versions of texts, and the *Comédie humaine* itself, as a collected edition, is surely the model for the New York Edition. Yet Balzacian revision scarcely produces the definitive polish that James seeks in his. Balzac in fact rarely revises in this sense: he rarely crosses out to propose a better version, he mainly adds—in great balloons of text that fill the margins of his proofs. Like Proust, for Balzac revision is largely the discovery that there is more to say on any given subject, more to dramatize in any situation. In fact, Jamesian revision is closer to Flaubert's practice, the progressive elimination of what seems to the novelist the approximate in favor of the *mot juste*: the precise term that will get it right.

Flaubert in fact makes an appearance toward the end of the preface, as the authority for reading fiction aloud—by which, I think, James mainly is concerned to justify to himself his practice of writing aloud, dictating his novels. "Gustave Flaubert has somewhere in this connection an excellent word—to the effect that any imaged prose that fails to be richly rewarding in return for a competent utterance ranks itself as wrong through not being 'in the conditions of life.'" I take this to mean that a novel that can be spoken aloud—"sounded," as James puts it earlier in the paragraph—is somehow more a part of real life, the life of speech. That is an interesting justification for a novelist as stylish and mannered as James, though it is certainly true that his late prose makes more sense if you read it aloud.

This plea for the spoken then modulates in the final paragraph of the preface into a claim for the imaginative verbal creation as ethical action in the world. The "whole conduct of life consists of things done," he says, to argue that there are no essential separations among kinds of acts we do. "The more we are capable of acting the less gropingly we plead such differences; whereby, with any capability, we recognize betimes that to 'put' things is very exactly and responsibly and interminably to do them." One hears an echo forward to J. L. Austin's *How to Do Things with Words*, the great exposition of performative language. James appears to argue for the performative function of the novel. Again, the reply may be to his brother: to write fiction like *The Golden Bowl* is a responsible and ethical act. It matches Flaubert's high conception of writing as a practice of perfection to Balzac's sense of writing as acting in the world.

It was some three years after writing this preface that James sat with in the basement of the Grafton Galleries while Roger Fry explained to him how such postimpressionists as Cézanne, Gauguin, and Seurat offered the pictorial equivalent of the Flaubertian and, by extension, the Jamesian novel. If James did not understand, this must probably be attributed to his continuing fidelity to a concept of representation that in the pictorial arts never quite led him to the experimental art of the early twentieth century. He was not so visually advanced. But in writing he did, with *The Golden Bowl* especially, reach some cognate form of expression. And in many ways it was a form of expression that flowed from a French tradition. It probably had its closest analogy in another French novelist and admirer of Balzac—Marcel Proust. The first volume of Proust's long novel, *Du côté de chez Swann*, published in 1913, was given to James by Edith Wharton the next year. There is no reliable record of his having read it: accounts of his doing so seem to have been invented by those who wanted to make such a fitting connection. James was reading little contemporary fiction at the time, and final illness was not far in the future. If he did read Proust's novel, we have no account of his reaction to it—one of those great missed encounters of literary history. The story of James's encounter with French modernism stops just short of the fulfillment we would ideally choose.

Epilogue: Chariot of Fire

"We remain rather persistently more aware of what is gone than of what is left," James wrote of French novelists in 1899, in an essay for *North American Review*. "There is in this quarter, evidently, a distinct chill in the air; there are empty places, gaps into space, the look of a field less occupied." His trip to France in 1899 was the last for a number of years—the American tour, illnesses, age, and the revisions and prefaces of the New York Edition supervened. But he went back to France in the spring of 1907, at the insistent invitation of Edith Wharton, who by now had become his most talented disciple and most flirtatious female friend. The Whartons in typical style had rented—from the Vanderbilts—an apartment at the heart of the Faubourg Saint-Germain, at 58 rue de Varenne, and had made their grand entry into the higher reaches of French society, in part through the good offices of Paul Bourget, the "inflamed Academician" as James now styled him—inflamed largely by his success and his self-importance. So James spent "a wondrous social fortnight in Paris, in the heart, and more or less in the lap, of the Faubourg St. Germain." With Edith as his guide he was making the acquaintance of that Faubourg he had often—in the manner of Balzac—portrayed without much real firsthand knowledge. The home of the Bellegardes of *The American*, of Madame de Vionnet in *The Ambassadors*, now welcomed James.

But the real revelation of the 1907 trip was motoring in Edith's automobile: "the wondrous cushioned *general* Car of your so wonderously india-rubber-tyred and deep-cushioned fortune," as he later styled it. The car—which James also repeatedly refers to as the "Chariot of Fire" (Edith then by extension became "the Firebird," after Stravinsky)— revolutionized the experience of time and space. As Wharton wrote in the first sentence of A *Motor Flight Through France*—her account of travels, partly with James—"The motor-car has restored the romance of travel." James declared to Howard Sturgis: "My three weeks of really *seeing* this large incomparable France in our friend's chariot of fire has been almost the time of my life. It's the old travelling-carriage way glorified and raised to the 100th power." The automobile worked its revolution in time and space, opening up landscapes hidden from the train traveler, bridging gaps between places that had once seemed separate, providing new perspectives at every turn of the road. It was, like the most daring postimpressionist art—and like the cinema just entering the world—a perspectival revolution.

No one understood this better than James's younger contemporary Marcel Proust, who devoted several passages of A *la recherche du temps perdu*—which would begin its publication six years following James's motor trip with the Whartons—to the way in which automobile travel changed the relations of time and space that lie at the heart of his novel. Art, Proust's narrator tells us, is modified by the motor car, "since a village which seemed to be in a different world from some other village becomes its neighbour in a landscape whose dimensions are altered"—which sounds very much like the modifications sought by Proust's fictional late-impressionist painter, Elstir. The narrator continues:

> In any case, to learn that there may perhaps exist a universe in which two and two make five and a straight line is not the shortest distance between two points would have astonished Albertine far less than to hear the driver say that it was easy to go in a single afternoon to Saint-Jean and La Raspelière. Douville and Quetteholme, Saint-Mars-le-Vieux and Saint-Mars-le-Vétu, Gourville and Balbec-le-Vieux, Tourville and Féterne, prisoners hitherto as hermetically confined in the cells of distinct days as long ago were Méséglise and Guermantes, upon which the same eyes could not

gaze in the course of a single afternoon, delivered now by the giant with the seven-league boots, clustered around our tea-time with their towers and steeples and their old gardens which the neighbouring wood sprang back to reveal.

Proust evokes a change in relations between the original cardinal points of his childhood imaginary, Méséglise ("Swann's Way") and Guermantes ("Guermantes' Way"), suggesting how motoring for the first generation to discover it wrought a revolutionary new understanding—a quasi-Einsteinian understanding—of the experience of time and place. A giant in seven-league boots, the motor gives a new kinetic experience of landscape, of the visual experience of phenomena and their interrelations. It prepares the celebration of speed and mobility promoted by the futurists, and the multifaceted presentation of objects associated in painting with the cubists, and in literature with Proust, Joyce, and Woolf.

For Proust, nearly thirty years younger than James, the motor car came in midcareer. For James it was a discovery of old age. There is no passage in James's writing that offers quite the equivalent of Proust's description of the kinetic transformations of landscape wrought by motoring. But there is a significant moment in a short story that appears to owe its genesis to Edith Wharton, though to equate the woman novelist in *"The Velvet Glove"* (1909) with Wharton would be a slur on the real person. The Olympian beauty who signs her novels "Amy Evans" acts as if she wants to seduce John Berridge—but it will turn out that what she really wants from him is a preface to the American edition of her novel. His discovery of that intention will put an abrupt end to his erotic arousal. But before this dire revelation, she takes him home from the soirée in which they have met in her motor car, driven by a "capped charioteer," by way of a night tour through Paris:

> *That* was knowing Paris, of a wondrous bland April night; that was hanging over it from vague consecrated lamp-studded heights and taking in, spread below and afar, the great scroll of all its irresistible story, pricked out, across river and bridge and radiant *place*, and along quays and boulevards and avenues, and around monumental circles and squares, in syllables of fire, and sketched and summarised, further and further, in the dim fire-dust of end-

less avenues; that was all of the essence of fond and thrilled and
throbbing recognition, with a thousand things understood and a
flood of response conveyed, a whole familiar possessive feeling appealed to and attested.

This rediscovery of Paris through the movement of the automobile
comes of course from an aroused Berridge. And one senses something
like that erotic response in James's evocations of his motor tour
through France with the Whartons. Just after his return to Paris, he
wrote to his Rye neighbors, George and Fanny Prothero: "I am pros-
trate under my so big impression (so big yet so detailed as the magical
monster the touring Panhard, makes it—the *only* way to travel at ease
and with power now) of the grand style and inordinate interest of this
incomparable France. Ah Grignon and Vézelay!—Ah the lovely rivers
and the inveterately glorious grub!" And in the midst of the tour, from
Pau in the Basses Pyrénées, he wrote to Jessie Allen that he was "immersed in a wondrous motor-tour through the centre and the wide and
entire south of this wonderful and most interesting country. . . . The
way our admirable motor and sane, discreet, deliberate American
chauffeur, *master* a country and make such a variety of experience of it
easy and intelligible reconciles me really to the monstrous process and
machine." The experience of motoring, to James as to Proust, is an intellectual discovery, a new perspective and understanding of the world.

Back in the summer of 1906, James expressed his envy of the Whartons' visit to George Sand's house in Nohant, claiming—in the high,
nearly mock-heroic style he often used with Edith—that "I've really
been for weeks in the disabled state, with the bleeding wound in my
side, produced by the Parthian shot of your own last—your fling back
at me, over your departing shoulder, of your unutterable vision of
the Nohant that I have all these (motorless) years so abjectly failed to
enlighten my eyes withal (for I am indeed convinced that it *must*, as
you say, enlighten & explain). Oh, if we could only have been enlightened & explained to together!" Returning to Nohant toward the
end of the letter, he asks for her account of the visit: "How you must
have *smelt* them all!" James's obituary piece for George Sand, back in
his *Tribune* contributions in 1876, was somewhat priggish about

Sand's collection of bohemian friends and lovers—including Alfred de Musset, Frédéric Chopin, Franz Liszt, and many others—but he never ceased to have a lively and largely prurient interest in the goings-on in Nohant.

Edith, devoted as she was to the Master, made sure that the 1907 motor trip headed quickly in the direction of Nohant. They explored the ground floor of the house, saw Sand's famous marionette theater, then wandered in the garden, "and looking up at the plain old house, tried to guess behind which windows the various famous visitors had slept," Wharton recalls. "James stood there a long time, gazing and brooding beneath the row of closed shutters. 'And in which of those rooms, I wonder, did George herself sleep?' I heard him suddenly mutter. 'Though in which, indeed—' with a twinkle—'in which indeed, my dear, did she *not*?'"

George Sand—the one famous novelist he had failed to meet in 1875–76, the implausible fabulist who yet knew the world of passion in a way no English writer did—remained the object of a largely sexual fascination on James's part. In 1912, a biography of Sand sent to him by Edith Wharton—which would furnish the matter of his final essay on Sand—led to a letter evoking their Nohant visit of 1907: "What a value it all gets from our memory of that wondrous day when we explored the very scene where they pigged so thrillingly together. What a crew, what moeurs, what habits, what conditions and relations every way—& what an altogether mighty & marvellous George!—not diminished by all the greasiness & smelliness in which she made herself (& *so* many other persons!) at home." How to understand this other than as a kind of Jamesian *nostalgie de la boue*: a fascination with the kind of promiscuous and public sexuality that he had always denied himself?

James returned to Paris once again, in the spring of 1908, again to stay with the Whartons, now on the right bank, at 3 Place des Etats-Unis. This was a brief visit, and the last. Thereafter, it was London and Rye, and illness, and then a return to the United States with his dying brother in the summer of 1910. That stay of course gave other chances for motoring from Edith Wharton's home base, The Mount, in Lenox, Massachusetts. But France remained a place he longed for, and French writers always of interest. And when the Great War broke out in 1914, his thoughts turned achingly toward the ordeal of France. In an essay written for *The Book of France*, a collective volume published in 1915, he put it that "what happens to France happens to all that part of ourselves which we are most proud, and most finely advised, to enlarge and cultivate and consecrate." The point is that France must for any fully sentient and civilized person stand first among cultures: "because of her treating us to the impression of genius as no nation since the Greeks has treated the watching world, and because of our feeling that genius at that intensity is infallible." Words elicited by a time of patriotic pledges of solidarity, no doubt, but also faithful to James's original and enduring French cultural allegiance.

Then there is the strange business of his deathbed dictation. Following a stroke, and then a second, in December 1915, he continued to summon his secretary—now Theodora Bosanquet—to his bedside: he had for years now been dictating all his fiction and much of his correspondence. On the morning of December 12, he dictated a passage that seemed to recall motoring with the Whartons, then evoked members of the Bonaparte clan. Then after lunch he dictated two letters from Napoleon to his brother and sister—the first signed Napoléone, the second Henry James. On the threshold of extinction, he apparently confused his identity with that of the French emperor, giving orders for the decoration of the Louvre and the Tuileries, demanding that his siblings live up to the fortune he has created for them.

It's of course impossible to know what mental processes created the Napoleonic identification, or what to make of it. It is nonetheless interesting that James at the very last evokes the French imperial grandeur that made such an impression on his childhood years—that first memory of Napoleon atop the column in the Place Vendôme, the view from his hotel balcony on the newly completed Tuileries, the visits to the Musée du Luxembourg and the Galerie d'Apollon and Salon Carré of the Louvre. "What he was unable to finish with the sword, I shall accomplish with the pen," Balzac is said to have proclaimed, seeing himself as the continuator of Napoleon's reorganization of France, and the perpetuation of French glory. It may be that the glory James wished for at death had a French gilding to it. In his last imaginings he traveled back to Paris.

Notes

Introduction

1 "in a manner of speaking, after the same thing": Virginia Woolf, *Roger Fry: A Biography* (London: Hogarth Press, 1940), 180.

2 his "major phase": see F. O. Matthiessen, *Henry James: The Major Phase* (New York: Oxford University Press, 1944). In terms of date of composition, *The Ambassadors* precedes *The Wings of the Dove*, though the latter (which failed to gain serial publication) was published in book form before the former.

3 from approximately the time of: I give here, as mostly elsewhere, the dates of publication in book form. Much of James's fiction was serialized in periodicals just prior to publication in book form.

5 "deep well of unconscious cerebration": see HJ, preface to *The American*, in *Literary Criticism* (New York: Library of America, 1984), 2:1055.

Chapter 1: To Paris

7 "a bright, cold, unremunerative, uninteresting winter": HJ, *The Complete Notebooks of Henry James*, ed. Leon Edel and Lyall H. Powers (New York and Oxford: Oxford University Press, 1987), 215.

8 earliest childhood memory: see *A Small Boy and Others* [1913] in HJ, *Autobiography*, ed. F. W. Dupee (New York: Criterion Books, 1956), 32.

9 Anthony Trollope: see "Anthony Trollope" in HJ, *Literary Criticism*, 2 vols. (New York: Library of America, 1984), 1:1332

10 "the superficial and external aspect of Paris": see *The Legend of the Master*, ed. Simon Nowell-Smith (New York: Charles Scribner's Sons, 1948), 99.

10   "as well as he can imagine doing": HJ, *Parisian Sketches*, ed. Leon Edel and Ilse Dusoir Lind (New York: New York University Press, 1957), 4.

10   "the modern Babylon": see WJ to HJ, July 5, 1876, in *The Correspondence of William James*, vol. 1: *William and Henry, 1861–84*, ed. Ignas K. Skupskelis and Elizabeth M. Berkeley (Charlottesville and London: University Press of Virginia, 1992).

10   "it suits me to a T": HJ to Lizzie Boott, December 31, 1875. Unpublished letter, used by permission of the Houghton Library, Harvard University, bMS Am 1094 (516).

11   "a sadly mutilated metropolis": *Paris and Northern France* (Coblenz: Karl Baedeker, 1872), vii.

12   "never known a cloud": *Parisian Sketches*, 40.

12   Chambord declared: originally issued July 5, 1871, Chambord's declaration was restated in a latter to the conservative newspaper *L'Union* on October 27, 1873. For the text of the declaration, see William Fortescue, *The Third Republic in France, 1870–1940* (London and New York: Routledge, 2000), 25–26.

13   "set on its feet": *Parisian Sketches*, 27.

13   "what they will make of it": *Parisian Sketches*, 84.

13   he wrote to his sister Alice on February 22, 1876: unless otherwise specified, all excerpts from letters are taken from HJ, *Letters*, ed. Leon Edel, 4 vols. (Cambridge, Mass.: Harvard University Press, 1974–84). Edel normalizes James's spelling and punctuation.

14   "who waits upon me": HJ to Henry James Sr., November 18, 1875.

14   "and I get on": HJ to Catherine Walsh ("Aunt Kate": his mother's sister), December 3, 1875.

15   "to make my conception concrete": HJ, preface to *The American*, in *Literary Criticism* 2:1055.

15   "your turkey & cranberries": HJ to AJ, December 24, 1875. Unpublished letter, used by permission of the Houghton Library, Harvard University, bMS Am 1094 (1571).

15 "my days are a blank": HJ to Mary Walsh James, January 11, 1876, in *Henry James: A Life in Letters*, ed. Philip Horne (New York: Viking, 1999).

15 "and a dinner party": HJ to Mary Walsh James, January 24, 1876.

16 "*j'en suis à 1000 lieues*": HJ to WJ, April 25, 1876.

16 "but with the remains of beauty": HJ to WJ, March 14, 1876.

17 his dismissal from Johns Hopkins University: on C. S. Peirce, see Joseph Brent, *Charles Sanders Peirce: A Life* (Bloomington: Indiana University Press, 1993) and Louis Menand, *The Metaphysical Club* (New York: Farrar, Straus and Giroux, 2001).

17 "to compel one's sympathy": WJ to HJ, December 12, 1875.

17 "economical rather than intellectual": HJ to WJ, December 3, 1875.

17 "I know the Théâtre-Français by heart!": HJ to WJ, July 29, 1876.

18 "turn over questions": on this and the later relations of HJ and C. S. Peirce, see Leon Edel, *The Life of Henry James* (New York: Lippincott, 1953; rpt. Avon Books, 1978), 2:233.

18 "much that was intolerable in him": see HJ, *Complete Notebooks*, 216.

18 "the civilization of the new": on the exchange of letters between HJ sr. and Turgenev, see F. O. Matthiessen, *The James Family* (New York: Alfred Knopf, 1947; rpt. Vintage Books, 1980), 549.

19 "Yours very truly, Iv. Tourgenieff": Turgenev to HJ, November 20, 1875. Unpublished letter, used by permission of the Houghton Library, Harvard University, bMS Am 1094 (453).

20 "encountered in a scribbler": HJ to Catherine Walsh, December 3, 1875.

20 "a true, ideal genius": HJ to Lizzie Boott, December 31, 1875. Unpublished letter, used by permission of the Houghton Library, Harvard University, bMS Am 1094 (516).

20 "in fine, angelic": HJ to William Dean Howells, February 3, 1876.

20   "an *amour d'homme*": HJ to WJ, February 8, 1876.

20   *"jusqu'à l'attendrissement"*: HJ to WJ, April 25, 1876.

20   "our sympathy with character": *Literary Criticism*, 2:988.

20   "the creatures he invokes": *Literary Criticism*, 2:1033.

21   "Puritan angularity": *Literary Criticism*, 2:982.

21   Turgenev's *Home of the Gentry*: this comparison to Lavretsky is discussed by Adrien Poole in his introduction to *The American* (New York and Oxford: Oxford University Press, 1999), xxi–xxii.

22   "weather-beaten old military man": HJ to HJ sr., December 20, 1875.

22   "uniform really of freedom of talk": *Literary Criticism*, 2:319.

22   *"je suis lancé en pleine Olympe"*: HJ to Thomas Sargent Perry, February 3, 1876.

23   "and their monkey!": HJ to Edmund Gosse, October 15 and 17, 1912.

23   "whore-house *de province*": HJ to William Dean Howells, February 3, 1876.

23   "he is intolerably unclean": *Literary Criticism*, 2:404.

23   "unclean things have been dropped": *Literary Criticism*, 2:556.

24   "mild & spiritualistic book today": WJ to HJ, December 12, 1875. See also WJ's letter to the editor of the *Nation*, October 29, 1875, in *Essays, Comments, and Reviews* (Cambridge, Mass.: Harvard University Press, 1987), 118–19.

24   "he signally failed": *Literary Criticism*, 2:158.

24   "a woman who was a little interesting": HJ to WJ, February 8, 1876.

25   "that one might compare with her": HJ to AJ, February 22, 1876.

25   "messages from mysterious regions": *Literary Criticism*, 1:974.

25   "see all round him intellectually": HJ to HJ sr., April 11, 1876.

26   "the Empire's legacy to France": *Parisian Sketches*, 9.

26 "to any such tune again": *Notes of a Son and Brother*, in *Autobiography*, 273–74.

27 "generally in evening costume": *Paris and Northern France*, 35.

28 "not elsewhere to be matched": *Parisian Sketches*, 66.

29 "individual bodies are pitifully real": *Parisian Sketches*, 20.

30 "brandishing her sword and heroically screaming": *Parisian Sketches*, 138.

30 "dreaming about his future": *Parisian Sketches*, 140.

31 "the sophistications of satiety": *Parisian Sketches*, 131.

32 "a melancholy collection": *Parisian Sketches*, 166.

32 "the sudden trill of the nightingale": HJ, *The American Scene*, ed. John F. Sears (London and New York: Penguin, 1994), 37.

32 "in a manner of speaking, after the same thing": Virginia Woolf, *Roger Fry: A Biography* (London: Hogarth Press, 1940), 180.

32 "(from the Italian point of view exotic) music of Aïda": *Parisian Sketches*, 175.

33 "she herself sings very little": HJ to HJ sr., April 11, 1876.

33 "but the rest were in ecstasy": HJ to HJ sr., November 11, 1876.

34 "the 'romantic' movement of 1830": *Parisian Sketches*, 82.

34 "'making up as you go along'": *Parisian Sketches*, 183.

35 "they produce a limited amount of illusion": *Parisian Sketches*, 185.

35 "she has given us ideas upon them": *Literary Criticism*, 2:724.

35 "simply hideous": HJ to Thomas Sergeant Perry, May 2, 1876.

35 "to its brutal indecency": *Parisian Sketches*, 135.

36 "to make his novel last longer yet": HJ to William Dean Howells, May 28, 1876.

36 he, had as it were, figured in a Zola novel: see HJ, *A Small Boy and Others*, in *Autobiography*, 187–88.

37   "that deals with only half of life?": *Literary Criticism*, 2:869.

37   "but no one intimately": HJ to William Dean Howells, April 4, 1876.

37   "the great Paris harmony": preface to *The American*, in *Literary Criticism*, 2:1058.

38   "the Comédie Française are to recite and sing": HJ to HJ sr., May 29, 1876. Unpublished letter, used by permission of the Houghton Library, Harvard University, bMS Am 1094 (1836).

38   "a complete mastery of the French tongue": HJ to WJ, June 22, 1876.

38   "in the midst of this Parisian Babylon": HJ to WJ, April 25, 1876.

39   "drawings (awful) by Goethe": HJ to Mary Walsh James, May 8, 1876.

39   "(I. S. likes him extremely.)": HJ to AJ, May 24, 1876.

40   insists that James and Zhukovsky were lovers: see Sheldon Novick, *Henry James: The Young Master* (New York: Random House, 1996).

40   *"ma guarda e passa"*: *Complete Notebooks*, 216.

41   *"afin de prendre part au grand oeuvre"*: HJ to AJ, April 25, 1880. On Wagner's Bayreuth, and Zhukovsky's contributions, see: Frederic Spotts, *Bayreuth: A History of the Wagner Festival* (New Haven and London: Yale University Press, 1994); Geoffrey Skelton, *Wagner at Bayreuth: Experiment and Tradition* (Rev. ed., New York: Da Capo Press, 1983)

41   "to describe them would carry me too far": HJ to Grace Norton, April 9, 1880.

42   "sturdy, thickset, simple and proud": Cosima Wagner, *Diaries*, ed. Martin Gregor-Dellin and Dietrich Mack, trans. Geoffrey Skelton (New York and London: Harcourt Brace Jovanovich, 1980) 2:432.

42   "It is all illusion": Cosima Wagner, *Diaries* 2:631.

42   "the exclusive king with his Wagner opera": *The Sacred Fount*, ed. Leon Edel (New York: Grove Press, 1953), 296. Wagner himself in

fact conducted the *Parsifal* prelude in private performance for King Ludwig of Bavaria on November 10, 1880.

43   masturbation guilt: see Kim Townsend, *Manhood at Harvard* (New York: Norton, 1996), esp. 52–54.

43   "unprecedented and resounding noise": Edel, *Life* 5:267. Theodore Roosevelt reciprocated HJ's view of him: see Townsend, *Manhood at Harvard*, 149.

44   "called 'epistemophilia'": see Freud on the "epistemophilic instinct," in "Notes Upon a Case of Obsessional Neurosis," in *Standard Edition of the Complete Psychological Writings* (London: Hogarth Press, 1955), 10:245; see also "Leonardo da Vinci and a Memory of his Childhood," *Standard Edition* 11:96.

44   "a dirty fellow": Townsend, *Manhood at Harvard*, 66.

45   "magazine rather than newspaper work": Whitelaw Reid to HJ, August 10, 1876, in *Parisian Sketches*, 218.

45   "especially for the money!": HJ to Whitelaw Reid, August 20, 1876, in *Parisian Sketches*, 219.

45   "more remuneratively otherwise": HJ to HJ sr., September 16, 1876.

45   "appreciably scanted": *Parisian Sketches*, 204.

46   "turrets & winding staircases": HJ to Lizzie Boott, August 19, 1876. Unpublished letter, used by permission of the Houghton Library, Harvard University, bMS Am 1094 (521).

46   "pretty as a *décor d'opéra*": HJ to MWJ, August 24, 1876.

46   "part of the *espada*": HJ to HJ sr., September 16, 1876.

46   "so huge an organism": *Literary Criticism*, 2:1059–60.

46   "turning English all over": HJ to WJ, July 29, 1876.

47   "excites my extreme wonder": HJ to William Dean Howells, May 28, 1876.

47   "serious and honest": HJ to William Dean Howells, February 21, 1884.

48   "general Balzac tradition": *Literary Criticism*, 2:319.

48   "so systematic and so articulate": *Literary Criticism*, 2:881.

48   "to meet any other": *Literary Criticism*, 2:319–20.

48   "eternal outsider": *Complete Notebooks*, 217.

49   *"affreusement bornés"* ["frightfully narrow-minded"]: HJ to Thomas Sargent Perry, February 3, 1876.

49   "horrible monotony of the new quarters": *Complete Notebooks*, 216–17.

49   "a simple voice from within": *Complete Notebooks*, 217.

50   "fascination upon the senses": *Bradshaw's Illustrated Guide Through Paris and Its Environs* (London: W. J. Adams, 1875), 4.

50   "fountain in a marble basin": *Literary Criticism* 2:1055–56.

51   "educative, formative, fertilizing": A *Small Boy and Others*, in *Auto-biography*, 197.

51   "on and on and slowly spread": A *Small Boy and Others*, in *Autobi-ography*, 198.

51   "sparing me preparations": preface to *The Ambassadors*, in *Literary Criticism*, 2:1312.

51   "seemed all depth the next" *The Ambassadors*, ed. Christopher Butler (New York and Oxford: Oxford University Press, 1985), 63.

CHAPTER 2: THE DREAM OF AN INTENSER EXPERIENCE

54   must have $150 per installment: HJ to F. P. Church, March 3, 1876.

54   "mutilations and disfigurements": HJ, preface to *The Golden in Bowl*, in *Literary Criticism*, 2:1337.

54   "fond perception of this truth": HJ, preface to *The American*, in *Lit-erary Criticism*, 2:1057. Subsequent references to this preface will be given in parentheses in the text.

56   "a threatening cry in the stillness of the night": *The American*, ed. William Spengeman (London and New York: Penguin Books, 1986), 312. All of my references are to this edition, which is a

reprint of the first English edition of 1879, essentially the same as the first American book edition of 1877, but with some corrections (James never saw proof on the American edition, thus the English version is considered definitive for the early, prerevision version of the novel). Subsequent references appear in parentheses in the text.

58 "innocence outraged and generosity betrayed": *The Golden Bowl*, ed. Virginia Llewellyn Smith (Oxford: Oxford World Classics, 1983), 471.

59 "Flaubert . . . admirably paints the moral": HJ, "Gustave Flaubert" (1902), in *Literary Criticism*, 2:333.

59 "at least serious and honest": HJ to W. D. Howells, February 21, 1884.

60 "than as a success however explained": "Gustave Flaubert," in *Literary Criticism*, 2:316.

60 the "wasted heritage" of the novel: HJ, "The Lesson of Balzac," in *Literary Criticism*, 2:120.

60 "the novelist's novelist": "Gustave Flaubert," in *Literary Criticism*, 2:329.

61 "*the* great sign of the painter of the first order": "The Lesson of Balzac," in *Literary Criticism*, 2:131–33.

61 on Turgenev: see HJ, "Ivan Turgenev," in *Literary Criticism*, 2:1033.

61 "Père Goriot, a hateful book": HJ, "The Life of George Eliot," in *Literary Criticism*, 1:1002.

62 "'views' upon life that she tries to feel": HJ, "*Daniel Deronda*: A Conversation," in *Literary Criticism*, 1:986.

63 "comparatively meagre human consciousness": "Gustave Flaubert," in *Literary Criticism*, 2:337, 336.

64 "so with this we will, at any rate, begin": "Charles de Bernard and Gustave Flaubert," in *Literary Criticism*, 2:170.

64 On "going behind," see the preface to *The Awkward Age*, in *Literary Criticism*, 2:1131, and my discussion of *The Tragic Muse* in the next

chapter. On the "penetrating imagination," see the preface to *The Princess Casamassima*, in *Literary Criticism*, 2:1102. For a study of Balzac's probing behind, his constant effort to discover the drama hidden behind facades and faces, see chapter 5 of Peter Brooks, *The Melodramatic Imagination* (New Haven: Yale University Press, 1976; rep. 1995).

66   "a 'case' in the most striking way": see "Guy de Maupassant," in *Literary Criticism*, 2:524.

66   "a case"; "imitation of observation": see "Emile Zola," in *Literary Criticism*, 2:871, 895.

67   "miss the mark": "Honoré de Balzac" (1875), in *Literary Criticism*, 2:64.

67   "able to put forth": "Honoré de Balzac" (1902), in *Literary Criticism*, 2:113.

68   "transparent screen": see Zola, "Lettre à Antony Valabrègue," August 18, 1864, in *Correspondance* (Paris: Editions du CNRS, 1978), 1:375–76.

69   "sink rather than sail": "Ivan Turgenev," in *Literary Criticism*, 2:1024.

74   as bad as they appear: On Newman as a "reader" of social codes, see chap. 2 of William W. Stowe, *Balzac, James, and the Realistic Novel* (Princeton: Princeton University Press, 1983). On the conflict of freedom and unfreedom in the novel, see chap. 2 of Richard Poirier, *The Comic Sense of Henry James* (London: Chatto and Windus, 1960).

74   "a sharp, fantastic crisis . . .": *The Ambassadors*, ed. Christopher Butler (Oxford: Oxford World Classics, 1985), 390.

74   "Venice all of evil": *The Wings of the Dove*, ed. Peter Brooks (Oxford: Oxford World Classics, 1984), 403.

76   "enjoy his advantage": preface to *The American*, in *Literary Criticism*, 2:1054–55.

77   "identification of a pirate": preface to *Portrait of a Lady*, in *Literary Criticism*, 2:1084.

CHAPTER 3: WHAT A DROLL THING TO REPRESENT

79 he took no sexual interest in her: Leon Edel, who first documented James's close friendship with Woolson, discusses it at length in *Henry James*; Colm Tóibín offers a fictionalized version in *The Master: A Novel* (New York: Scribner, 2004).

80 "don't do the British matron!": HJ, *The Tragic Muse*, ed. Philip Horne (London and New York: Penguin Books, 1995), 22. Subsequent references to this work will appear in the text.

84 "the production of an ill-made play": HJ, "The London Theatres," in HJ, *The Scenic Art: Notes on Acting and the Drama, 1872–1901*, ed. Allan Wade (New Brunswick: Rutgers University Press, 1948), 108.

85 "almost anywhere than at the theatre": "The London Theatres," in *The Scenic Art*, 101.

85 "moral timidity": HJ, "The Art of Fiction," in *Literary Criticism*, 1:63.

85 "the great relation between men and women": HJ, "The Future of the Novel," in *Literary Criticism*, 1:107.

88 "negative capability": see John Keats to Richard Woodhouse, October 27, 1818, in *English Romantic Writers*, ed. David Perkins (New York: Harcourt, Brace and World, 1967), 1219–20.

88 Diderot: see Denis Diderot, "Paradox of the Actor," in *Selected Writings on Art and Literature*, trans. and ed. Geoffrey Bremner (New York and London: Penguin, 1994).

89 Rousseau: see "Letter to M. d'Alembert on the Theatre," in *Collected Writings of Rousseau*, ed. Roger D. Masters and Christopher Kelly (Hanover and London: University Press of New England, 2004), 251–352.

93 Milly Theale's "pink dawn of an apotheosis: see *The Wings of the Dove*, ed. Peter Brooks (Oxford: Oxford World Classics, 1984), 157.

94 "my only salvation": HJ, *Complete Notebooks*, 167.

94 "theatre for the second half": preface to *The Tragic Muse*, in *Literary Criticism*, 2:1109–10.

94   "as the novel may permit itself ": preface to *The Tragic Muse*, in *Literary Criticism*, 2:1112.

94   "I never 'go behind' Miriam": preface to *The Tragic Muse*, in *Literary Criticism*, 2:1113.

96   "its fullest worth in the Scene": preface to *The Wings of the Dove*, in *Literary Criticism*, 2:1297–98.

97   " intensification of interest": preface to *The Golden Bowl*, in *Literary Criticism*, 2:1322.

97   "only a relation to painting": *Painter's Eye*, 143.

98   "a poem or a piece of music is": *Painter's Eye*, 185.

98   "romantic to the imagination": "The Théâtre Français," in *Scenic Art*, 73–74.

98   "superior to the thing itself ": *Literary Criticism*, 2:340.

CHAPTER 4: FLAUBERT'S NERDS

102   "Honor will be preserved, but nothing else": Gustave Flaubert to Léonie Brainne, October 2, 1875. Unless otherwise specified, all excerpts from letters are taken from Gustave Flaubert, *Correspondance*, ed. Jean Bruneau (Paris: Bibliothèque de la Pléiade, 1980–98). Currently in four volumes, volume 5 (which picks up in 1876) is expected soon. For letters from 1876 to Flaubert's death in 1880, see Flaubert, *Oeuvres complètes* (Paris: Club de l'Honnête Homme, 1971–75): vols. 12–16 contain the correspondence. Translations here and elsewhere are my own. There is a good English selection in two volumes: *The Letters of Gustave Flaubert*, trans. and ed. Francis Steegmuller (Cambridge, Mass.: Harvard University Press, 1980)

103   "kind of encyclopaedia of modern Stupidity": GF to Adèle Perrot, October 17, 1872.

103   "That's what really frightens me . . .": GF to Ivan Turgenev, July 29, 1874.

104   "strange work": GF to Louis Bouilhet, September 4, 1850.

104 "everything generally approved": GF to Louise Colet, December 16, 1852.

104 "something perverse and puerile done for a wager": HJ, "Correspondance de Gustave Flaubert," in *Literary Criticism*, 2:306.

104 "the comprehensive *bêtise*, of mankind": *Literary Criticism*, 2:300.

105 to sit by chance on the same bench: GF, *Bouvard et Pécuchet*, ed. Stéphanie Dord-Crouslé (Paris: Garnier/Flammarion , 1999), 47. My references are to this edition; translations are mine. The latest English version is: *Bouvard and Pécuchet*, trans. Mark Polizzotti (Normal, Ill.: Dalkey Archive Press, 2005), 3. For the reader's convenience, I will give references to the French in ( ), to the Polizzotti translation in [ ].

107 their absurdity becomes apparent: on Flaubert's "stupidity," see Jonathan Culler, *Flaubert: the Uses of Uncertainty* (Ithaca: Cornell University Press, 1974).

108 "Voice of Science": see Roland Barthes, *S/Z*, trans. Richard Miller (New York: Hill and Wang, 1974), 205–6.

116 "a mass of citations without order": Guy de Maupassant to Caroline Commanville, July 30, 1881.

116 "completely done" and ready to go into the second volume: letter of April 1879, cited by Dord-Crouslé in her introduction to *Bouvard et Pécuchet*, 24.

116 at the head of the *Dictionnaire*: all citations from the *Dictionnaire des idées reçues* are taken from the Garnier/Flammarion edition of *Bouvard et Pécuchet*, 404 ff.

120 to recover its "wasted heritage": see HJ, "The Lesson of Balzac," in *Literary Criticism*, 2:120.

120 "present everywhere and visible nowhere": GF to Louise Colet, December 9, 1852.

121 "the moral and useful meaning of one's work": George Sand to GF, January 12, 1876.

121 "wholly serious and sad": GF to Edma Roger des Genettes, June 19, 1876.

121   "the deepest imaginative hue": HJ, "Gustave Flaubert," in *Literary Criticism*, 2:321.

122   "touching, loving, a little masterpiece": "The Art of Fiction," in *Literary Criticism*, 1:57.

123   "the tranquillity of the church": GF, *Un Coeur simple*, in *Trois Contes* (Paris: Garnier, 1956), 26; translations are my own. For a decent English version, see *Three Tales*, trans. Robert Baldick, (London and New York: Penguin, 1961), 30. Again, French page numbers are given in ( ), references to the Baldick translation in [ ].

124   stuffed parrot from the Rouen museum: for the most entertaining account of this episode, see Julian Barnes, *Flaubert's Parrrot* (London: Jonathan Cape, 1984).

127   "shows in him but ill": *Literary Criticism*, 2:338.

127   "the excellence of his soul was slow in coming": GF, *L'Education sentimentale* (Paris: Garnier/Flammarion, 1969), 48; in English: *Sentimental Education*, trans. Robert Baldick, rev. by Geoffrey Wall (London and New York: Penguin, 2004), 6.

128   "so handsomely paid for it": *Literary Criticism*, 2:332.

128   no evidence that Flaubert paid any attention: a search of Flaubert's correspondence does not find any mention of the young American novelist who came to call in 1875.

CHAPTER 5: THE QUICKENED NOTATION OF OUR MODERNITY

129   "to stare and to try to recollect": HJ, *Harper's Weekly*, August 21, 1897; repr. as "London Notes" in *Notes on Novelists* (1914), in *Literary Criticism*, 1:1407.

129   "to give and the other to gain": HJ, *Literary Criticism*, 1:1408.

130   "Un héros intellectuel," Bourget called Flaubert: see *Studies in European Literature, being the Taylorian Lectures, 1889–1899* (Oxford: Clarendon, 1900), 274.

133   "a divine little light to walk by": HJ, *Complete Notebooks*, 261.

134   of Joyce, of Woolf, of Proust: see Edel, *Life*, 4:15.

135 "down two floors to the-paving stones": HJ, *What Maisie Knew* (London and New York: Penguin, 1985), 190.

140 knowledge about sex: see the essay by Barbara Johnson on the similar problem faced by Arnolphe in Molière's *School for Wives*: "Teaching Ignorance," *Yale French Studies* 63 (1982): 165–82.

140 "what then on earth was I?": HJ, *The Turn of the Screw*, in *The Turn of the Screw and The Aspern Papers* (London: Penguin, 1986), 260.

142 "in the heart of man": HJ, *The Golden Bowl*, ed. Virginia Llewellyn Smith (London and New York: Oxford, 1999), 553.

143 "the loser's knowledge of the robber": Edgar Allan Poe, "The Purloined Letter," in *The Complete Tales and Poems of Edgar Allan Poe* (New York: Vintage, 1975), 209.

144 "the small expanding consciousness": HJ, preface to *What Maisie Knew* [and *The Pupil* and *In the Cage*], in *Literary Criticism*, 2: 1157.

144 "their scant unredeemed importances—namely *appreciable*": *Literary Criticism*, 2:1162–63.

147 "his subject may cast up": *Literary Criticism*, 2:1169–70.

147 "my *only* salvation": HJ, *Complete Notebooks*, 167.

148 his first amanuensis, William MacAlpine: *Complete Notebooks*, 407.

149 "after the same thing": Woolf, *Roger Fry: A Biography* (London: Hogarth Press, 1940), 180.

149 "they have only a relation to painting": HJ, *The Painter's Eye*, 143.

149 "just as a poem or a piece of music is": HJ, *The Painter's Eye*, 143.

150 by a skeptical intelligence: on the interpretive controversies elicited by *The Turn of the Screw*, see the material collected in *The Turn of the Screw*, ed. Deborah Esch and Jonathan Warren (New York: Norton, 1999).

151 "it demanded and consumed": HJ, *In the Cage*, in *Selected Tales*, ed. John Lyon (New York, Penguin, 2001), 322.

151 "gaps and blanks and absent answers": HJ, *Selected Tales*, 369. For a

more extended discussion of this novella, see Peter Brooks, *Realist Vision* (New Haven: Yale University Press, 2005), 180–97.

153 "the sounded void of his life": HJ, *The Beast in the Jungle*, in *Selected Tales*, 460.

153 "he flung himself, face down, on the tomb": HJ, *Selected Tales*, 460–61.

154 lends itself fully to this kind of reading: see especially Eve Kosofsky Sedgwick, "The Beast in the Closet: Henry James and the Writing of Homosexual Panic," in *The Epistemology of the Closet* (Berkeley: University of California Press, 1990), 182–212.

154 *Wisstrieb*: see Sigmund Freud on "the epistemophilic instinct" in "Notes on a Case of Obsessional Neurosis," in *Standard Edition*, 10:245.

CHAPTER 6: THE DEATH OF ZOLA, SEX IN THE FRENCH
NOVEL, AND THE IMPROPER

156 a deathbed confession: the confession came from a stove-fitter in 1927, and was reported by a friend of his to the newspaper *Libération* in 1953; it can probably never be confirmed or disconfirmed. See Frederick Brown, *Zola: A Life* (New York: Farrar Straus Giroux, 1995), 792–93.

156 "a moment in the history of human conscience": see Brown, *Zola: A Life*, 796.

157 "inflamed Academician": see Edel, *Life*, 5: 341—Academician, because Bourget had been elected to the Académie Française.

157 "really a hero": HJ to Henry Brewster, February 11, 1898.

157 "made and stamped and left him": HJ, "Emile Zola," in *Literary Criticism*, 2:874.

158 "Lourdes, Paris, Rome," came Zola's reply: *Literary Criticism*, 2:886.

159 "*imitation* of observation that we possess": *Literary Criticism*, 2:893.

159 "experience by imitation": *Literary Criticism*, 2:896.

159   "representation imitated": *Literary Criticism*, 2:130.

160   "the New York inspiration": HJ, *The American Scene*, ed. John F. Sears (New York: Penguin, 1994), 64.

161   "a bad thing for the novel itself": *Literary Criticism*, 2:869.

161   "a kind of technical intrepidity": *Literary Criticism*, 2:889.

161   "Zola's mastery resides": *Literary Criticism*, 2:894.

163   "the dreams of an ambitious hairdresser": *Literary Criticism*, 2:65.

163   "this particular helplessness of immersion": *Literary Criticism*, 2:113.

163   "realistic to the eye and romantic to the imagination": *Scenic Art*, 73–74.

164   "the natural food of novelists": *Literary Criticism*, 2:110.

164   "the long rope, for acting herself out": *Literary Criticism*, 2:131.

164   "not by knowing that he loved": *Literary Criticism*, 2:131–32.

165   to sample English womanhood: see Edel, *Life*, 3:173.

165   "no exaggeration is possible": *Literary Criticism*, 2:528.

166   "mystifying to the moralist": *Literary Criticism*, 2:529.

166   "a perfectly dead wall": *Literary Criticism*, 2:531.

166   "governs conduct and produces character": *Literary Criticism*, 2:547.

166   "he reacts against his weaknesses, his defeats": *Literary Criticism*, 2:548.

167   "if it be sufficiently general": *Literary Criticism*, 2:549.

167   "without petticoats and trousers": *Literary Criticism*, 2:530.

168   "the third and the fourth lovers": *Literary Criticism*, 1:120.

168   "other obsessions than the sole sexual": *Literary Criticism*, 1:121.

169   bring the full weight of his damning analysis to bear: see Edith Wharton, *A Backward Glance* (New York: D. Appleton-Century, 1934), 181–84.

170   "these persons aren't married": HJ to Paul Bourget, February 23, 1888. Translation from James's French is my own.

170   "to exasperate you in what I write": Paul Bourget to HJ, March 7, 1888. Unpublished letter, used by permission of the Houghton Library, Harvard University, bMS Am 1094 (60). Translation from Bourget's French is my own.

171   "give them *rapport* and sense": HJ to Edith Wharton, March 13, 1912.

172   "Bottom to Bottom, however sublime": HJ to Hendrik Andersen, November 25, 1906. See, in addition to letters in the Edel selection, this and others collected in HJ, *Beloved Boy: Letters to Hendrik C. Andersen, 1899–1915*, ed. Rosella Mamoli Zorzi, introduction by Millicent Bell, afterword by Elena di Majo (Charlottesville and London: University of Virginia Press, 2004).

172   "to have a good deal more": HJ to Hendrik Andersen, July 20, 1906.

173   "from your tenderest HJ": HJ to Hendrik Andersen, October 18, 1906.

173   "a joyish sense of childish defilement": Hugh Stevens, *Henry James and Sexuality* (Cambridge and New York: Cambridge, 1998), 122.

173   modern concept of the homosexual: see Michel Foucault, *The History of Sexuality*, trans. Robert Hurley (New York: Random House, 1978), 1:42–43. Work that has been done in the wake of Foucault's argument includes: David M. Halperin. *One Hundred Years of Sexuality* (New York: Routledge, 1990), 15–40; Ed Cohen, *Talk on the Wilde side : Towards a Genealogy of a Discourse on Male Sexualities* (New York: Routledge, 1993); Jonathan Ned Katz, *The Invention of Heterosexuality* (New York: Dutton, 1995), especially 51–54.

175   speech enunciated in the novel by Strether to Little Bilham: see *Complete Notebooks*, 141.

175   "possibilities I didn't *embrace*": HJ to Hugh Walpole, August 21, 1913, in *Dearly Beloved Friends: Henry James's Letters to Younger Men*, ed. Susan E. Gunter and Steven H. Jobe (Ann Arbor: University of Michigan Press, 2001).

CHAPTER 7: FOR THE SAKE OF THIS END

178   "no Oxford, nor Eton, nor Harrow . . .": HJ, *Nathaniel Hawthorne* (London: Macmillan, 1879), in *Literary Criticism*, 1:351–52.

179   "vainer brother is already in the Academy": see R.W.B. Lewis, *The Jameses* (New York: Farrar Straus Giroux, 1991), 547. William's correspondence regarding the Academy is in the archives of the Academy of Arts and Letters, New York, N.Y.

179   "to embark on a 'fourth manner.'": WJ to HJ, October 22, 1905.

180   "sooner descend to a dishonored grave than have written": HJ to WJ, November 23, 1905.

181   "daughter all intensely American": *Complete Notebooks*, 75.

181   "our love and joy and sympathy": HJ, *The Golden Bowl*, ed. Virginia Llewellyn Smith (London and New York: Oxford World Classics, 1999), 170. All subsequent references are to this edition, which is a reprint of the first English edition of 1905, and appear in parentheses in the text.

183   "the consciousness of but two of the characters": HJ, preface to *The Golden Bowl*, in *Literary Criticism*, 2:1323.

183   dismisses it as "superficial": *Literary Criticism*, 2:1324.

185   see *The Ambassadors*, see *The Wings of the Dove*: see the famous lines of Strether to Little Bilham in *The Ambassadors*: "Live all you can, it's a mistake not to" (Oxford: Oxford World Classics, 1985), 153; in *The Wings of the Dove*, it's the doctor, Sir Luke Strett, who urges Milly Theale to live, an admonition that includes "gentlemen" (Oxford: Oxford World Classics, 1984), 309.

191   "chatters with his finger-tips; betrayal oozes out of him at every pore": see Sigmund Freud, *Fragment of the Analysis of a Case of Hysteria* ["Dora"], in *Standard Edition*, 7:77–78.

200   "oblique view of my presented action": *Literary Criticism*, 2:1322.

201   "majesty of irresponsible 'authorship'": *Literary Criticism*, 2:1323.

201   "highly susceptible of registration": *Literary Criticism*, 2:1323.

202 "unworthy of it": *Literary Criticism*, 2:1337.

202 "brief remainder of these remarks": *Literary Criticism*, 2:1336.

203 " 'in the conditions of life' ": *Literary Criticism*, 2:1339.

203 the great exposition of performative language: see J.L. Austin, *How to Do Things with Words* (Cambridge, Mass.: Harvard University Press, 1962).

EPILOGUE: CHARIOT OF FIRE

205 "the look of a field less occupied": HJ, *Literary Criticism*, 1:119.

205 "the lap, of the Faubourg St. Germain": HJ to Jessie Allen, March 28, 1907.

206 "deep-cushioned fortune": HJ to Edith Wharton, October 4, 1907. For the James-Wharton correspondence, see *Henry James and Edith Wharton: Letters, 1900–1915*, ed. Lyall H. Powers (New York: Scribner, 1990).

206 "the romance of travel": Edith Wharton, *A Motor Flight Through France* (New York: Charles Scribner's Sons, 1908), 1.

206 "raised to the 100th power": HJ to Howard Sturgis, April 13, 1907.

207 "the neighbouring woods sprang back to reveal": Marcel Proust, *In Search of Lost Time*, trans. C. K. Scott Moncrieff, and Terence Kilmartin, rev. by D.J. Enright (New York: Modern Library, 2003), 4:538.

208 "feeling appealed to and attested": HJ, *Complete Stories, 1898–1910*, ed. Denis Donoghue (New York: Library of America, 1996), 752.

208 "the inverately glorious grub!": HJ to George and Fanny Prothero, April 13, 1907.

208 "the monstrous process and machine": HJ to Jessie Allen, March 28, 1907.

208 "enlightened & explained to together": HJ to Edith Wharton, July 2, 1906.

209 "in which indeed, my dear, did she *not?*": Edith Wharton, *A Backward Glance* (New York: D. Appleton-Century, 1934), 308.

209 "herself (& *so* many other persons!) at home": HJ to Edith Wharton, March 13, 1912.

210 "that genius at that intensity is infallible": HJ, "France," in *Within the Rim and Other Essays, 1914–1915* (London: W. Collins, 1918), 89–91.

210 "I shall accomplish with the pen": anecdote recounted by Balzac's publisher, Edmond Werdet, in *Portrait Intime de Balzac* (Paris: Dentu, 1859), 331; see Graham Robb, *Balzac* (New York: Norton, 1994), 142.

Bibliography

By Henry James

(For novels discussed, I have generally used
readily available paperback editions.)

The Ambassadors, ed. Harry Levin. London: Penguin, 1986.

The American, ed. William Spengeman. New York: Penguin, 1986.

The American Scene, ed. John F. Sears. London: Penguin, 1994.

Autobiography (*A Small Boy and Others* [1913], *Notes of a Son and Brother* [1914], *The Middle Years* [1917]), ed. Frederick W. Dupee. New York: Criterion Books, 1956.

Beloved Boy: Letters to Hendrik C. Andersen, 1899–1915, ed. Rosella Mamoli Zorzi, introduction by Millicent Bell, afterword by Elena di Majo. Charlottesville and London: University of Virginia Press, 2004.

Collected Travel Writings, ed. Richard Howard. New York: Library of America, 1993.

The Complete Notebooks of Henry James, ed. Leon Edel and Lyall H. Powers. New York and Oxford: Oxford University Press, 1987.

Complete Stories. 4 vols. New York: Library of America, 1996–99.

Dearly Beloved Friends: Henry James's Letters to Younger Men, ed. Susan E. Gunter and Steven H. Jobe. Ann Arbor: University of Michigan Press, 2001.

The Golden Bowl, ed. Virginia Llwellyn Smith. Oxford: Oxford World Classics, 1983.

Henry James: A Life in Letters, ed. Philip Horne. New York: Viking, 1999.

Henry James and Edith Wharton: Letters, 1900–1915, ed. Lyall H. Powers. New York: Scribner, 1990

Letters, ed. Leon Edel. 4 vols. Cambridge, Mass.: Harvard University Press, 1974–84.

The Letters of Henry James, ed. Percy Lubbock. 2 vols. New York: Charles Scribner's Sons, 1920.

Literary Criticism, ed. Leon Edel. 2 vols.: 1. *Essays on Literature, American Writers, English Writers*; 2. *French Writers, Other European*

Writers, The Prefaces to the New York Edition. New York: Library of America, 1984.

The Novels and Tales of Henry James ("The New York Edition"). New York: Charles Scribner's Sons, 1907–17.

The Painter's Eye: Notes and Essays on the Pictorial Arts, ed. John L. Sweeney. Cambridge, Mass.: Harvard University Press, 1956.

Parisian Sketches: Letters to the New York Tribune, 1875–76, ed. Leon Edel and Ilse Dusoir Lind. New York: New York University Press, 1957.

The Sacred Fount, ed. Leon Edel. New York: Grove Press, 1953.

The Scenic Art: Notes on Acting & the Drama, 1872–1901, ed. Allan Wade. New Brunswick: Rutgers University Press, 1948.

Selected Tales, ed. John Lyon. New York, Penguin, 2001.

The Tragic Muse, ed. Philip Horne. London and New York: Penguin, 1995.

The Turn of the Screw and The Aspern Papers, ed. Anthony Curtis. London: Penguin, 1986.

What Maisie Knew. ed. Paul Theroux and Patricia Crick. London and New York: Penguin, 1985.

The Wings of the Dove, ed. Peter Brooks. Oxford: Oxford World Classics, 1984.

Within the Rim and Other Essays, 1914–15. London: W. Collins, 1918.

Other Sources

Theodora Bosanquet, *Henry James at Work*. London: Hogarth Press, 1924.

The Correspondence of William James, vol 1: *William and Henry, 1861–84*, ed. Ignas K. Skupskelis and Elizabeth M. Berkeley. Charlottesville and London: University Press of Virginia, 1992.

Edgar A. Harden, *A Henry James Chronology*. Basingstoke: Palgrave Macmillan, 2005.

William James, *Essays, Comments, and Reviews*. Cambridge, Mass.: Harvard University Press, 1987.

The Legend of the Master, ed. Simon Nowell-Smith. New York: Charles Scribner's Sons, 1948.

R.W.B. Lewis, *The Jameses: A Family Narrative*. New York: Farrar, Straus and Giroux, 1991.

F. O. Matthiessen, *The James Family: A Group Biography*. New York: Alfred A. Knopf, 1947; rpt. Vintage, 1980.

BIOGRAPHIES

Leon Edel, *The Life of Henry James*. 5 vols. New York: Lippincott, 1953; rpt. Avon Books, 1978.

Fred Kaplan, *Henry James: The Imagination of Genius, A Biography*. New York: William Morrow, 1992.

Sheldon M. Novick, *Henry James: The Young Master*. New York: Random House, 1996.

ON JAMES

F. W. Dupee, *Henry James*. 1951; rpt. Garden City: Anchor Books, 1965.

Edwin Sill Fussell, *The French Side of Henry James*. New York: Columbia University Press, 1990.

Philip Grover, *Henry James and the French Novel: A Study in Inspiration*. New York: Barnes and Noble, 1973.

Lawrence B. Holland, *The Expense of Vision*. Princeton: Princeton University Press, 1964.

F. O. Matthiessen, *Henry James: The Major Phase*. New York: Oxford University Press, 1944.

Mona Ozouf, *La Muse démocratique. Henry James ou les pouvoirs du roman*. Paris: Calmann-Lévy, 1998.

Richard Poirier, *The Comic Sense of Henry James*. London: Chatto and Windus, 1960.

Adrian Poole, "Introduction," *The American*. New York and Oxford: Oxford University Press, 1999, xxi–xxii.

John Carlos Rowe, *The Other Henry James*. Durham and London: Duke University Press, 1998.

Eve Kosofsky Sedgwick, "The Beast in the Closet: Henry James and the Writing of Homosexual Panic," in *The Epistemology of the Closet*. Berkeley: University of California Press, 1990, 182–212.

Hugh Stevens, *Henry James and Sexuality*. Cambridge: Cambridge University Press, 1998.

William W. Stowe, *Balzac, James, and the Realistic Novel*. Princeton: Princeton University Press. 1983.

Adeline R. Tintner, *The Museum World of Henry James*. Ann Arbor: University of Michigan Research Press, 1986.

Colm Tóibín, *The Master: A Novel*. New York: Scribner, 2004.

Viola Hopkins Winner, *Henry James and the Visual Arts*. Charlottesville and London: University Press of Virginia, 1970.

Pierre A. Walker, *Reading Henry James in French Cultural Contexts*. DeKalb: Northern Illinois University Press, 1995.

Ruth B. Yeazell, *Language and Knowledge in the Late Henry James*. Chicago: University of Chicago Press, 1976.

ON PARIS AND FRENCH HISTORY

Bradshaw's Illustrated Guide Through Paris and Its Environs. London: W. J. Adams, 1875.

D. W. Brogan, *The French Nation, from Napoleon to Pétain*. New York: Harper and Brothers, 1957.

T. J. Clark, *The Painting of Modern Life: Paris in the Art of Manet and His Followers*. New York: Alfred A. Knopf, 1984.

William Fortescue, *The Third Republic in France, 1870–1940*. London and New York: Routledge, 2000.

Jérôme Grondeux, *La France entre en République, 1870–1893*. Paris: Livre de Poche "références," 2000.

Robert L. Herbert, *Impressionism: Art, Leisure, and Parisian Society*. New Haven and London: Yale University Press, 1988.

Ross King, *The Judgment of Paris*. New York: Walker and Co., 2006.

Jean-Marie Mayeur, *Les Débuts de la IIIe République, 1891–1898*. (Nouvelle Histoire de la France Contemporaine, vol. 10) Paris: Editions du Seuil, 1973.

Philip Nord, *The Republican Moment*. Cambridge, Mass.: Harvard University Press, 1995)

Philip Nord, *Impressionists and Politics: Art and Democracy in the Nineteenth Century*. London and New York: Routledge, 2000.

Paris and Northern France. Coblenz: Karl Baedeker, 1872.

Theodore Zeldin, *France, 1848–1945*. 3 vols. Oxford: Clarendon, 1973–79.

OTHER WRITERS AND ISSUES

J. L. Austin, *How to Do Things with Words*. Cambridge, Mass.: Harvard University Press, 1962.

Julian Barnes, *Flaubert's Parrot*. London: Jonathan Cape, 1984.

Roland Barthes, *S/Z*, trans. Richard Miller. New York: Hill and Wang, 1974.

Albert Béguin, *Balzac visionnaire*. Geneva: Skira, 1946.

Paul Bourget, *Mensonges*. Paris: Alphonse Lemerre, 1887.

———. *Le Disciple*. 1889. Paris: La Table Ronde, 1994.

Joseph Brent, *Charles Sanders Peirce: A Life*. Bloomington: Indiana University Press, 1993.

Victor Brombert, *The Novels of Flaubert*. Princeton: Princeton University Press, 1966.

Peter Brooks, *The Melodramatic Imagination*. New Haven: Yale University Press, 1976; rpt. 1995.

———. *Realist Vision*. New Haven: Yale University Press, 2005.

Frederick Brown, *Flaubert: A Biography*. Boston: Little, Brown, 2006.

———. *Zola: A Life*. New York: Farrar Straus Giroux, 1995.

Ed Cohen, *Talk on the Wilde Side*. New York: Routledge, 1993.

Philip Conisbee and Denis Coutagne, *Cézanne in Provence*. New Haven and London: Yale University Press, 2006.

Jonathan Culler, *Flaubert: the Uses of Uncertainty*. Ithaca: Cornell University Press, 1974.

Raymonde Debray-Genette, ed. *Flaubert*. Paris: Firmin-Didot, 1970.

Denis Diderot, "Paradox of the Actor," in *Selected Writings on Art and Literature*, trans. and ed. Geoffrey Bremner. New York and London: Penguin, 1994.

English Romantic Writers, ed. David Perkins. New York: Harcourt, Brace and World, 1967.

Gustave Flaubert, *Bouvard et Pécuchet*, ed. Stéphanie Dord-Crouslé. Paris: Garnier/Flammarion, 1999.

———. *Bouvard and Pécuchet*, trans. Mark Polizzotti. Normal, Ill.: Dalkey Archive Press, 2005.

———. *Correspondance*, ed. Jean Bruneau. 4 vols. Paris: Bibliothèque de la Pléiade, 1980–98.

———. *The Letters of Gustave Flaubert*, trans. and ed. Francis Steegmuller. Cambridge, Mass.: Harvard University Press, 1980.

———. *L'Education sentimentale*. Paris: Garnier/Flammarion, 1969.

———. *Oeuvres complètes* 16 vols. Paris: Club de l'Honnête Homme, 1971–75.

———. *Sentimental Education*, trans. Robert Baldick, rev. by Geoffrey Wall. London and New York: Penguin, 2004.

Michel Foucault, *The History of Sexuality*, vol. 1, trans. Robert Hurley. New York: Random House, 1978.

Sigmund Freud, *Standard Edition of the Complete Psychological Works*, ed. James Strachey. vols. 7 and 10. London: Hogarth Press, 1955, 1964.

David M. Halperin, *One Hundred Years of Homosexuality*. New York: Routledge, 1990.

Jonathan Ned Katz, *The Invention of Heterosexuality*. New York: Dutton, 1995.

Barbara Johnson, "Teaching Ignorance," *Yale French Studies* 63 (1982): 165–82.

R.W.B. Lewis, *Edith Wharton: A Biography*. New York: Harper and Row, 1975.

Louis Menand, *The Metaphysical Club*. New York: Farrar, Straus and Giroux, 2001.

Jacques Neefs and Claude Mouchard, *Flaubert*. Paris: Balland, 1986.

Edgar Allan Poe, "The Purloined Letter," in *The Complete Tales and Poems of Edgar Allan Poe*. New York: Vintage, 1975.

Marcel Proust, *In Search of Lost Time*, trans. C. K. Scott Moncrieff and Terence Kilmartin, rev. by D. J. Enright. New York: Modern Library, 2003.

Graham Robb, *Balzac*. New York: Norton, 1994.

———. *Strangers: Homosexual Love in the Nineteenth Century*. London: Picador, 2003.

Jean-Jacques Rousseau, "Letter to M. d'Alembert on the Theatre," in *Collected Writings of Rousseau*, ed. Roger D. Masters and Christopher Kelly. Hanover and London: University Press of New England, 2004.

Richard Shone, *The Art of Bloomsbury: Roger Fry, Vanessa Bell and Duncan Grant*. London: Tate Gallery Publishing, 1999.

Geoffrey Skelton, *Wagner at Bayreuth: Experiment and Tradition*. Rev. ed. New York: Da Capo Press, 1983.

Frederic Spotts, *Bayreuth: A History of the Wagner Festival*. New Haven and London: Yale University Press, 1994.

Studies in European Literature, being the Taylorian Lectures, 1889–1899. Oxford: Clarendon, 1900.

Kim Townsend, *Manhood at Harvard*. New York: Norton, 1996.

Ivan Turgenev, *Fathers and Sons*, trans. Richard Freeborn. Oxford: Oxford World Classics, 1991.

———. *Spring Torrents*, trans. Leonard Schaprio. London: Penguin Books, 1972.

———. *Virgin Soil*, trans. Constance Garnett. New York: New York Review of Books, 2000.

Geoffrey Wall, *Flaubert: A Life*. London: Faber and Faber, 2001.

Cosima Wagner, *Diaries*, vol. 2 (1878–83), ed. Martin Gregor-Dellin and Dietrich Mack, trans. Geoffrey Skelton. New York and London: Harcourt Brace Jovanovich, 1980.

Edmond Werdet, *Portrait Intime de Balzac*. Paris: Dentu, 1859.

Edith Wharton, *A Backward Glance*. New York: D. Appleton-Century, 1934.

———. *A Motor-Flight Through France*. New York: Charles Scribner's Sons, 1908.

Virginia Woolf, *Roger Fry: A Biography*. London: Hogarth Press, 1940.

Emile Zola, *L'Assommoir*. Paris: Gallimard/Folio, 1978.

———. *La Débâcle*. Paris: Gallimard/Folio, 1995.

———. *Son Excellence Eugène Rougon*. Paris: Gallimard/Folio, 1982.

Acknowledgments

I began working on this book during a year at Oxford in 2001–02, but its subject has been of interest for decades. In fact, James and French literature was the concern of my undergraduate senior thesis, written from much ignorance but with the encouragement and guidance of Richard Poirier. Since that time, I have come back to James often, sometimes in response to specific occasions: the request for an essay on *The American* by Martha Banta many years ago, and the invitation from Virginia Llewllyn Smith to edit the Oxford World Classics edition of *The Wings of the Dove*. My year in Oxford gave me a chance to teach Flaubert alongside a true Flaubertian, Adrienne Tooke, as well as conversation with Terence Cave, Malcolm Bowie, and Ann Jefferson. I was aided along the way by helpful librarians at the Bodleian, Oxford, Alderman Library at the University of Virginia—special thanks to Bryson Clevenger—and Houghton Library, Harvard, where Leslie Morris and Susan Halpert were of the utmost help. Thanks are owing also to many students over the years with whom I have discussed James, in the classroom and outside it. Among them special thanks are due to William Stowe, Susan Winnett, D. A. Miller, and Lina Steiner for the intensity of their response to James. Other friends and colleagues have responded to calls for help and conversation: Jacques Neefs, Yvan Leclerc, Michael Holquist, Leah Price, Max Byrd, and Marie-Claude de Brunhoff. I have made use of the talents of three research assistants in this project: Miranda Gill, who expertly rummaged the library of the Taylorian Institution, Oxford, at my behest; Hannah Sullivan, who endured James's handwriting and read through many unpublished letters from and to him held at the Houghton Library; and Elizabeth Sheehan, who helped in the late stages of manuscript preparation at the University of Virginia. I was fortunate in enlisting the services of such impeccable scholars. And my good fortune extended to finding in Hanne Winarsky at Princeton University Press an editor enthusiastic about my project and a very great pleasure to work with, and to the gentle copyediting of Jon Munk. Finally, thanks to the three joyous people I live with, Rosa, Anna, and Clara.

Index

acting: in Eliot's *Daniel Deronda*, 82;
in *The Golden Bowl*, 189; in *The
Tragic Muse*, 83, 87–88, 89, 90, 93,
96, 99. *See also* theater
aesthetics: in *The Ambassadors*, 51; in
The American, 57, 69, 81; in Eliot,
62; and expressionist impulse, 150;
in Flaubert, 122; in *The Golden
Bowl*, 194; in *The Tragic Muse*,
81, 85
Aldrich, Thomas Bailey, 80
Alexander, George, 132
All-Kinds-of-Fur (folk tale), 200
American novel, 59
Americans, 29, 30, 38, 43, 49, 74
Andersen, Hendrik, 87, 154,
171–73
Anglo-American culture, 145
Anglo-Saxon culture, 171
antisemitism, 156
Appleton, Thomas, 38
Ariadne (mythic figure), 196
art: in *The American*, 57, 69, 80, 81;
and Andersen, 171–73; and automobile, 206–7; and beauty, 31; HJ's al-
legories of, 150; HJ's comments on,
28–32; impurity of, 98; medium of,
149, 150; morality of, 84; negative
capability in, 83, 85, 87, 88; and
representation, 81, 90, 97, 98–99,
148; in *The Tragic Muse*, 80, 81, 83,
84, 85, 91, 92–93, 167
Atlantic Monthly, 7, 14, 36, 53, 54
Aumale, Duc d', 16
Austen, Jane, 59
Austin, J. L., *How to Do Things with
Words*, 203
author, 61, 120, 167, 201, 202

Baedeker, Karl, 11, 27
Balzac, Honoré de, 46, 53; and *The
Ambassadors*, 51; and *The American*,
55, 69, 70, 72, 74; and Bourget, 171;
character in, 64, 119, 120, 163–64,
166; Eliot on, 61–63; and expressionism, 98, 149; and Flaubert, 2,
64, 97, 108, 127, 167; "going behind" by, 64; and *The Golden Bowl*,
188, 192, 202; HJ's critical evaluation of, 59–61, 64, 119–20, 161–64,
175, 177, 178; HJ's essays on, 8,
59–61, 66, 68, 159, 161, 161–64,
175, 177, 178; HJ's faithfulness to,
100; HJ's lessons from, 78; as HJ's
model, 8, 97; and HJ's modernism,
5; and HJ's perspectivalism, 4; and
In the Cage, 147; intensity of art in,
64; and matter behind social life, 94;
melodrama of, 34, 93, 121; observation in, 66; realism in, 66, 68, 77,
163; and reorganization of France,
210; representation in, 63, 68; and
revision, 202; Taine on, 164; translations of, 177–78; visionary streak in,
66–67; and *What Maisie Knew*, 139,
144; writers in tradition of, 48; writing as acting in, 203; and Zola, 159;
works: *Comédie humaine*, 162, 178,
202; *La Cousine Bette*, 60, 61, 120,
164; *La Duchesse de Langeais*, 73; *Illusions perdues*, 67, 162; *Les Parents
Pauvres*, 63; *Le Père Goriot*, 61, 63;
Two Young Brides, 162
Bartet, Julia, 82
Barthes, Roland, 108
Barye, Louis, 29
Bastien-Lepage, Jules, 30

59; and HJ's visits with Flaubert,
101; *Home of the Gentry*, 21; and
Roderick Hudson, 48; *Sportsman's
Diary*, 18; *Virgin Soil*, 21
Turgenev, Madame Nikolai, 38, 40
Turgenev, Nikolai, 40

United States, 14

Verdi, Giuseppe: *Aïda*, 32–33;
Requiem, 32, 33
Versailles, 11, 13
Viardot, Louis, 19, 20, 33
Viardot, Pauline, 19, 20, 33
violence: in *The American*, 56–57; in
The Golden Bowl, 194
vision: in *The American*, 69, 70;
unfamiliar angles of, 134. *See also*
observer/observation
visionary, the, in Balzac, 66–67
Voltaire (François-Marie Arouet), 103

Wagner, Cosima, *Diaries*, 42
Wagner, Richard, 5, 40–41; *Parsifal*,
41, 42; *The Ring*, 33, 39
Wagnerian lovers, 195, 198
Waldmann, Maria, 32
Wallon Amendment, 12
Walpole, Hugh, 154, 172, 175
Wharton, Edith, 157, 168–69, 170,
204, 205–6, 207, 209; *A Motor
Flight Through France*, 206
What Maisie Knew, 99–100, 119, 144,
174, 200, 201
Whistler, James McNeill, 5, 32, 97–98,
100, 149
Wilde, Oscar, 4, 81, 165, 173
window(s), 68. *See also* representation
Wittgenstein, Ludwig, 155

women, 21, 24, 67, 161, 196, 200
Woolf, Virginia, 1, 4, 32, 134, 148–49,
155, 187, 207
Woolson, Constance Fenimore, 4, 40,
79, 80, 155
word play, 87
Wormeley, Katherine Prescott,
177–78

Zhukovsky, Pavel Vasilievich (Paul
Joukovsky), 16, 19, 20, 33, 37–44,
79, 154, 173–74
Zhukovsky, Vasilij Andreevich, 39
Zola, Emile, 5, 131; artistry of, 66, 69;
and Balzac, 159; and *The Beast in
the Jungle*, 157, 158; and Cézanne,
149; death of, 156; didactic theme
in, 66; on Droz, 35; and Flaubert,
36; HJ's critical evaluation of, 35–37,
47–48, 59, 157–60, 161, 175, 178;
HJ's essays on, 36–37, 157–60, 161,
178; HJ's introduction to, 22; HJ's
lessons from, 78; and impressionism,
31; indecency in, 36–37; intensity of
art in, 59; and New York City, 160;
observation in, 66, 159; as parochial,
49, 78; realism in, 36, 109, 161;
representation in, 149, 159; return
of repressed lessons from, 52; sex/
sexuality in, 174; and *The Tragic
Muse*, 95, 96; visit to HJ in London
by, 132, 157, 158; windows in, 68;
works: *L'Assommoir*, 36, 37, 159; *La
Débâcle*, 36, 159–60; *Le Docteur
Pascal*, 158; *Germinal*, 36, 156, 159;
J'accuse, 157, 158; *Nana*, 36–37, 95,
96, 161; *Les Rougon-Macquart*, 157,
158; *Son Excellence Eugène Rougon*,
35, 36; *Les Trois Villes*, 158